GARLAND STUDIES ON

INDUSTRIAL PRODUCTIVITY

edited by
STUART BRUCHEY
ALLAN NEVINS PROFESSOR EMERITUS
COLUMBIA UNIVERSITY

T0347950

JAPANESE INDUSTRIAL TRANSPLANTS IN THE UNITED STATES

ORGANIZATIONAL PRACTICES AND RELATIONS OF POWER

ATSUSHI SUMI

Routledge
Taylor & Francis Group

LONDON AND NEW YORK

First published 1998 by Garland Publishing, Inc.

2 Park Square, Milton Park, Abingdon, Oxfordshire OX14 4RN
52 Vanderbilt Avenue, New York, NY 10017

Routledge is an imprint of the Taylor & Francis Group, an informa business

First issued in paperback 2018

Library of Congress Cataloging-in-Publication Data

Sumi, Atsushi, 1958–
   Japanese industrial transplants in the United States : organizational practices and relations of power / Atsushi Sumi.
      p.   cm. — (Garland studies on industrial productivity)
   Based on the author's dissertation completed in 1997.
   Includes bibliographical references and index.
   ISBN 0-8153-3211-4 (alk. paper)
      1. Corporations, Japanese—United States—Management—Case studies. 2. Industrial management—United States—Cross-cultural studies. 3. Comparative management. I. Title. II. Series.
HD70.U5S85 1998
338.8'8952073—dc21

                                                        98-38338

ISBN 13: 978-0-8153-3211-4 (hbk)
ISBN 13: 978-1-138-87934-8 (pbk)

For Tilda

Contents

Tables and Figures

Preface

As the title of this book indicates, my study concerns organizational practices of Japanese transplants in the U.S., and the day-to-day struggles at the workplace between managers and workers, both American and Japanese. At the same time, this book reflects the trajectory of my own lifecourse since I came to the United States as a foreign student 15 years ago, and implicitly reflects my lifecourse in Japan before I came here.

I was raised the son of an industrialist's family where my father was a typical "company man" in the manufacturing environment. He dedicated his life to his company, six days a week for more than 30 years. It was my daily experience to observe my father leave for work by 6:30 a.m. and return home late—at ten or eleven o'clock every night. Because of *tukiai* (obligatory personal relationships) my father would routinely join other company men and his business associates for drinks and dinner. When he arrived at home he would immediately go to bed, and the next morning, begin the routine again . . . six days a week. On Sundays, he would play golf or go fishing with his fellow workers and subordinates from his workplace.

During my university years in Tokyo, I majored in economics. Most of my colleagues, upon graduation, were recruited by and absorbed into the various business institutions in Japan. In my junior year at Keio University, I had an opportunity to discuss Ruth Benedict's work, *The Chrysanthemum and the Sword* in a seminar with Professor Terao. I still strongly recall that my encounter with her insightful work was actually a turning point in my academic interest toward American anthropology.

When I was in graduate school in the U.S. I was drawn to

somehow bridge "anthropology" and "industrial work." When I was at the point of choosing a topic for my dissertation in 1989, the anthropological study of Japanese industry, therefore, seemed to me a possible area of exploration. It seems, in fact, an irony that I chose this topic, because when I left Japan in 1983, deciding not to seek employment with a Japanese company, it was, at least, an expression of my own sense of rebellion against the company man's way of life, epitomized in my father's day-to-day lifecourse. In this sense, I have gone full circle in the trajectory of my life in the U.S.

This book is mostly based on my dissertation completed in 1997. I must mention, however, that this study did not have a particular structure or emphasis on power relations when it started. Although I had a general focus on the issue of transferability of organizational practices from Japanese home plants to their U.S. subsidiaries, I began my research lacking a cohesive thesis. My fieldwork, therefore, was a process of exploration in order to seek some integrative framework with anthropological "spice."

This anthropological spice, of course, never came easily to me. Staring at a heap of cassette tapes (120 of them) that I collected from the interviews, I felt almost desperate, not clearly knowing where I was going both in my research and in my life. In the process of transcribing indeed endless interviews with managers and workers, however, some pattern finally started emerging. One of these patterns was "complaints"—by both managers and workers, and by both Japanese and Americans—clearly relating to issues of power and control. I considered myself lucky to ascertain this pattern, although this inspiration came to me only six months before my dissertation defense.

For this book, I particularly tried to refine the text, especially quotes from interviews. I also updated some of the information and literature from my dissertation. In addition, I gathered further information from some former employees of the case study company, and presented this new data in the epilogue. In presenting informants' voices, I paid special attention to safeguarding their confidentiality. Interviews with Japanese employees were conducted in Japanese, and I translated them to English. Any errors remain solely my own.

A.S.
May 1998

Acknowledgments

I would like to express my sincerest thanks and deepest gratitude to Dr. Louise Lamphere, my teacher and "academic mother," whose unfailing mentorship, expertise, guidance, and support brought me to this point in time. Her tolerance and strictness, patience and forgiveness were, and still are, invaluable to me. I am also grateful to Dr. Les Field, Dr. John Condon, Dr. Robert Rehder, who helped and advised me throughout the process of research and writing while I was a graduate student. I would also like to acknowledge my former teacher, Dr. Philip Bock.

Since 1997 I have been an adjunct assistant professor at the University of New Mexico. I would, therefore, like to extend my appreciation to the University, particularly to the staff and faculty of the anthropology department, for their on-going support and the use of resources in facilitating the completion of this project.

I want to express my sincere appreciation to my beloved mentor in Japan, Professor Makoto Terao of Keio University. For stimulating my interest in American anthropology, I thank Dr. John Zeugner, a visiting professor from the U.S. during my undergraduate years at Keio University.

My fieldwork for the original dissertation, especially the second phase, was funded by the US-Japan Center at the University of New Mexico; I am grateful to the staff for supporting my project during that period. In addition, it was necessary to develop networks among business people in the manufacturing environment. I extend my gratitude to those who kindly offered assistance in opening doors to both Japanese transplants and American companies: Professor Yoshi Turumi of the Pacific Basin Center Foundation, Dr. Everett Rogers of the University of New Mexico, Mr. Inagaki of JETRO (Japan External Trade Organization), Mr. Smoke Price of Human Factors and Ergonomics Society, students and staff of the School of Labor and Industrial Relations at Michigan State University, and members of the APICS (American Production and Inventory Control Society). I also want to express my thanks to Roger McConochie and Jean Canavan, practicing anthropologists, who helped me while I was in the Midwest.

Although they remain anonymous in my dissertation, I am deeply grateful to all the people I interviewed. Without their willingness and cooperation, this study would not have been possible. Especially, I want to express my sincere gratitude to employees at my case study company. I am fortunate to have been able to have extended dialogues with some of the key informants in this study, even after the completion of my original dissertation. Only because of this lasting rapport was I able to gather more profound information about the case study company. I want to express my admiration for their openness and courage to speak out.

Transcribing of 150 hours of taped interviews was, literally, a never-ending process. I want to thank Dr. Miguel Leatham, for his many hours of transcription, and Debbie Conner for her contribution to this process.

Difficulties I had during the actual process of writing this dissertation in a second language were simply beyond description. I wish to extend my deepest appreciation and admiration to Tilda Sosaya, my editor, for her insightful comments and critical feedback on this study, especially regarding the presentation of ethnographic accounts. As a second language speaker, her communication skills and competency in the English language have been truly invaluable to me. I must also express my appreciation to her two loving daughters, Ann-Marie and Noelle, for their patience and understanding during the many hours of editorial work.

Finally, and most importantly, I want to express my deepest gratitude to my parents in Japan, Chiharu and Terue Sumi, for their support and trust in me. Although they can never fully understand my choices, it was their lives and examples that provided the reflection of many people I encountered throughout the process of my fieldwork.

Introduction

In this part of the United States, I have always been a winner, you know. I am white, a male, educated, and this is really the first time when I've worked somewhere and meet people who feel that they are better than me, just because they are something . . . just because they are Japanese. It's real easy to over react to that.

Manufacturing manager at a Japanese-owned company

The contemporary world is immersed and encompassed by the overarching effects of big business, industry, capitalism and the quest for profit. Since the latter decades of the nineteenth century, the United States had become an industrial giant, facing little competition on the world market. Since World War II, however, Japan's industrial efforts have led Japan to the top ranks of the global economy.

During the 1950's products labeled "made in Japan" were considered by the American consumer to be second-rate, hardly a threat to American industries. By the 1960's a noticeable shift had begun to occur. Japanese industries were making quantum leaps in the quality of their consumer products. American industry was stretching its collective neck to view the changes occurring far across the Pacific. In two short decades since the devastation of most of Japan's viable industries during World War II, this small, island nation was rapidly rising and expanding economically. Western industrialists began to search the heart of the Japanese business culture in an attempt to understand how and why so much could have been accomplished in such a relatively short period of time.

Throughout the 1970's Japanese automobiles were increasingly visible everywhere on American highways from the Atlantic to the Pacific. Following the oil crisis of 1973 Japanese industrialists began to shift manufacturing facilities to foreign soil in order to further their competitive abilities on the world market, not only in the automotive industry, but in the burgeoning field of consumer electronics.

During the 1980's and into the 1990's, Japanese industrialists extended their operations throughout the world to both industrialized and developing countries. This has created a unique environment where Japanese management must deal with employees of many different cultures. Cross-cultural encounters on both the organizational level and in the workplace have expanded especially in the United States, where there are 1,275 Japanese "transplants" in the manufacturing sector. When I gathered information for this study in 1993 and 1994, there were eight Japanese automotive assembly transplants in the U.S., more than 320 Japanese-owned or Japanese-American joint venture automotive suppliers, 72 Japanese-owned or Japanese-American joint ventures in steel, and 21 Japanese-owned rubber and tire plants (Kenney and Florida 1993).

Based on extensive interviews with managers and workers in Japanese-owned and American companies, and one case study of a Japanese-owned manufacturing company, I tried to elicit the employees' experience at the workplaces of Japanese-owned companies in the United States. Throughout the course of these interviews I attempted to ascertain what, if any, organizational practices were intrinsically Japanese, and, if so, how might they differ from organizational practices in the home plants. In addition, I tried to discover how such practices might be taking root in the U.S. transplants. Negotiations of power relations between American and Japanese employees were also an important issue in my research. In dealing with the issue of power relations, I examined forms of control, particularly how management control is exerted over employees at the workplace.

Research on Japanese and American business organizations has been frequently undertaken by many management professionals and consultants. The number of books and articles in the popular press in this area is indeed countless. However, research on business organizations and industrial relations has rarely been conducted by anthropologists. Although I can trace the roots of anthropological studies on business and industrial organizations to the work of Lloyd Warner and to the Hawthorne studies during the 1930's (Baba 1986), there have been only a few anthropological studies that provide a framework for understanding Japanese organizations in the past 50 years (Benedict 1946; Abegglen 1958; Rohlen 1974; Kondo 1990). It was only about a decade ago when social scientists began talking about "organizational culture" in their analyses of organizations. Shortly afterwards, mainly because of the Japanese business influence, people in the popular press began using the term "organizational culture" or "corporate culture" in their countless articles about foreign and American companies. In fact, the popularity of the term "organizational culture" is largely the result of the American response to Japanese business success (Jordan 1994).

Nonetheless, it is important to point out that in the majority of books and articles in the mass media or management journals, "culture" is treated either as a peripheral factor or as some mysterious entity that explains everything in organizations. My concern is mainly with the influence of culture on behaviors in organizations and on management practices. However, there is always a great danger in making general statements about culture. Generalizations on the cultural level often result in normative descriptions of employees' behavior, ignoring all the multiple layers of meanings (or experience) associated with actions and events in the everyday process of cross-cultural interactions in organizations. One of the toughest challenges for me in presenting this work was to cope with the variety of information from informants as well as various and often contradictory findings from the previous works of other social scientists. During my fieldwork, some employees even said, "If you talk to 100 employees, you will get 100 different answers."

It is by no means an easy task to account for the differences and similarities of management practices between Japan and the U.S., let alone to account for the differences and similarities of Japanese and American culture. For instance, in many studies of management practices in Japan, the practice of consensus decision-making, called "ringi," has been emphasized as one of the most salient characteristics. However, the interview data from my fieldwork indicate that it is, in fact, quite common for a manager in Japan to give an "order," to a subordinate production engineer, saying, for example, "Why don't you go to the sales department to learn what the customers really want." In this case, this production engineer really is obliged to go and work for the sales department. The idea of consensus may exist as a "norm" in the company, but in reality everyday decision-making is a top-down process.

The traditionally emphasized characteristic of harmony in Japanese organizations can also give a somewhat misleading image of everyday worklife in Japan. The interview data from my fieldwork also indicate that it is quite common for team members in Japan to make overt criticisms of one another, and sometimes even criticize the president of the company. This frequently happens within a homogeneous group setting, in which all members belong to the same company or to the same work group. Again, the idea of harmony certainly exists on the normative level, but the real picture seems to be far more complex.

Observing work behaviors of both the Japanese and Americans, it seems easier to say that Japanese organizations have been more effective than their American counterparts because employees are treated better in Japanese organizations than American organizations, and because Japanese workers are more docile and obedient than American workers. Even some of the most recent studies on the organizations of work and production in Japanese companies in Japan and their subsidiaries in the United States tend to present the implicit picture of Japanese employees as happy, satisfied, well-motivated, and willing employees. Yet some of the literature and parts of my interview data actually show how both managers and workers in the production area are dissatisfied, pressured, and stressed out in Japanese companies both in Japan and the U.S. All in all, the level of dissatisfaction among workers in Japan seems quite high.

My fieldwork indeed gave me a good sense of the diversity of experiences among employees as well as among companies. Even among companies in the same industries, the characteristics of an organization and the conditions of the workplaces are vastly different depending on the size and history of organizations, the types of industries, kinds of production lines, the organization's geographical location, and the surrounding local-level political economy.

In this study, the sample size is relatively small. In the first phase of my fieldwork I conducted one (1) case study of a small to medium size company (118 employees). In the second phase I visited eight (8) Japanese-owned medium to large size companies, one (1) medium size joint-venture company, two (2) foreign-owned, and two (2) U.S.-owned medium to large size companies in the Midwest and California. Among these fourteen (14) companies, seven (7) are high-tech related, one (1) is the headquarters of an automobile manufacturer, and the six (6) remaining companies are automotive parts suppliers. In addition, I also used the relevant data from my preliminary fieldwork among automobile manufacturers and their parts suppliers in the Midwest.

Considering the diverse experiences among manufacturing organizations and the small sample size in this study, I will not attempt to generalize my findings. Rather, based on the findings from the case study, I will present the tendencies that are unique in the process of the transfer of the management practices from Japan to the U.S., and the everyday interactions between Japanese and American employees at the workplace level.

I should also note that this study differs from many other studies in anthropology where anthropologists typically work with the social groups with less political and economic power. Anthropologists traditionally studied foreign, "exotic," communities that have been relatively isolated from the influences of the surrounding world capitalism. In the United States a great majority of anthropologists tend to study either less industrialized foreign societies or the social groups of less political and economic power in their own society, such as ethnic minority groups. In these studies, anthropologists, like it or not, usually represent a social group of more political and economic power than the social group that is being studied. In the studies of business organizations, on the other hand, companies have more control over anthropologists in terms of when, how, and for what duration anthropologists conduct their research. This is true whether anthropologists focus either on management or on labor in their studies.

This power relation between the anthropologist (or any researcher) and the company heavily influences the process of the fieldwork. It affects both how the anthropologist enters the field (i.e., company) and how the anthropologist forms strategies to get around in the company. In addition, it affects the behaviors of the anthropologist in the field. As a result, the fieldwork processes in this study are very different from the majority of studies in anthropology. I will explore this matter in the fieldwork chapter (Chapter Two).

Finally, all names of informants and companies in this study have been changed to protect privacy and confidentiality. It is my hope that the message of this book provides employees in binational organizations the insight to improve the conditions of daily worklife, and further, provides theoretical insight to the studies of organizational behavior and industrial work.

The book is divided into eight chapters. In the first chapter I deal with the theoretical framework and the relevant social science literature. I look at the body of literature on the development of Japanese practices in Japan, as well as the literature on Japanese transplants in the United States. Chapter Two deals with the methods I employed for data collection, and the process of data gathering during my fieldwork. The main theme of Chapter Two is to address the issue of access to professional work organizations in anthropological fieldwork, and to show how my nationality and my Japanese cultural background affected the process of data collection in both positive and negative ways.

The third chapter examines the transferability of eight salient characteristics of organizations of production in Japanese factories, which Murakami and Rohlen outlined (Murakami and Rohlen 1992), among four (4) Japanese-owned, and one (1) joint-venture auto-related transplant companies in the Midwest. In contrasting the characteristics of the companies in the Midwest, Chapter Four also examines the transferability of those eight Japanese elements among three (3) high-tech related transplant companies and one (1) corporate headquarters of an automobile manufacturer in California.

Chapter five, six, and seven, deal with the case study of Suntech Corporation (pseudonym), a Japanese-owned high-tech manufacturing company in New Mexico. In Chapter Five, I examine the transferability of these eight Japanese elements to the U.S. subsidiary in New Mexico. In chapters six and seven, I explore the issue of a corporate culture specific to the case study company and interactions between Japanese and American employees by examining forms of management control at the workplace. I am concerned especially with the ways and means management control is exerted over American workers by the Japanese managers and how both American managers and workers respond to the different kinds of management control.

Finally, the concluding chapter reflects on the transferability of organizational practices from Japan to the United States in general, on the social and cultural differences at the workplace, and on the significance of corporate structural level influences on everyday interactions among employees at the workplace.

Japanese Industrial Transplants in the United States

CHAPTER 1

Problem and Literature

There has been an enormous amount of interest and concern among social scientists as to the reasons behind Japan's economic success and the high productivity of their industrial organizations. Much attention has been paid, especially, to Japanese business practices and their distinctive characteristics, such as the lifetime employment practice, the team based work organization and work process, and the organization of unions. In the broadest terms, these organizational features and industrial policies, along with the social, economic, political, and cultural context of Japan have frequently been considered to be at least partly responsible for their impressive levels of industrial performance (Abegglen 1973; Cole 1979; Dore 1973).

During the last few decades, Japanese industrialists extended their operations throughout the world, including both industrialized and developing countries. This has created a unique environment, in which Japanese management has had to face employees of many different cultures. This cross cultural encounter of management and workers has been especially prevalent in contemporary North America. In 1990, 43.8 percent of the total Japanese direct investment in foreign countries was made in North America (JETRO 1992). During the 1980's and continuing into the 1990's, 1,275 Japanese "transplants" established manufacturing operations in the United States (Kenney and Florida 1993). The number of total employees in Japanese-owned companies in the U.S. was 244,008 in 1994 (JETRO 1995).

This study will assess the degree of transferability of Japanese organizational practices to the United States within the automobile and high technology industries. In addition, I will examine how organizational practices of Japanese-owned firms are evolving in the

U.S. and how they differ from either the management practices of Japanese firms in Japan, or those of American firms in the U.S.

The study of the transferability of the organizational practices of Japanese organizations raises two basic questions. First, what are the organizational practices of Japanese companies? Second, if such "Japanese" organizational practices exist, are they transferable to the United States?

Throughout the past few decades many social scientists have focused on the distinguishing characteristics of the organization of work and production among Japanese companies, such as the practice of lifetime employment, the system of pay and promotions, consensus decision-making processes, small group activities such as QC circles, labor-management relations, and so on. It is important to note here that the existence of those characteristics varies to a large extent depending on the size of organizations. As well documented by now, those characteristics only apply to large organizations in Japan. On the other hand, the majority of smaller scale companies are often contractors or suppliers for large companies and do not have a policy of lifetime employment (Cole 1976; Kenney and Florida 1993). Even in large organizations women and part-time employees are often excluded from this practice in Japan.

Though the empirical evidence regarding the significant characteristics of industrial organizations in Japan is still somewhat uneven, most social scientists generally agree on the following as the elements distinguishing large Japanese industrial organizations in the postwar period (Murakami and Rohlen 1992):

(1) lifetime employment (or long tenure of employment)
(2) seniority-based wage and promotion systems
(3) elaborate welfare, bonus, and other benefits systems
(4) company-based labor unions
(5) considerable inter-job mobility within a firm and emphasis on internal promotion
(6) small group activities at the shop floor level
(7) intensive training and socialization by the management
(8) attention to developing a corporate culture and managerial philosophy

These characteristics mentioned above (especially 2-8) can only be realized when there is a specific labor agreement between employer and employee. In the context of the labor market in Japan, this specific agreement, while it is not contractual, is the practice of lifetime employment. Therefore, lifetime employment is the crux of these elements that often constitute "Japanese management practices." Some experts even mention that the Japanese will make every effort to maintain these principles in the foreseeable future, and that the changes going on in employment practices are not designed to destroy the present system but to increase its flexibility (Mroczkowski and Hanaoka 1989). In essence, therefore, the study of transferability of the Japanese management practices to the U.S. entails examining the above mentioned characteristics in Japanese-owned companies in the United States.

My fieldwork data gave me a good sense of how the management practices of medium-sized Japanese-owned firms in the U.S. are different from those of home plants in Japan. The data generally indicate some of the major differences in the areas of small group activities on the shop floor, team based work processes, training programs, and labor-management relations. Many Japanese managers generally wish these practices to be as similar to those at their home plants as possible. Nonetheless, the process of implementing these practices is a continuous struggle mainly because of the social and cultural differences between Japan and the U.S. In Japan these practices are usually not highly structured except for those in large Japanese factories. In the U.S. Japanese managers perceive the need to implement those practices more systematically for American workers. In reality, however, the training programs, small group activities, and team based work processes on the shop floor have been unsuccessful, in part because of the lack of understanding among Japanese managers of the differences between the two cultures, and partially because of their lack of preparation for implementing those practices in a foreign environment. In this study, I will argue that the medium-sized Japanese-owned firms in the U.S. have implemented different small group activities, teams, and training programs that emphasize more on-the-job and more systematic training because of the social and cultural differences.

In examining the transferability of management practices, it is necessary to look at how employees (especially American employees) respond to the new Japanese environment on the shopfloor level. Here, power relations, particularly the relations between Japanese managers and American employees on the one hand, and the relations between the parent company in Japan and its U.S. transplant on the other hand, become important. The interview data generally demonstrate that there is a strong emphasis among Japanese on the length of employment, commitment to the company, and the attitudes toward company's work at least on the level of management ideals. However, these Japanese emphases often frustrate American employees, especially middle-level managers and engineers in everyday worklife at the workplace. Using the case study, I explore the issue of power relations by examining how management control is exerted by the Japanese managers over both American managers and workers, and how they (American managers and workers) respond to the exertion of control by Japanese managers. When examining forms of control at the transplants, I will employ Richard Edwards' definition of managerial control as "the ability of capitalists and/or managers to obtain desired work behavior from workers" (Edwards 1979:17).

In his discussion of power, Eric Wolf differentiated between structural power on the one hand, and organizational and tactical power on the other hand (Wolf 1990). In the same manner, it is helpful to distinguish corporate structural level control from management control on the shopfloor level. In my study, I use the term "corporate control" when I refer to structural level relations, such as the relationships among the parent company, its corporate headquarters, and its U.S. transplant. On the other hand, I use the term "management control" when I refer to the workplace level relations among employees in one company, such as the relationships between Japanese managers and American workers.

This power/control dimension is a significant factor in behavior in corporations at both the organizational and individual levels. It is a factor in the behavior of subordinates toward superiors in any office, as well as the behavior of multinational corporations in the world system (Jordan 1994). It is an especially important factor when the organization is binational, and the workforce is multicultural.

Finally, it is important to note that the analysis of the transferability of Japanese management practices to the North American industrial environment implies the following question. How significant are cultural factors in the process of transferring the Japanese practices? How influential are cultural factors on behaviors in organizations and on management practices? How much can social scientists explain the diversity of experiences among Japanese-owned firms in the United States by simply utilizing a "cultural" analysis?

In this study I will contrast the characteristics of automobile industries in the Midwest with those of high-tech industries in California. Automobile industries in the Midwest possess unique characteristics. Compared to high-tech industries, for example, there is a larger proportion of blue-collar workers. The percentage of racial and ethnic minorities in the total workforce is small in the Midwest. Those minorities tend to be primarily African-Americans and Asians in the production area, or at the lower-level of management. In contrast, the characteristics of high-tech industries in California are very different. The presence of many immigrant professionals and the small portion of blue-collar workers in these industries have influenced the organization of work and production, management practices, and the interaction among employees at the workplace.

In this book, I use the term, "culture" as separate from "structure," such as social institutions and social groups, and the relationships among these institutions and groups. I use the term "culture" as "historically situated and emergent, shifting and incomplete meanings and practices generated in webs of agency and power" (Ong 1987: 2-3). In my study, I view the processes of cultural change not as "unfolding according to some predetermined logic (of development, modernization, or capitalism) but as the disrupted, contradictory, and differential outcomes which involve changes in identity, relations of struggle and dependence, including the experience of reality of itself" (Ong 1987: 3).

It is important to note here, however, that the "folk" definitions of culture in my study always differed from the way I conceived the concept of culture. As I mention in the fieldwork chapter, my informants, both Japanese and American employees, defined "culture" in their own ways and often perceived culture in terms of the differences and similarities between such monolithic concepts as "Japanese culture" and "American culture." I, therefore, have used these folk definitions of culture in my own text as perceived by my informants.

My central argument in this study is that culture does not explain everything about Japanese transplants. Culture is only one of many significant factors influencing organizational practices and behaviors in these industrial organizations. Other significant factors of fundamental importance are the size and history of organizations, the kinds of industry, the organization of production lines, the firm's geographical location, the racial and ethnic composition of local laborforces, and the surrounding local, as well as the national-level, political economy. While culture has been of primary importance, it is my contention that relations of power and conflict on the corporate structural level are equally significant in the daily worklife at Japanese transplants in the U.S. In fact, these struggles on the corporate structural level have a profound impact on the workplace, even greater perhaps, than do the more obvious circumstances of social contrasts and cultural differences.

REVIEW OF THE LITERATURE

In order to examine the transferability of management practices of organizations in Japan to the United States, it is first necessary to see the development of organizational form and management practices of Japanese firms in Japan in an historical framework. Second, it is necessary to identify the differences of organizational form and management practices between Japan and the United States. In this section, after this ground work, I focus on the literature on Japanese transplants in the U.S. regarding the extent to which particular practices have been transferred, and to what extent power relations have been examined in these transplants.

1. Development of the Management Practices in Organizations in Japan

When looking at a large number of studies on the development of management practices in Japanese organizations, I argue that most of the studies on Japanese factories are basically interested in describing and explaining what is uniquely Japanese about both the social structure and culture of Japanese industrial organizations. There is little disagreement among social scientists in identifying the characteristics that are often considered uniquely Japanese in industrial organizations in Japan. However, as Fruin shows, there has been disagreement about the development of the management practices and organizational forms of Japanese organizations (Fruin 1994).

In one of the pioneering studies in this area, Abegglen identified three organizational elements—lifetime employment, seniority-based wage and promotion systems, and enterprise unions—as distinctive characteristics of organizational forms in Japan. He saw Japanese employment practices as based on a paternalism rooted in the traditional Japanese collectivist values of pre-war society of Japan (Abegglen 1958). From this perspective those distinctive characteristics of Japanese work organization are all expressions of feudal, patriarchal, and agrarian values that are carried over from the pre-war society into the post-war, industrial era. In short, he employed a cultural-historical interpretation of the distinctive characteristics of Japanese organizations.

Another important study was carried out by Robert Cole. Cole (1971) employed a structural-functional framework in his study of blue-collar workers at a diecast company. He found that the characteristics of Japanese employment practices have little to do with the culture and history of Japan and more to do with the rational managerial response to the labor shortage of the Japanese labor market and the scarce economic resources of Japanese society. For Cole, those characteristics of Japanese organizations that are often seen as "distinctive" and "different" from organizations in the West, are in fact the functional equivalents of Western structures and institutions.

Dore (1973) characterized the employment practices and distinctive characteristics of Japanese organizations as "welfare corporatism." In his study, Dore disagreed with Cole's position that distinctive characteristics of management practices and organizational forms of Japanese institutions are functional equivalents of the West. Instead, he posited a late development hypothesis to explain those distinguishing characteristics of industrial activities in Japan. He argued that Japan's late industrial development compared to the West resulted in different management practices and organizational forms in Japan. For him, characteristics such as the "egalitarian" structures, consensus management practices, and the labor-management relations are the result of effective industrial policies by the Japanese government in the course of the industrial development of Japan. He emphasized the role of ideology in the process of industrialization. The fact that Japan learned from the successes and failures of the West had a profound effect on how new institutional practices were implemented. In his framework the late-learning effect which accompanied the late industrial development of Japan resulted in Japan's more "advanced" organizational forms and practices, such as the practice of lifetime employment, the team-based organizations of work and production, and the consensus labor-management relations.

Marsh and Mannari examined organizational forms and management practices from a totally different angle. Based on the broad perspective of modernization theory, they argued that the characteristic organizational forms and practices in Japanese organizations, such as the long-tenure of employment, seniority-based wage and promotions, a strong sense of commitment and loyalty to the company, and employees' strong identification with their companies will eventually become less significant, and will diminish in the future as Japanese society converges more toward Western European and North American societies (Marsh and Mannari 1976).

Cole was influenced by the work of Dore, and modified his viewpoint in his later works (Cole 1979, 1989). Although Cole still continued to see the development of the Japanese practices through a structural-functional model, he emphasized the role of macro-institutional factors, such as the industrial policies by the government, on the way new practices are realized. In the same manner, in his comparative analysis of QC circles in Japan and the U.S., he emphasized the significance of social and cultural factors on the way QC circles are implemented in different environments. For Cole, the same QC circle or organization will not be realized in the same way in Japan and the U.S. mainly because of social and cultural differences.

Another important work in this context is Johnson's study on the role of the state in the course of the industrial development of Japan (Johnson, C. 1982). He characterized Japan as a capitalist "developmental state" as opposed to the United States, a capitalist "regulatory state." He emphasized the role of government in directing the private as well as other public sectors during the course of the postwar economic development of Japan. For Johnson, the contrasting characteristics of institutions in Japan and the West are mainly due to the different role of the state of Japan, and Japan's late industrial development. From this perspective, the above-mentioned distinguishing characteristics of industrial organizations in Japan can be explained in terms of the macro institutional factors, such as the industrial policies by MITI (Ministry of International Trade and Industry). Regarding the practice of lifetime employment, he contends in his later work that this practice has nothing to do with Japanese culture, and that it grew out of the enormous insecurities faced by Japanese workers during the late 1940's and 1950's. It did not become a prominent feature of Japanese management, he argues, until after the Mitsui Miike coal mine strike of 1960 (Johnson, C. 1988).

Finally, it is important to note here that my own view is based on the meticulous historical scholarship of Andrew Gordon, who examined the emergence of the employment system in a historical context in terms of the relations of power and conflict among labor, capital, the Japanese state, and the U.S. Occupation forces (Gordon 1985). For Gordon, the distinguishing characteristics of Japanese organizational forms and management practices, such as an informally guaranteed long-term employment, seniority-based wage and promotion systems, and enterprise unionism were neither a simple reflection of the traditional values of the pre-war society of Japan, nor the mere invention of management, but gradually became a set of organizational forms and practices through the labor-management struggles during the 1920's, the 1930's, and the late 1940's—shortly after Japan's defeat in World War II.

Gordon saw that Japanese labor relations moved through several distinctive stages between the 1850's and 1950's. He argued that paternal ideology was gradually articulated as a managerial response to the workers' anti-firing struggles from the turn of the century (1900), through the end of World War I (1917). For him, it was during the inter-war years (1917-1939) between World Wars I and II, when this paternal ideology was reshaped into the more familiar form of Japanese labor-management practices regarding the issue of job security, such as the practice of lifetime employment.

When Japan surrendered to the Allied forces in 1945, the pre-war ruling class was discredited, and the widespread working class discontent turned into labor militancy. Labor's initial demands during this struggle were mainly for a living wage based on age, seniority, and family, the contractually guaranteed job, and the equal union participation (Gordon 1985: 414). On the other hand, the management response to labor demands was the seniority wage with important exceptions, the implicit job guarantee for some (especially male, regular employees), and weak secondary unions (Gordon 1985: 414). Capitalists and the General Headquarters of the U.S. Occupational Force also saw Japanese unions as a springboard for communism and eventually wiped out the radical unions. This basically resulted in Japanese organizations' "unique" characteristics, such as the lifetime employment practice, the system of seniority-based wage and promotions, and company unions.

Based on Gordon's examinations, Kenney and Florida contended that the team-based organization of work and production was also partly the result of workers' struggles, referred to as "production control," of the late 1940's when workers occupied factories, ousted top management, and continued to produce and sell the products using stocks that management had hoarded (Kenney and Florida 1993: 28). They see the root of the Japanese system of team-based work organization in the process of "production control" where shop floor workers and line managers had to cooperate to keep plants running.

Smith also shares a similar point of view and contends that what are generally characterized as distinctive features of the Japanese management system, such as lifetime employment, a comprehensive system of benefits, and enterprise unions, are a product of specific circumstances in the history of the development of Japanese capitalism (Smith, W. 1994: 156).

It is not only Western scholars who saw the development of organizational forms and practices in Japan as a historically specific organizational response to the labor conditions of the postwar period. Taira argues that the practice of permanent employment was not simply an outcome of the paternalistic values of the Japanese pre-war society but emerged as a concrete set of practices during the postwar period. It emerged as Japanese industrialists' response to cope with the high degree of labor mobility in the postwar period and to exert more effective control over the laborforce (Taira 1988, 1993).

Koike also notes that "company unions" were produced during the late 1940's and early 1950's by the union-busting policies by the U.S. Occupation forces, Japanese industrialists, and the Japanese government. Those company unions were known for their weak ties to other company unions within the same industry, and had a strong sense of allegiance to the firm (Koike 1977).

My contention is that the distinctive characteristics of Japanese industrial organizations are not simply the products of Japanese "culture" but emerged through the historically unique processes of the interaction between social and cultural factors and the political economy of Japan. This view will inform my basic argument in this study that culture is only one of many significant factors influencing behaviors in organizations and the organizational practices of Japanese transplants in the United States. These factors include the size, history, geographical location, nature of production in a company, the relations of power and conflict at both the workplace and corporate structural levels, and the local as well as the national level political economy.

2. Differences between Japanese and U.S. Management Practices

Whether characterized as "company paternalism" rooted in the traditional values of Japanese prewar society (Abegglen 1958), "welfare corporatism" (Dore 1973), or "the outcome of bitter postwar class struggles" (Kenney and Florida 1993), virtually all observers agree that the basic management practices and organizational forms that are often labeled as "Japanese management" are lifetime employment practice and the team-based organizations of work and production. Here I contrast the characteristics of management practices in large Japanese organizations with those of traditional Fordist organizations in the U.S. I account for the differences between large Japanese organizations and Fordist organizations in the light of management control.

Edwards differentiated three forms of management control—simple (or direct) control, technical control, and bureaucratic control (Edwards 1979). While simple, or direct control involves the manager's personal exercise of power over workers, bureaucratic control involves the institutionalization of simple and technical control into hierarchical power. Technical control, for example, refers to the process whereby manufacturing machinery or the assembly line regulate the speed of work. Burawoy refers to management control in Japanese factories as "hegemonic despotism," in which managers exercise a high degree of direct and indirect control over workers' lives (Burawoy 1979). He sees the Japanese production system as designed to build worker dependence and submission by extending managerial control more completely over the worker. A similar view is the "management-by-stress" thesis which sees the Japanese system as a faster and more exploitative form of the Taylor-Fordist system, illustrated by a fast and intense work pace and concomitant internal pressure from work teams (Parker and Slaughter 1987). Kamata wrote about life on the Toyota assembly line in the early 1970's, describing in detail the intense work pace, illustrating clearly how the working conditions in the factory were constantly rationalized by the company (Kamata 1982). In contrast, Dore argues that the crucial elements of management control in Japanese organizations are encapsulated in the form of "welfare corporatism" where employees' needs are met by the company through the elaborated benefits packages and "egalitarian" organizational structures (Dore 1973). In addition, some of the scholars in Japan see the practice of lifetime employment as a central element of management control. They see that the practice of lifetime employment in large firms works to foster employees' commitment, dedication, and a sense of loyalty to the company. This practice serves to align employees' interests with those of the company, and in so doing, eventually fosters employees' identification with the company (Koike 1988; Shimada 1983). Sullivan and Peterson also contend that lifetime employment is offered within a rhetorical context of loyalty and benevolence based on cultural values, and that the impact of the practice is to increase the control of employees by the company (Sullivan and Peterson 1990).

Kenney and Florida conceptualize a new model of the organization of work and production in the Japanese factory. What they term "the innovation-mediated production system" taps workers' intelligence and knowledge of production, and harnesses workers' intellectual capabilities more effectively than any other organization of work and production (Kenney and Florida 1993). For them, the innovation-mediated production system is fundamentally different from the mass production system in traditional Fordist factories in the West, where the premise of the system is based on the separation of physical and intellectual labor. In their analysis of the innovation-mediated production system, they point to corporate control ("management control" in my study) that differentiates this production system from any other organization of work and production. In a similar vein,

Johnson refers to the different nature of Japanese capitalism where labor means "human capital," not simply workers who are engaged in manual labor (Johnson, C. 1988; also Shimada 1983). Hull and Azumi, exploring an alternative to Marx's alienation thesis that suggests a positive correlation between technological advancements and worker alienation, show that this does not apply to the high-tech factories in Japan. In their study, those high-tech factories demonstrate that "more advanced technologies can be introduced effectively to the extent that employees are interpersonally integrated with their employing organization and are neither de-skilled nor rendered powerless in the workplace" (Hull and Azumi 1988).

In this production system the control mechanism implicit in group social processes is maximized to increase the total work accomplished. The underlying objective in the innovation-mediated production system, is management control aimed at motivating workers and aligning the interests of the workers with those of the company. It is also directed toward creating a social context where workers will readily supply their ideas or suggestions. Kenney and Florida refer to various types management control in Japanese factories as follows:

> A key element of this form of corporate control involves establishing an identity between workers and the corporation—creating what might be termed a 'corporatist hegemony' over work life. Such identification makes workers feel as though they are a part of an over-arching corporate entity. As such, it creates implicit and subtle forms of coercion and motivation, spurring workers to work hard, think for the company, and assist in motivating fellow workers . . . Japanese corporations establish extensive means of social control, and indeed, socialization to ensure that workers identify with the company. These include company activities, corporate socializing, company-sponsored sports events, and even company towns like Toyota City. Corporations became 'total institutions' exerting influence over many aspects of social life. In this sense, they bear some resemblance to other forms of total institutions such as religious orders or the military (Kenney and Florida 1993: 271).

One of the most powerful forms of coercion and motivation is peer pressure. However, peer pressure in Japanese factories goes beyond the team-based organization of work and production. The source of peer pressure in a company indeed goes far beyond the factory walls. It is combined with other social pressures from family members, relatives, neighbors, peer groups of a school from which one graduated, and even society at large. One of the elements that closely relate to peer pressure is the notion of "*sekentei*"(one's social face within the community). In Japan, peer pressure is one of the major elements of social control in influencing the individual's behavior both inside and outside organizations. It is a powerful source for the conformity of the individual employee to the company's norms, and furthermore, to the social norms of Japanese society. This system of social controls is usually hidden beneath the surface of formal descriptions of Japanese society. Nakane (1967, 1974) described and analyzed the social structure of Japanese society in terms of vertical and horizontal structures. In her framework of Japanese society, vertical structures refer to, for example, the relationships between a parent and a child, and a boss and a subordinate. Horizontal structures, on the other hand, refer to the relationships between individuals with the same attributes. Peer groups are major elements in these horizontal structures. Although her study has its significance for the analysis of formal structures, her primary focus on formal, vertical structures obscured the significance of horizontal structures in Japanese society. Furthermore, it is usually along these horizontal structures where various forms of social controls are at work.

There also exist elements of control in the socialization processes. As Murakami and Rohlen pointed out, the intense socialization of new employees by management is one of the significant characteristics of Japanese firms (Murakami and Rohlen 1992). As Rohlen showed in his anthropological study of a Japanese bank, socialization consists of direct inculcation of employees by the management as to the rules, regulations, norms, and values of the company. In Japanese firms, socialization happens and is reinforced constantly through various formal and informal processes, such as orientation activities, in-house training, job rotations, ongoing counseling, after-hour activities, weekend and various company-sponsored activities (Rohlen 1974). Employees are thus socialized to fit into the company's "mold" through these everyday interactions with, for example, "*sempai*" (senior veteran workers) and the peer workers. Cole also notes in his observation of

Toyota Autobody that employees grow to fit in the company's mold through everyday interactions and ongoing counseling with the superiors (Cole 1979).

Finally, discipline is also a crucial element of control in any organization (Kenney and Florida 1993). It is an integral part of control especially on the level of the shop floor. In contrast with American firms where "right" and "wrong" are clearly distinguished, they are often less formalized in Japanese firms. It is not usually codified in detail as a document. Discipline under normal conditions usually takes the form of counseling, or informal conversations with superiors and peers for the purpose of altering or improving inappropriate behavior. Punishment, such as termination, is only used when the behavior does not improve.

It is important to note that control in Japanese organizations does not stop here. The above mentioned social controls in Japanese organizations are indeed the same type of social control illustrated by Ouchi in his analysis of Z-type organizations which consist of many "industrial clans" (Ouchi 1981). In his analysis, the social control mechanisms in Japanese organizations are similar to those of pre-industrial societies. Anthropologists, however, have pointed out that those social control mechanisms of preindustrial society in fact serve for "anti-production," which holds a society (or group) below its potential productive capabilities (Sahlins 1958; Kaplan and Ziegler 1985). Sahlins has pointed out that this anti-production tendency is overcome when political incentives are imposed by hierarchical methods of social control (Sahlins 1972). In the context of Japanese industrial organizations, when higher productivity is achieved, it is usually "because some hierarchical methods of social control are linked to the industrial clan-like groups" (Kaplan and Ziegler 1985: 85). As I mentioned in the Introduction, the data from my research clearly indicate that there is a hierarchical control system in Japanese organizations. At this point, it is evident that management control in Japanese industrial organizations involves simple control, various type of horizontal control such as team and peer pressure, and hierarchical control.

In contrast, the way management control is exerted on workers is significantly different in the traditional Fordist organizations in the United States. Management control in the traditional Fordist factory usually takes the form of technical and hierarchical control. When compared with factories in Japan, this resulted in radically different social conditions in Fordist factories. As Braverman showed, the premise of the Fordist organization of work and production is Taylorian scientific management (Braverman 1974). The scientific management movement was founded on the premise that control over labor processes must pass into the hands of management through control over the decisions that are made in the course of work.

There are two principles that are involved in the scientific management movement. First, the labor process is dissociated from the skills of workers. It is management who owns the knowledge of work processes that have been possessed by workers before. The traditional knowledge of work has been broken down and reduced to countless rules, laws, and formulas. Second, scientific management divided the work to be executed into different processes, each requiring a different degree of skill, or of physical strength so that management could pay the higher skilled workers higher wages, and lower skilled workers lower wages. The resulting form was an organization with extensive system of job classifications and replaceable workers. The system of job classifications accompanied countless formal rules over the allocation of work and behaviors in the organization (Kenney and Florida 1993: 273). In response to the management policy of pushing and coercing employees to work harder, workers and their unions formed a clearly separated identification from the management. The characteristic resulting from this environment was a highly differentiated "class hierarchy" among white- and blue-collar employees with antagonistic labor-management relations.

In the context of Fordist factories in the U.S. where management control is exerted through countless job classifications and formal rules to force employees to work harder, workers and their unions had to fight for control over the choice of days when they would come to work. Regarding the social aspects in this vein, Kenney and Florida mention as follows:

> Unions developed an elaborate contractual structure and grievance mechanism to protect employees from management's attempts to exert social control by limiting absences and days off. Labor contracts devoted extensive portions of the agreement to the rights of

workers to have sick days and to have vacation days and to have significant discretion in the use of the days they wished to take off. Thus, control of the disposition of a worker's time was constantly disputed. Employees could take days off whenever they chose, read magazines on the shop floor, take unauthorized breaks, and so on (Kenney and Florida 1993: 274).

As opposed to Japanese firms where management control is often exerted through social mechanisms such as everyday interactions including ongoing counseling, teams, peer pressure, and various company activities, control in Fordist organizations is exerted through formal rules and countless job classifications. Such power/control issues often surface through labor-management conflict.

Regarding discipline in American firms, there is often, a clear codified, distinction of "right" and "wrong." Wrong or improper behavior is subjected to punishment, such as suspension or dismissal. The severity of punishment is often written in documents such as corporate manuals (for example, attendance policy). In many cases such punishment is practiced solely for punishment's sake without any accompanying guidance for the improvement of the behavior, and perhaps, to make an example of the errant employee.

Finally, it is important to note that the contrasting ways management control is exercised in Japanese firms and American Fordist firms manifests in the following differences. First, in the Fordist organizational environment, layoffs are quite common when the economic climate of the company declines (Hoerr and Zellner 1990) because labor is seen as a dispensable commodity. Second, small group activity on the shop floor in Japanese factory aims not just at the satisfactory execution of a given task, but emphasizes improving all aspects of the company. This is because job descriptions and job classification systems in Japan are not narrowly defined, and tasks are shared by many workers (Watanabe 1991). Third, generally speaking, the loyalty and commitment to the corporation among American employees are far less than those of Japanese employees (e.g., Blau and Boal 1987; Cole 1979; Lincoln 1989; Shimada 1984; W.E. Upjohn Institute for Employment research 1973). It is reported that dissatisfaction among Japanese employees is much higher than among American employees (Lincoln 1989). In her study of a Japanese automobile factory, Osako found that Japanese employees indicated a high degree of commitment to and identification with the company despite their dissatisfaction with the immediate job and wages (Osako 1977). Fourth, the limitations American workers place on worklife (e.g., prioritizing family and private life before work) also demonstrates a significant contrast in attitudes toward worklife among employees of Japanese companies.

The actual number of working hours in the manufacturing industry in Japan is 44 hours/week in contrast to 38 hours/week in the U.S. (Japan Institute for Social and Economic Affairs 1989). The actual difference in number of working hours is much greater when considering the after-hours activities in Japan. The differences in work hours is just a small indication of the differences of worklife between Japan and the U.S. Workers in Japan usually do not have a vehicle like American labor unions for voicing dissatisfactions and, therefore, they remain loyal to the company because "exit" is extremely difficult at both the company-level and the society-level (Hirschman 1970). As Kenney and Florida pointed out, the phenomenon of "corporate hegemony" where the corporation plays an over-arching role in most aspects of employees' life has been certainly rare in the North American industrial environment.

3. Studies on the Transfer and Organizational Practices of Japanese Transplants

The empirical evidence regarding the transfer of Japanese organizations is mixed. Some experts declare that Japanese practices will not work outside of Japan because they are a product of Japanese culture. Others insist that Japanese companies will modify their practices to the conditions of the local environment. Some even emphasize how successfully Japanese management practices are taking root in the United States.

In his pioneering study, Abegglen basically perceived every aspect of Japanese management practices in cultural terms (Abegglen 1958). This cultural explanation has had a major influence on the thinking of social scientists to this day.

Among early studies on the transferability of Japanese organizational forms and practices, Yoshino mentioned that the successful operation of Japanese management practices is dependent on the unique social and cultural conditions of Japanese society. For him, therefore, this represented a fundamental difficulty in transferring Japanese practices to the outside environment (Yoshino 1967).

Regarding the transferability of Japanese practices, Dore commented that transfer of one particular aspect of management practices would fail because every practice is interrelated to every other one and integrated into a whole (Dore 1973).

Cole was originally pessimistic about the possibility of the transfer. He thought there were social and cultural factors that influenced the way Japanese industrialists solved problems. However, in his study of quality-control circles, he gradually saw some possibility that Japanese QC circles could be implemented in a different environment (Cole 1979).

Ishida points out the different patterns of transfer. He argued that part of the practices which "benefit" employees such as the elaborated benefits structure, job security, and participatory management practices seem to be transferred more easily. On the other hand, some of the practices, like the long-term commitment and loyalty to one company, and group-oriented practices, cannot be easily transferred and require significant adaptation (Ishida 1981). However, as Murakami and Rohlen discuss later, job security and the long-term commitment and loyalty to the company are, in reality, two sides of the same coin and difficult to separate (Murakami and Rohlen 1992).

Bartlett and Yoshihara mention the social and cultural constraints of the Japanese organizational process that cannot be transferred to the outside operation. They point out that the discussion-intensive, group-oriented process, the people-dependent, communication intensive management process, the limited strategic role of subsidiaries, and culturally constrained management mentality (e.g., ethnocentric bias) should present serious obstacles when transferred to a foreign environment (Bartlett and Yoshihara 1988). Gibney also mentioned that a heavy emphasis on cooperation and harmony is not likely to be easily transferred to the multiracial and multicultural American society (Gibney 1988).

On the other hand, many contend that some of the unique characteristics of Japanese management practices, such as the team-based work processes and participatory management practices in general, are successfully transferred and are taking root in the North

American environment. There is now a sizable literature that emphasize successful aspects of Japanese transplants.

Johnson and Ouchi (1974) observed that some of the important aspects of Japanese practices have been transferred to the United States, such as (1) emphasizing flow of information and initiative from the bottom up; (2) making top management the facilitator of decision making rather than the issuer of edicts; (3) using middle management as the impetus for, and shaper of, solutions to problems; (4) stressing consensus as the way to make decisions; (5) paying close attention to the personal well-being of employees (Johnson and Ouchi 1974).

Hatvany and Pucik (1980) show that Japanese-owned firms in the U.S. are, on the whole, achieving higher productivity and employee satisfaction than their American counterparts and that much of this success is directly attributed to the use of a variety of Japanese management techniques. In particular, they find a secure employment policy, a unique company philosophy that emphasizes human resources, policies transcending immediate profit, open communication between management and workers, work groups, and company sponsorship of organized activities have all contributed to such success.

Starr and Bloom (1985) examine the extent to which Japanese management techniques are in use among Japanese-owned firms in the U.S. Although traditional elements of the Japanese management practices, such as lifetime employment, consensus decision-making, and training programs are not generally found, many of what can loosely be regarded as Japanese management techniques are in practice. They find, for example, long-term planning, an emphasis on teamwork, information-sharing between management and workers through various meetings such as QC circles and suggestion systems that offer prizes and bonuses. They conclude that Japanese-owned firms in the U.S. place great value on their human resources.

Starr and Hall (1987) also find that while Japanese firms display an external orientation in the U.S. market (e.g., increasing reliance on American vendors) which allows them to operate and grow much like an American firm, they still appear to maintain a more traditional Japanese environment internal to the organization. This environment includes participatory management techniques such as QC circles and suggestion systems and statistical quality control. They conclude that Japanese-owned firms in the U.S. have begun to act very differently from both their counterparts in Japan and the U.S.

Ito Kinko (1987), in her study of Japanese transplants in the U.S., also researched the process of adaptation of Japanese business organizations to the American industrial environment. She concluded that Japanese transplants were successful in adapting to this environment. She seems to have reached this conclusion mainly because the issue of power relations was a peripheral concern in her study. Her research provided, however, additional insight because she was one of the few native Japanese to undertake the study of Japanese transplants in the U.S. Her conclusions, lacking the reference of these power control issues were quite opposite from my own. Her conclusions were based upon the more personal and individual factors such as job satisfaction, cooperativeness, and worker loyalty.

Wakabayashi and Graen report all transplants that they studied emphasize the following functional goals through a variety of managerial practices (Wakabayashi and Graen 1991: 163-168):

(1) Training and development: They found training and education programs similar to firms in Japan, such as on-the-job training, job rotation, off-the-job training in the company's *"kenshu"* (training) house. They also found that average training hours per employee is longer in transplants than in their home plants in Japan.

(2) Welfare programs: They found extensive benefit programs including a variety of medical and fringe benefits, as well as attendance gifts, awards, and a family festival.

(3) Human relations: They found activities to support a friendly atmosphere among employees, such as sports tournaments, club and hobby activities, company picnics, parties and ceremonial meetings, gift giving and birthday cards.

(4) Organizational communication: They found an extensive intra-organizational communication network, such as a morning team meeting on the shop floor, a weekly team leaders' meeting, a weekly middle managers' meeting, and a monthly senior managers' meeting. In addition, they found Japanese managers volunteering to wander around the shop to talk to both associates and team leaders. Managers at one company are required to spend three days a year working with associates at the shop floor on the company's "plant familiarization days"

(Ibid.: 164).

(5) Equal treatment: They found in all of the transplants that equal treatment of employees was practiced. This involved an equal access to space in parking lots, dining halls, rest rooms, and spaces in open-plan offices. It also involved the use of uniforms, calling everyone an associate, setting the same pay day, and providing equal opportunities to participate in the company's social events.

(6) Employee participation: They found that QC activities are not common. Only one company used QC's as a means of morale enhancement. They also found that these activities have different functions from those in Japan where they are more tuned into cost reductions and improvements in actual production processes.

(7) Organizational commitment: All transplants they visited had a no layoff policy. The policy was clearly announced. The authors see the no layoff policy of the U.S. transplants a "functional equivalent" of the lifetime employment practice in their home plants in Japan. In this policy they observed the company's effort to strengthen long-term employee-employer linkages. They also note, however, that layoffs could happen in exceptionally hard economic downturns.

Many social scientists also found significant differences between Japanese firms in the United States and their American-owned counterparts. Case studies of the NUMMI plant in Fremont, California, offered good examples of the successful transfer of the Japanese organizational forms and practices to the United States (Gelsanliter 1990; Rehder 1988). Comparing NUMMI with GM-Van Nuys plant, Brown and Reich showed that even the labor-management relations in Japan are successfully transferred (Brown and Reich 1989).

A study carried out by the MIT International Motor Vehicle Program offered a unique characterization of the organizational forms and practices of Japanese firms, which is now popularly called the "lean production" system (Womack, Jones and Roots 1990). The concept of lean production basically refers to the efficiency of Japanese organizations of work and production in automobile industries. The defining characteristics include efficient use of resources, low inventories, just-in-time production in the factory, a rapid product development cycle, and efficient staffing. Compared with the traditional method of craft production and mass production, the system extensively employs teams of multi-skilled workers at all levels of organization and uses highly flexible and automated machines to produce volumes of products in enormous variety within a short time period (Ibid. 1990). Lean production, therefore, involves frequent job rotations and sharing of responsibilities, which results in a so-called "flatter" organizational hierarchy. The authors see that the method of manufacturing in automobile industries in the United States and Europe are converging toward the lean production model. They further see that lean production is transforming every aspect of worklife, such as professional career patterns, interpersonal relations among employees, and traditional labor-management relations as lean production diffuses into other industries and spreads globally.

A group of social scientists in Japan conducted a study on Japanese transplants in the consumer electronics, semiconductor, and automobile industries in the United States. Their findings were that automotive transplants have been the most successful in transferring Japanese organizational forms and practices, while consumer electronics transplants showed a tendency to conform to the traditional American environment, and semiconductor transplants fall into middle positions (University of Tokyo, Institute of Social Science 1990).

Milkman, in her study on Japanese-owned factories in California, also found that many Japanese-owned firms (especially outside of the automobile industry) do not rely on Japanese practices, such as teamwork, quality circles, or flexible job classification systems. Instead, they tend to rely on more traditionally American modes of management, such as large numbers of job classifications (Milkman 1991). Except highly complex and capital-intensive operations such as auto assembly, most of the Japanese-owned factories in the U.S. are branch plants of large home plants, and engage in relatively simple assembly operations. Due to the size and the kinds of operation in a factory, "the training and other costs of implementing the Japanese model seem to be foregone, and American-style work organization and management practices prevail instead" (Milkman 1991: 6). Regarding labor-management relations, she mentioned that Japanese-owned firms resist unionization efforts just like many other American-owned firms, especially in electronics industries. The distinctiveness of labor-management relations among Japanese-owned firms in the U.S. is, therefore, open to question (Milkman 1991: 8).

It is important to note here that some social scientists have criticized the lean production model. Though he agreed with the accuracy of surface-level description of the model and its efficiencies, Rehder pointed out that analyses of the lean production model neglected its negative consequences to the social and worklife of employees, such as high stress levels during the work day and the extensive use of group pressure (Rehder 1991), and posits the following question: "If the Japanese lean system so highly values and develops its human resources, why is it also associated with overstressing its employees and [groups over] their individual . . . freedoms?"(Rehder 1992) Based on the study at the Mazda automotive assembly plant in Flat Rock, Michigan, Bobson also examined the lean production model in terms of power distribution and conflict resolution in both union and non-union environments. Bobson pointed out the lean production model's potential for "unilateral management control"(Bobson 1993).

Kenney and Florida also see the lean production model as providing a static, ahistorical view of the Japanese system (Kenney and Florida 1993). For them the model fails to specify the underlying forces and relations of production that underpin the organizations of work and production in Japan, such as the historical trajectory, the balance of class forces, and the structural, organizational, and institutional patterns (Kenney and Florida 1993: 25). Instead, the authors offer an insightful view on the organization of work and production of Japanese firms. In this monumental study, they suggest that Japanese organizational forms and practices constitute a new model of "innovation-mediated production" toward which companies all over the world are converging. As I suggested briefly before, the authors see this new mode of production as originating in post-war Japan, and representing a basic alternative mode of production to the traditional mass production system. In their view, the innovation-mediated production system involves such characteristics as a transition from physical skill and manual labor to intellectual capabilities or mental labor, the increasing importance of social or collective intelligence as opposed to individual knowledge and skill, an acceleration of the pace of technological innovation, the increasing importance of continuous process improvement on the factory floor and constant revolutions in production, and the blurring of the lines between the R&D lab and the factory (Kenney and Florida 1993: 14). Furthermore, the authors see the model as not culturally bound to Japan, but as crystallized through historical conditions, class struggles, structures unique to the political economy of Japan, and, hence, transferable to foreign environments.

Based on this conceptualization of innovation-mediated production, the authors extensively examine the reality of the transfer of Japanese organizational practices in the Japanese automotive transplants, automotive parts, steel, and rubber transplants, as well as transplants of consumer and high-technology electronics. Their findings basically confirm the above mentioned general trend in the transfer of Japanese organizational forms and practices to the United States. In automotive assembly transplants, the authors found extensive use of work teams, job rotation, long-term employment guarantees, Kaizen (continuous improvement), quality-control circles, and a high rate of suggestions from the shop floor level. They see the successful transfer of Japanese production organization to the United States. In transplants of automotive parts suppliers, the authors also found the successful implementation of a Japanese-style just-in-time subcontracting system. In most of the joint-venture companies in steel industries, the authors observe the attempt to implement aspects of Japanese production organization, such as reduced numbers of job classifications and work teams of the traditional Taylor-Fordist factories. They found that such efforts of restructuring the organization come from both top managers and union officials, while meeting considerable opposition from both middle-level managers and shop floor senior workers who see the ongoing set of organizational practices as an integral part of their own existence (Kenney and Florida 1993: 188). The authors acknowledge, however, that the joint-venture companies in the steel industries are tending to be taken over by Japanese capital as the Japanese automotive assembly transplants become more successful and dominant. These findings basically support their view that Japanese corporations are re-creating a spatially concentrated automobile-steel-rubber production complex in the United States (Kenney and Florida 1993: 215-217).

On the other hand, in the transplants of consumer and high-technology electronics, the authors did not find as many significant characteristics of Japanese organizational forms and practices as in the transplants of heavy industries and automotive assembly. They saw a tendency in the electronics transplants to have far more job classifications, to use fewer work teams and job rotation, to have more rigid reporting hierarchies, and to reproduce the traditional distinctions between blue-and white-collar workers (Kenney and Florida 1993: 258). Similar to Milkman, they concluded that the electronics transplants exhibit greater evidence of "fitting in" to the American environment.

There is other evidence that reflects the Japanese emphasis at least on management ideals, if not on the actual transfer of Japanese practices to the United States. Compared to the typical hiring processes among American-owned firms which consist mainly of the evaluation of an applicant's job history, the process of hiring in Japanese-owned firms is usually more far reaching. It involves written tests for literacy and technical skills, as well as long-lasting, probing interviews. For instance, it is reported that American applicants for the lowest-paying jobs on the shop floor went through at least 14 hours of testing at the Toyota plant in Georgetown Kentucky (The Wall Street Journal 1987). The use of a mock assembly line and simulation of the workplace have also been reported (The Wall Street Journal 1987). This information shows that Japanese-owned firms in the United States are careful about selecting local American workers, indicating the existence of particular Japanese expectations toward American workers, such as cooperation skills in the team environment, at least on the level of the management ideals.

The non-unionized Japanese transplants, like many other American-owned firms, emphasize their opposition to labor unions. In 1989 workers at the Nissan plant in Smyrna, Tennessee voted against United Auto Workers' representation (The Wall Street Journal 1989; Gelsanliter 1990). In 1991 unions have been defeated in decertification votes at Sony plants in Illinois and Hawaii (The Wall Street Journal 1991). Starr and Hall report a decrease in the number of union-represented employees among Japanese-owned firms (union employees averaged 27 percent of all employees they studied in 1985, down 4 percent from 31 percent in 1982; 1987:17). Moreover, Misawa (1987) notes that Japanese firms are adopting a number of management strategies in an attempt to forestall labor unions. These include: (1) providing better working conditions than the local norm, (2) locating in states where the extent of unionization is low, and (3) introducing suggestion systems and workers' participation in decision-making. As Milkman (1991) pointed out, however, whether this anti-unionism constitutes distinctive elements of Japanese organizational form or not is, indeed, questionable. Nearly all of the transplants' parent companies in Japan are unionized. Kenney and Florida also point to the fact that a fairly large number of Japanese steel, rubber and tire, and automobile assembly transplants have effectively implemented Japanese practices to a unionized environment in the U.S., while electronics transplants have experienced great difficulty working with American unions and are resisting unionization effort (Kenney and Florida 1993: 285). In addition, Trevor shows that Japanese firms are implementing Japanese practices in their unionized transplants in England where unions are far more powerful than in the United States (Trevor 1988). Kenney and Florida point out that Japanese transplants are not opposed to unions per se, but are opposed to "forms of alternative worker identification, including traditional American unions, which create a separate sphere of identity for workers and disrupt the alignment between worker and company" (Kenney and Florida 1993: 285). There is a study that points to the functional similarities of the unions' participation between the West and Japan (Kruvilla, Gallagher, Fiorito and Wakabayashi 1990). The real picture of the various aspects of industrial relations in Japanese transplants is thus fairly complex. It seems at least to be true that the presence of adversarial labor unions posits a serious challenge for Japanese transplants in the United States.

The studies of Japanese transplants also point out many problems that have surfaced in the workplace. Generally speaking, most of the problems that are identified at the workplace are based on social and cultural differences between Japan and the United States. Yoshino (1976) reported that Japanese nationals always occupy key positions in U.S. subsidiaries and that even Japanese-American employees recruited in the U.S. become more functionaries and interpreters, regardless of seniority and experience. Johnson elucidates several problem areas. He found that Americans were frustrated by either a fast or slow process of localization of personnel in the company, that is, hiring Americans for important positions. Regarding the relations between the subsidiary and its parent company in Japan, he found a tendency toward parochialism at the home office made effective communication with subsidiaries more difficult. He also found difficulties in integrating the American and Japanese staff into coherent teams. In addition, when recruiting American employees, he found Japanese managers' tendency to prefer senior American managers in their forties or fifties with substantial professional experience. According to Johnson, this creates problems because those senior American managers usually do not have sufficient interpersonal skills that are often taken for granted in the workplace in Japan (Johnson, R. 1977). Tsurumi (1978) mentioned the Japanese "grapevine" connections among Japanese personnel which tend to exclude American employees. Starr and Hall (1987) also noted that the exclusive network among the Japanese employees may be increasingly uncomfortable for American employees who desire opportunities to break into the "family circle" of the Japanese employees.

A report on Mazda's Michigan plant also provides information on various problems, including high rates of injury on the shop floor, discontent among workers, and labor-management conflict (Fucini and Fucini 1990). Joseph and Suzy Fucini describe in detail the initially high expectations and gradual disappointment of American employees over matters such as safety and health, discrimination, work stress, and loss of autonomy. This work represents a case study on the adaptability of Japanese practices to the highly-unionized, urban environment. Sullivan also mentions that "highly authoritarian but benevolent" Japanese practices are successfully transferred to the transplants in "the Southern locales where workers find benevolent dictatorship congenial," but not to the transplants in urban areas (Sullivan 1992). Brannen, though she acknowledges that success or failure to implement Japanese practices in the United States can not be explained simply by "cultural" differences between the two countries, emphasizes that cultural factors, such as differences between American and Japanese attitudes toward work, are a critical factor in implementing new practices in Japanese transplants in the United States (Brannen 1991). Similarly, Kleinberg, an anthropologist, shows some cognitive differences between Japanese and American employees in important areas, such as "concept of the job," which resulted in "the prominent subcultural groupings of American and Japanese" at the workplace

(Kleinberg 1994). She also points out the tendency among Japanese employees to share strategic information almost exclusively, and that American employees get lost and frustrated in a binational company which is going through a significant restructuring (Kleinberg 1994). In an exploratory study based on a structured interview technique among five Japanese companies in the United States, Dillon also suggests that cultural differences are the greatest barrier in integrating Japanese and American work forces at the workplace (Dillon 1992).

In relation to the frustration among American employees at the workplace, some studies also referred to the discrimination against American employees. Cole and Deskins reported that three Japanese-owned firms, Mazda, Honda and Nissan, and fifty-one Japanese auto parts manufacturers in the U.S. have hired significantly fewer black workers than eight new GM plants (Cole and Deskins 1988). A growing number of sexual harassment and discrimination cases are appearing among Japanese-owned firms in America, which employ an estimated 100,000 American women (Rehder 1989; Yates 1992). Women in managerial positions account for only two percent of the total workforce among Japanese-owned firms (Starr and Hall 1987). Rehder (1989) also reports that Honda of America had to pay 6 million dollars to 377 female and black employees as a result of past discrimination in hiring and promotion. Regarding the Japanese automobile assembly, steel, and rubber and tire transplants complex, Kenney and Florida comment that rural areas in the Midwest also allow Japanese transplants to avoid hiring large numbers of African-Americans, or members of other racial and ethnic minority groups (Kenney and Florida 1993: 282). However, I should note here that there is a significant variation in minority hiring by company (Kenney and Florida 1993), and that all of the studies focus on the issue of discrimination only in Japanese transplants instead of comparing hiring practices with those of American-owned or other foreign-owned companies.

Another recent study conducted by a group of Japanese and American researchers (Abo, ed. 1994) explores the processes of transfer of the Japanese management and production systems to the United States. Compared to previous studies on the lean production model, the authors acknowledge the significance of national contexts in influencing the processes of production innovation, and thus argue that the attempt to transfer the core elements of the Japanese production systems, such as work organization, production control, supplier networks, and procurement to the U.S. context would face a tension with the environment set by national-specific conditions, resulting in a system that differs from the original system in Japan. Therefore, the authors further argue that because of the differences of the industrial environment between the U.S. and Japan, the management and production systems in the transplants result in a hybrid form or even, in some cases, the adoption of American style practices. In addition, the authors find that the adoption of American style practices is more prevalent among the consumer electronics related transplants than among the automobile related transplants in the United States.

All in all, the empirical data presented above does not allow any definitive conclusions about the reality of the organizational forms and practices of Japanese transplants in the United States. Despite all the positive reports about how successfully Japanese practices are taking root in the U.S., it is also crucial to recognize many other recent studies that report emerging social and cultural problems in the workplace.

Finally, I should note here that studies on power relations in Japanese transplants in the United States are very few. Although some of the recent materials in the popular press are beginning to look at the issue of the organizational culture and its effect on management practices and organizational change, very few works have seriously dealt with the issue of power and organizational culture. Some recent reports on Japanese transplants deal with aspects of power relations at the workplace between Japanese and American employees. As I mentioned, Joseph and Suzy Fucini (1990) described how American employees are trying to negotiate power relations with Japanese management at Mazda's Michigan plant mainly through the check-and-balance processes between the union and Mazda management, but are failing to create a "third-culture plant." Gelsanliter (1990) also deals with the power relations in terms of union-management relations; his main focus is to show how Japanese automotive manufacturers are successfully transplanting the Japanese practices to their new facilities in rural areas in the Midwest. Kenney and Florida (1993) deal with power relations between Japanese and American employees in terms of corporate control on the theoretical level. They examine corporate control in Japanese transplants in terms of how Japanese management is trying to socialize American workers, how the company is trying to instill a sense of the corporate family and a sense of loyalty and dedication to the company, and how they are trying to transform the American union into a cooperative "partner." They also look at workplace control in terms of absence and attendance policies, peer discipline, and the implication of hiring temporary workers. They finally refer to community control in terms of how transplants are trying to instill their "corporate hegemony" in American civil society in the long term. They did not distinguish between corporate and management control, and used the term, corporate control, to examine forms of control at the workplace level at the transplants. In this sense, their use of this term rather implied management control in my study.

Although not directly related to the study of transplants, Kondo's study of the workplace at a small business in Japan is worth mentioning. In this study, Kondo explores the process whereby members of a small family-owned business in Japan construct (or craft) selves and gendered identities in the web of power, hierarchy, and discipline. She tries to present the processes of "crafting selves" in the domain of work with multiple, shifting voices, and in doing so, she explores what "company" or "family" means to workers, and what it means to work in a small factory in Tokyo in the late seventies and early eighties (Kondo 1990).

Kondo's work has a significance, and actually does have much relevance to this work. My study begins by examining the transferability of the eight elements of what is generally perceived as the "organizational practices of Japanese companies" in Japan to the industrial environment in the U.S. The main purpose of these analyses, however, is to explore the "processes" of everyday practices at the transplants whereby Japanese and Americans, both managers and workers, interact in the web of power relations in their attempt to form a hybrid corporate culture. In presenting these processes, I tried to elicit those shifting, multiple voices of the many managers and workers I interviewed across the country. Kondo's work offers this study an insightful model and a point of view regarding the ethnographic presentation that often points to many and diverse subtleties and contextualities of the various situations and relationships I examined.

In the following chapter I will examine the process of data collection in order to address issues relating to anthropologists' access to professional work organizations. In addressing these issues, I will explore how my social and cultural status—a Japanese graduate student in the United States—influenced the process of fieldwork in both Japanese-owned and American-owned firms.

CHAPTER 2

Fieldwork in the Organizational Context

I gathered the information for this study from a case study of a Japanese-owned company in the Southwest, from July through October of 1992, and from my research trip to the Midwest and California during the Summer of 1993. In addition to one case study company, I studied nine (9) Japanese-owned and four (4) non-Japanese companies. The primary source of data is a series of semi-formal interviews with managers and workers. Most of the interviews were tape-recorded and later transcribed. I conducted 72 interviews and collected about 150 hours of taped interviews. In addition, I did participant observation whenever possible. My fieldnotes on what I observed and on activities that I shared with employees, as well as my own ideas and reflections comprise an important part of the primary data. A secondary source of data involves formal written documents of the various companies regarding management policies and procedures, and informal documents such as a company's employee newsletter. I also relied on government documents, articles in the press, and the secondary literature on the subject during the fieldwork.

In this chapter, I will address the issue of access to professional work organizations in the fieldwork process of anthropology. One of the crucial characteristics of the fieldwork in my study was the difficulty for conducting long-term participant observation at the workplace, one of the salient characteristics of anthropological fieldwork. This aspect of fieldwork, the access issue, has not been discussed extensively among the previous literature on work organizations. Only a few anthropologists in the area of organizational study recently started addressing the importance of this issue. Baba called for more attention to this issue as anthropologists became more involved in researches in the private sector and in policy-making processes (Baba 1994). Coleman also addressed the need of more methodological attention to the issue of access in anthropology (Coleman 1996). In addition, when discussing this issue, it is particularly important to examine how social and cultural factors, such as a researcher's social status and cultural background, influence the processes of data gathering in the organizational context. In the following section, I will discuss how my social status as a graduate student and my Japanese cultural background influenced my fieldwork process. First, I will look at the process in which I sought access to Japanese transplants and American firms. Second, I will look at the actual process of data collection inside these companies.

BETWEEN TWO CULTURES

As a foreign student I had had already spent at least eight years in graduate school in a university in North America when I started my fieldwork in the summer of 1992. Eight years of living in the U.S., and studying anthropology in the western educational system had already greatly influenced my perceptions of myself and others and my world view in general. I will not provide a detailed examination of how American and Japanese "cultures" had influenced me and my world view during those eight years because this is not the main purpose of this study. However, cross-cultural experience, over the course of time, especially one that bridges Western and non-Western cultures, significantly modifies our perceptions of the "self" on the individual or personal level. There are many ways of describing these social and cultural influences that my experience of living in the U.S. had given me. Here I want to note that my unusual and atypical lifecourse itself was also an alienating factor from associating myself closely with Japanese business people.

One of the crucial elements that significantly affected my fieldwork process was that I had spent such a long time in the U.S. by then, and did not belong to any institution or corporation in Japan. At the case study company, Suntech [1], this was a constant underlying factor when I was interacting with Japanese employees. Three Japanese engineers, whom I mention in chapter three, were more or less close to my age. Moreover, one of them was a graduate from the same school in Japan that I had graduated from. He (Masao) and I happened to graduate from the same school in Tokyo in the same year. All these engineers were married, and two of them had brought their wives with them to the U.S. All of them played golf on weekends. On the other hand, I had been single, and had been in graduate school during all the years that they had been experiencing corporate life in Japan and were becoming an integrated part of the corporation. When I met Masao's wife at the company's picnic she told me, "Sumi-san, you should start thinking about getting married and settling down. It is not good that you stay single too long. In case of marriage, you'd better think about 'naijo no kou.'" "*Naijo no kou*" in Japanese refers to the benefits that man can get from a wife who can skillfully handle her domestic chores and, at the same time, is able to support her husband's success in his social world. When she told me this, she meant specifically that I should marry a traditional Japanese woman from the appropriate social class, who would be responsible for all family matters and would help me to succeed in my career. As a Japanese I was, of course, aware of the importance of that concept. At the same time, I was also well aware how my own life had diverged from the traditional Japanese mainstream lifestyle.

The interview with Masao at Suntech also gave me an opportunity to see in retrospect the trajectory of my life in the U.S., and showed me how far I had departed from my own social and cultural tradition. I wrote as follows in my fieldnote after the interview.

> It was a very strange experience to interview with [Masao] today. As usual I used Bill's room to conduct my interview. I was waiting for him in the room. When he came in he slightly bows and says, "Ah, domo domo."[3] I was kind of surprised to see that the way he does this comes so naturally. Already he somewhat reminds me of my father. [Masao] and I sat across Bill's work desk face to face. He was wearing a nice gray business suit. Although not as formal as his, I was also wearing a dark business suit. Both of us were wearing a tie on white shirts. Both of us wear glasses. Yet, we feel so far away from one another. I sensed a kind of defense in him. I sensed something that is quite familiar. Some sort of competition among the peers in Japan. The interview with him was not as great as I was

expecting. Most of his responses were quite formal and very proper. Most answers from him were similar to what I get from reading books. Dumb! Nothing special or intriguing in his responses. He really did not reveal himself. This is so familiar to me. Businessmen try not to reveal themselves easily. This is almost opposite from what I want to get in my life. He referred to 'security' many times. He says he doesn't have to worry about the tenure of his employment at Suntech. He doesn't think he will be out of his job unless he makes seriously bad mistakes in the future. This is not likely to happen, he says. He told me that he could not even imagine what my life in America is like. I could imagine what his corporate life is like in Japan. I tried to explain what my life is like here as much as possible, but I am not sure how well he understood. He looked like he was looking at an empty hall when listening to me. I cannot believe that he and I were once at the same school in Tokyo ten years ago. I am stunned to realize that there is no way for me to go back there at that point. Gosh! Where am I going?

Another alienating element was the assertion of my self in a social (group) setting. It is usually true for most Japanese, myself included, that we have been raised learning the importance (or appropriateness) of conforming to dominant variables in a social setting, such as conversational topics, modes of dress, and deferring to elders and superiors. In this sense, the concept of *"wa"* (harmony) still exists as a respected social norm today even though the real picture can vary significantly depending upon the various cohorts participating in everyday life in Japan. In a corporate setting, these dominant variables tend to be set by *"sempai"* (the seniors and the experienced) or *"jyousi"* (the bosses). In Japan, asserting one's self is not really considered positive in social occasions. People tend to see the person who is self assertive as selfish, egotistic, and a troublemaker. On the other hand, my eight years of experience in American graduate school had taught me the importance of asserting myself as clearly as possible. When I did not assert myself enough in social occasions in the U.S., I was usually left out of conversations, and ended up feeling that my existence was not even recognized in the situation. During my fieldwork, I was trying to be assertive with American employees, while I was less assertive with Japanese managers and engineers. Except for a very few senior level managers who had years of experience of dealing with Americans, most of Japanese employees interacted with me in a traditional Japanese manner.

Anthropologists are trained to be cultural brokers when they are in the field. For me, going back and forth between Japanese and American cultures had been the skill that I needed to develop in my everyday life in this country, at least on the level of individual interaction. During my fieldwork, it was relatively easier for me to go back and forth between the two cultures in the formal situations where every participant's role and expectation were clearly defined. For instance, I happened to act as a an interpreter and a liaison at a managers' meeting that was attended by both American managers and Japanese engineers. In this kind of formal situation, I did not have much difficulty in switching my degree of assertiveness when I was talking with American managers and the Japanese about the business matters. On the other hand, I experienced more difficulties in the informal situation, such as lunch time, a casual chat in a cafeteria, or at the company picnic. I probably have to admit, on the personal level, that my American experience had overshadowed my interaction style with others. When I was informally interacting with the Japanese employees during lunch time, and when I was talking about myself and what I was doing in this study, I tended to be more self assertive, and more talkative even in Japanese. It was during this kind of situation when one Japanese informant told me, "Sumi-san, you sound like you're speaking English even when you speak Japanese." Fortunately enough, this "distance" between them and me did not impede my fieldwork processes. They must have, however, perceived me as a somewhat strange Japanese. At the case study company, Suntech, I was lucky enough to have Mr. Shibata, the plant manager, who lived in the U.S. for a log time and was experienced in dealing with Americans and was, therefore, tolerant enough to accept me as I was.

In this context I have to note that the fact that I am Japanese worked for me and against me. Generally speaking, it worked for me in Japanese transplants, and worked against me in most of the American-owned companies. In Japanese transplants the familiarity of American employees with some of the Japanese culture helped me to start off the fieldwork. Because of the presence of Japanese employees, many Americans in Japanese transplants have had at least some cross-cultural encounters with the Japanese. Most American employees in Japanese transplants have more or less been socialized into each company's unique corporate culture which involves some elements of Japanese culture. For example, many American employees in transplants were used to listening to English with a Japanese accent. Of course, there were some American workers in any Japanese transplant companies who do not need to interact with the Japanese employees and, therefore, were not familiar with Japanese accented English. On the other hand, most of American employees above the supervisor level were more or less able to deal with English spoken with a foreign accent, because they needed to interact with the Japanese employees in their everyday work. This was particularly true in my case study company, Suntech, in New Mexico.

Because the size of the company was very small, most of American employees interacted with some of the Japanese managers and engineers on daily basis. At Suntech many American employees seemed to have learned some greeting phrases in Japanese through interacting with the Japanese managers and engineers. When I was waiting for an appointment at the lobby, or when I came across some Americans in the hallway, some of them were curious, wanting to try their Japanese with me, and said in Japanese "*konnichiwa*" (Good afternoon), "*yokoso*" (welcome), or "*ogenkidesuka?*" (How are you doing?). Although these were small events in everyday experience of my fieldwork, they made a big difference at the initial stage of my fieldwork, at least when I was being introduced to American employees. In contrast, when I was in American-owned companies, I had to spend more time and exert greater effort to explain who I was and what I was doing because most American employees (or at least American employees with whom I interviewed) were not familiar with my cultural background.[2]

In addition, the fact that I am a native Japanese made a significant difference in the kinds of information I obtained in my interviews with Japanese managers when we talked in Japanese. Their responses were strikingly different when we spoke English. It is true that for most Japanese, no matter how long they have been living in this culture and speaking English, they tend to feel more comfortable when speaking Japanese. When speaking Japanese they were much more able to elaborate events and to carry on more extensive conversation. This was especially the case for most Japanese managers who came to this country only a few years ago.

In general, two specific Japanese speakers at Suntech switched languages from Japanese to English when an American employee approached. This happened frequently in my interviews. It was often quite surprising to recognize how they changed and how I changed. There is unique and often very subtle distinction between *"uti"* (inside) and *"soto"* (outside) in cultural categories in Japan. When I speak Japanese with Japanese managers, I encountered little difficulty in getting into the *"uti"* area, where a lot of *"honne"* (in-depth feeling or information) is revealed. This was especially true in the interviews with Japanese upper-level managers. They tend to be quite open and honest in Japanese if they felt comfortable with the person with whom they are talking. Even interviews with American managers in Japanese transplants were mostly very successful. Both American and Japanese employees in Japanese transplants were less afraid of me than many employees in American-owned companies. All in all, most managers of Japanese-owned companies were very cooperative with me in my study.

In explaining why this was the case in most Japanese transplants, I want to note the relations of power as the most significant factor. In this study, the relations of power specifically refer to the various forms of corporate and management control in the Japanese transplants. Although most of the Japanese transplants in this study were "American" companies in legal terms, they were wholly Japanese-owned subsidiaries of parent companies in Japan. In this sense, the main corporate decision making power belongs to the Japanese. At Suntech, Mr. Shibata, a top plant manager, was a Japanese, though he was under the employment system of the "American" company, Suntech America. Among the Japanese transplants in this study, there were always Japanese presidents as well as Japanese in the positions of upper level managers. In these situations I found my interviews with American employees were very successful. This clearly indicated to me the differentiation of power in the Japanese transplants, where American employees feel that it is better to cooperate with a request from their Japanese bosses for their own sake. In Japanese transplants, the request by the Japanese managers to cooperate with my study was never forced upon American employees. American employees always could say no to their bosses. Indeed some of them whom I did not meet in my fieldwork might have said no. However, it is quite reasonable to interpret that American employees had agreed to cooperate with me because this would make a positive impression upon their Japanese bosses in their everyday worklife.

As I mentioned, there is certainly a cultural factor operating upon the cooperation of American employees who had been pre-socialized into some aspects of Japanese culture before my arrival at the company. At the same time, this cooperation from American employees in the Japanese transplants certainly indicates the existence of corporate or management control that influences the behavior of employees in any organization.

Finally, I have to note two significant exceptions to the American employees' cooperation in the Japanese transplants. First of all, I should note one American employee in the corporate headquarters of a Japanese automobile manufacturer in California, totally revoked the interview after the fact. The interview with her turned out to be a very difficult one. During my previous fieldwork, communications with American informants in the Japanese transplants were basically fairly smooth. She was actually the first American informant with whom I had severe difficulties in communicating. By the time I interviewed her, she had been working for the company for several years under her Japanese boss. Although the interview with her was extremely difficult, I thought I was getting very interesting information because she was primarily revealing her negative image of the Japanese. When she pointed to the fact that the Japanese system of production requires only mediocre workers, I was, in fact, totally agreeing with what she was talking about. As I describe in the case study chapter, management control in the Japanese production system basically demands workers to be regular, steady, and standardized, instead of becoming a super star worker. For her, this nature of management control made her think that the system requires only mediocrity. Although she pointed to quite an intriguing point about management control in the Japanese factories, she revoked this interview the next day without giving me any substantial explanation. She was obviously afraid that her negative comments about Japanese organizations might get back to the company, thereby affecting her career, directly or indirectly.

I also had another Japanese company in California that canceled our appointment for an interview. Before my research trip to California I had called the company and talked with a Japanese manager who consented to cooperate with me and my interview plans. On the day of the appointment he did not show up. I was making all the appointments for the interviews through the US-Japan Center at the University of New Mexico at that time. I called the Center that day only to find out that he had faxed a cancellation letter to the center on the same day of the appointment. In the previous conversation with him on the phone, he had told me that meeting with me might be helpful because his company was considering relocation to New Mexico. This company, however, never relocated to New Mexico.

Although I had two cases where I had difficulties in data collection, I did not meet further obstacles to gathering information in most of the Japanese transplants, including the case study company, Suntech. In contrast, the fact that I am Japanese worked against my research in many of the American companies I approached. First of all, getting in the door of American companies was extremely difficult for me, compared to my experience with Japanese-owned companies. Managers were equally busy in any other company, but in general were less interested in, and more protective about what I was proposing for my research. A few managers were interested in my study, and I was only able to visit the companies where these kind of managers existed. In fact, especially in the Midwestern area, I perceived strongly a sense of competition between American and Japanese automotive-related industries. I was, of course, expecting this might be the case.

It was relatively easier to gain access to large American-owned companies than small or medium/medium-large companies. I tried to gain access to some smaller American auto suppliers in the Midwest, and did not have any success. In larger organizations, it was relatively easier to gain access to managerial people. This was partly because these companies usually have public relations departments and human resources professionals who are used to dealing with outside researchers. My experience at one American-owned company in the Chicago area demonstrates clearly that the national-level competition between the U.S. and Japan had certainly limited the possibility of data collection in the company. At this company I had to sign a company-designed confidentiality agreement. Although I had prepared my own consent forms regarding the confidentiality of the interview, they did not accept them. I was not allowed to tape record any interview. Among all the companies I visited during the summer of 1993, this was the only one that severely restricted my access to information. However, they may have had tight security for good reasons. One informant at the company told me that they had hired some Japanese engineers in the past who told them that they got tired of the corporate life in Japan and wanted to be in a different environment. They left the company in a few years, and the company found out that they had returned to their previous employers in Japan. This company was, therefore, extremely sensitive about revealing any production-related information to outside researchers. The following is a short quote from an employee newsletter of the company.

> As competition in the electronics industry becomes more fierce, corporations as well as governments are spying on their competitors to gain an edge in the marketplace. Often, it is the lack of security awareness that these industrial spies prey upon when stealing information.

The above quote shows how sensitive my research could be, and therefore, how difficult it was for me to collect in-depth information about American companies and about business organizations in general. It was a significant experience in my fieldwork that I had to deal with the wide gaps between Japanese and American perceptions of each other including stereotypes at the workplaces in both the Japanese transplants and the American-owned firms. These wide gaps in the perceptions of Japanese and Americans are often expressed at the workplaces in such a way as "Japanese" versus "American." These wide gaps were especially strong in the automotive-related industries in the Midwest, though this was also an everyday experience in many high-tech, consumer electronics industries in California. Even at the case study company where my fieldwork proceeded relatively smoothly, the wide gaps in the perceptions between "Japanese" and "American" was evident everywhere at the workplace everyday. These gaps in American and Japanese perceptions of one another and about how work tasks should be accomplished often manifested as potential frustrations between Japanese and American employees, if not in overt conflict in everyday worklife. I will be dealing with this matter in more detail in the following chapters on the case study, the Midwest, and California respectively.

Finally, I want to note that the fieldwork process is also related to the development of the theoretical framework for the study. My experience of going back and forth between the wide perceptual gaps of "Japanese" and "American" in business organizations indeed gave me a good opportunity for developing a framework. I mentioned that I started the research without a broad theoretical framework. When I was starting the interviews at the case study company, I was not considering examining the power relations between Japanese and American employees, nor was I thinking about employing a political economy framework. The second phase of the fieldwork taught me, however, the importance of power relations, specifically forms of corporate and management control, in shaping individual behaviors in organizations. In addition, taking account of the power relations at the organizational-level actually meant that I was compelled to account for the political as well as economic factors at the national-level in the study. The second phase of the fieldwork, therefore, has illustrated the importance of closely examining the macro-level factors of political economy in addition to the micro-level cultural analysis at the workplace in the study of binational industrial organizations. The theoretical framework for this study, therefore, actually developed out of the fieldwork process.

PRELIMINARY FIELDWORK

This study originally began in December of 1991, when I conducted preliminary fieldwork in Kentucky. I visited two manufacturing companies—one was a joint-venture automotive parts supplier and the other an automotive assembly plant. At that time, although one Japanese-owned company had informally allowed me to study the company, I did not have an extensive network of contacts in Japanese-owned firms. Moreover, this company was still too small in size (15-20 employees) to conduct fieldwork because the facility had just started its operation and was still engaged in the start-up phase. I had not yet clearly articulated the problem for the study, and I needed to do preliminary fieldwork to build a foundation for the research so that I could frame a concrete research design. Fortunately, my father had at that time some personal connections to Japanese managers at one joint-venture automotive supplier in Kentucky, and through his connections I was able to arrange meetings with two Japanese managers at the company. One manager also referred me to one of the top Japanese managers of an automotive transplant in the same region.

As a student of cultural anthropology I was interested in collecting in-depth, qualitative data on the Japanese-owned companies in the United States, instead of relying on previous data collected from brief surveys. Achieving such data in any environment is generally quite difficult for many researchers, as they are perceived basically as "outsiders." This difficulty is compounded by the fact that people in any business environment tend to be occupied with their own work and have little free time for interviews, and perceive them as an unimportant interruption.

My initial intention in visiting these two firms in Kentucky was to request permission to enter the company as an employee and do participant observation at the workplace for a certain period of time- for example, one year if possible, if not, at least 6 months. At that time I had hoped to conduct "anthropological fieldwork," and naturally thought of working with one particular firm and doing participant observation from inside the company, like the majority of anthropologists do in their fieldwork. When anthropologists select a site, they usually remain for one or two years, and collect information. Neither of these companies were willing to allow me to do this. I conducted extensive and lengthy interviews with the managers at the auto supplier company (5 hours) and explored many issues, such as the differences in work styles between Japanese and American employees.

In contrast, the meeting with a top Japanese manager at an automobile assembly plant turned out to be quite a difficult experience for me. My intention of entering the company to do research for a year was totally out of question. He told me that he received requests to conduct research from many other institutions including the mass media almost every day. The most he had ever done in the past, he said, was to take a few hours for the interviews. His concern was basically time, cost, and safety. The company cannot afford to ignore the loss of work time caused by outside researchers, especially, a researcher like me, who wished to talk to production workers. In terms of cost, he told me that the company would have to pay workers for the hours spent for the interviews, which was totally unrealistic from his point of view. For company safety, I needed to be accompanied by production supervisors because of the high powered equipment on the shop floor. The company obviously could not afford to assign someone to be with me all the time. He said, "Our company can get sued in this country if you get injured in the plant." The conversation below shows the general attitudes of corporations toward anthropological research.

> *Tanaka:* (pseudonym) About a year ago a group of professors from Harvard and MIT asked to do some research in our plant . . . they were professors, you know? All the time we could afford for them was 2-3 hours.
>
> *Sumi* [myself]*:* I see.
>
> *Tanaka:* This tremendously lowers the productivity of the plant.
>
> *Sumi:* . . .
>
> *Tanaka:* As a *"sempai"* [4] I tell you this . . . I think what you are talking about is very unrealistic . . . I can't imagine any company that lets you in if you keep saying this. Honestly, I wonder if you can make it anywhere with this idea.
>
> *Sumi:* I see . . .
>
> *Tanaka:* I guess I know what you want . . . in a nutshell . . . you want to know how do we or I think of Americans deep in the heart . . . is this right?
>
> *Sumi:* Yes, it is.
>
> *Tanaka:* This takes extremely long time, you know . . . two or three years at least. You can't get what you want in a few months . . . and you have a very ambitious plan.
>
> *Sumi:* . . .
>
> *Tanaka:* Have you read the book, *The Chrysanthemum and the Bat*? That book is made of episodes. This must have required a great amount of time and work.
>
> *Sumi:* I see . . .
>
> *Tanaka:* Doing this kind of thing in business world is very disrupting to work. Don't you think so? [Asking another manager who was sitting next to me]
>
> *Other manager:* Well, right. Like this, I have been with him all morning and couldn't do my work.
>
> *Other manager:* [Speaking to me] You have to change your approach.

Facing the reality of the business world, I was totally powerless. This meeting only proved my naiveté about conducting research in a corporate environment. Shortly before my visit to Kentucky, I had made the same request to one automotive assembly transplant in Ohio. The answer from the company was exactly the same. All I could do in this visit was conduct exploratory interviews with two managers and was given a one hour tour of the plant at the supplier company, a one hour meeting with a top manager, and one hour of exploratory interview with a Japanese employee at the auto assembly company. In addition, I could share an after-hour get together with one Japanese manager at the supplier company. All in all, the possibility of conducting participant observation study in a company as an employee was extremely unlikely at that time.

At one point during my research, I had a chance to talk to the chairman of a Japanese company on the phone. After living in the United States for more than 20 years, he was about to go back to Japan. He was very interested in cultural anthropology and told me as follows:

> After fighting through everyday life with Americans for more than 20 years, I've come to think that ultimately things get anthropological, humans work together through confrontation. There is something in it, something that is more than merely Japanese or American. However, the most serious weakness you have is the fact that you are a researcher. There are a lot of things you can't see unless you work with us day after day for 10-20 years. Now I am thinking about writing a book.

The top manager of my case study company stated to me that he was thinking of writing a book as well. In the field of anthropology it sometimes occurs that a researcher is employed by a company. This is often the case with American researchers in American companies. However, Japanese-owned companies in the United States are quite reluctant to hire outside researchers on any level, including positions for assembly line work. Moreover, they do not see any reason for hiring someone for academic research purposes. When they need consultants, they tend to rely on large, established consulting firms, mainly for financial evaluations or legal consulting, not for human resources issues.

As a Japanese graduate student in an American university in the U.S., I did not fit into any part of their employment system. If I were going to be employed by Japanese-owned companies, the "proper" route would be to become employed by the parent company in Japan right after graduation from university in Japan and, once employed, I would be expected to remain with the company until I retired. Working for the company only for the purpose of my fieldwork (possibly for 12 months) and leaving the company after my research was done would be out of the question for Japanese companies.

Also, my legal status in the United States as a foreign student basically excluded me from any possible formal employment in companies for the purpose of conducting participant observation. I also sought the possibility of working as a translator or a general assistant for Japanese-owned companies. This also turned out to be difficult not only because I was a foreign student, but also because Japanese managers were accustomed to having women serve in such positions.[5]

Furthermore, not only was it impossible to gain formal entrance to a company for the purpose of conducting participant observation, but it was extremely difficult even to access any companies through more informal means. By formal entrance to a company, I refer to the acquisition of some form of employment or official status as a researcher conducting 10-12 months of participant observation at the workplace. On the other hand, informal entrance to a company refers to accessing a company through personal friendships, or through temporary jobs such as translating for a few days when some important guests from Japan visit the company. When I was conducting my preliminary fieldwork in 1991, Japanese presence among the local business community in New Mexico was very low and, therefore, I did not have an extensive network among them which might have enabled me to access companies more easily.

My bitter experience in Kentucky taught me several things. First, in my study, participant observation would necessarily be minimal, but interviews were quite possible. Second, gaining access to managers, especially to higher level managers, would be much easier than to shop floor supervisors, let alone line workers, because higher level managers have more control of their own time. In addition, this may be at least in part because higher-level managers do not want lower-level employees to represent the company. The managers see themselves as more suited to represent the company to outsiders. Third, the interviews with Japanese managers in the Japanese language can reveal much more in-depth information about their worklife and their relations with Americans.

The difficulty in gaining access to lower-level employees, especially to shop floor supervisors and production workers, posed a serious problem in formulating an anthropological research design. I went back to Albuquerque and decided to focus on the interviews as the central element of my research design. There was one company that was available for the case study. This case study company seemed to be the only place where I could conduct even the minimum amount of participant observation and interviews with production workers. In order to supplement the narrowness of the case-specific data from the case study company, I also decided to study other Japanese-owned firms, as well as American-owned firms, in different regions of the United States. Recognizing that I had little power to negotiate a fieldsite in a firm and to conduct long term fieldwork, focusing on the interviews seemed to me the only available realistic choice at that time. I had to grab the opportunity to access companies whenever and wherever possible. Therefore, I did not make a random sampling for the companies I studied. I had to rely on my personal connections to open doors to the various companies. This aspect of the data collection, namely, the difficulty in entering the field (company), is significantly different from the majority of quantitative-oriented research on organizations that rely primarily on surveys, let alone many other anthropological studies that deal with social groups (or countries) of less economic and political power.

I decided to focus on high-tech and automobile-related industries and then started the next fieldwork process—a case study of one Japanese-owned high-tech related company. In this case study and the following plant visits in the Midwest and California, I planned to examine the transferability of "Japanese organizational practices" to the United States. I decided to examine company policies regarding the systems of pay and promotion, the training of employees, policies dealing with the diversity of the American workforce, and the internal dynamics at the workplace by exploring how workers participate in the processes of implementing those management policies. Among all the companies, the training processes and affirmative action policies were focal points of examination. From reading many studies about Japanese companies either in Japan or transplants in the United States, I had learned that the training of employees has been of major interest to numerous researchers. I was interested in the various training practices in a holistic sense, involving both technical and non-technical training. The intention of my research design, in examining the non-technical training practices, meant especially looking at how companies attempt to raise the workers' sense of commitment and how companies try to retain workers. Overall, I had a holistic interest in examining the organizational practices of Japanese transplants in the United States.

A CASE STUDY

I gained access to the case study company, Suntech, and its people through one Japanese top manager. After this introduction, the human resource staff was able to connect me with almost anyone that I needed to interview. I started the interviews in July, 1992. Although the company had allowed me to conduct research at the plant when the facility started its operation in October, 1989, I had to show the research design to the top manager of the plant and get more specific permission for conducting the interviews. I did not have much difficulty in obtaining consent from the company this time mainly because I had focused on the interviews in my research design. One anticipated problem was the interviews with production workers. The top Japanese manager of the facility was especially concerned with the time I might spend interviewing them because they get paid by the hour (non-exempt).[6] I was told not to disrupt employees during their working hours. On the condition that I interview non-exempt employees after work hours on a voluntarily basis, he further asked me to limit the interview time to a maximum of one hour with each of them.[7] The company compensated those who cooperated with overtime pay. Having access to hourly workers was, indeed, the most difficult aspect of my research. Workers on the production line had little control over when they were able to talk with me. They were also unwilling to remain after work hours to be interviewed, preferring instead to attend to their personal lives. As compared to accessing hourly workers, it was much easier for me to access managerial staff. Although they tend to be overworked, especially in the manufacturing environment, once I was introduced to them by the top manager, they were cooperative and flexible in arranging an interview schedule with me.

At the beginning of the study, I was introduced to several department managers by a top manager of the facility as a doctoral student in anthropology at the University of New Mexico. This did not mean, however, that everybody in the company understood my role. At the initial stage of the case study I was told by his secretary that I should wear formal clothes, including a tie, when I visited the company. My formal position was a "visitor" of the company. Everytime I visited the company I had to mention the purpose of the visit to the receptionist and wait in the lobby. To most of the employees,' therefore, I looked like a typical visitor from Japan. Some American employees, as they told me afterwards, wondered if I was a new employee from the parent company in Tokyo, or perhaps some sort of "special employee" from the parent company for the purpose of investigating some highly confidential problems.[8] The data collection went smoothly despite this initial misunderstanding. Basically, most of the managers and workers enjoyed the interview with me, partly because they were curious, and partly because both Japanese and American employees needed an outlet for their frustrations about work experiences.

Telling me all their frustrations about work had a positive function in the employees' worklives. Many employees told me that they felt better after expressing some of their problems and frustrations about their jobs. Some employees even characterized me as a "corporate counselor.[9]" My attitude of listening patiently to what they said and being sympathetic to their problems appealed to many employees at the company. Some American managers, however, remained skeptical. The fact that I was introduced to the company by the top Japanese manager and the fact that I was Japanese had positive as well as negative effects. It was positive in the sense that I gained more cooperation from Japanese employees and that they tended to reveal more in-depth information (*"honne"*), especially about their everyday interactions with American employees at the workplace.

On the other hand, it was more difficult to extract informal, in-depth information from American employees about their opinions of management practices and the company. Some employees were cautious about telling me their negative opinions of the company (if they had any), and instead, tended to emphasize the positive aspects of everyday worklife and how they were satisfied with the company. They were obviously concerned that the information might reach the top manager.[10]

Nonetheless, some lower-level employees who obviously had problems with their immediate American supervisors, were eager to tell me every difficulty they had in their daily worklife at the company. They thought that the complaints would reach directly to the top manager if they disclosed everything to me. Some employees tended to reveal all of their problems to me, hoping that their working conditions would eventually improve if the top manager knew what was really going on at the lower end of the organizational hierarchy.

Some American managers who were frustrated with the ongoing management practices of the company remained skeptical of my interviews at the initial stage of the research. They thought I was representing corporate headquarters because I was introduced by the top manager of the plant who was a Japanese. Since the plant was a new facility, the management of this new plant was not permitted much control in determining everyday practices. Instead, most of the decision making was coming from the corporate headquarters.[11] Some American managers in the production area were especially frustrated because of the corporate control coming from headquarters. Suntech America had been a sales subsidiary company of the parent company in Japan (Suntech Japan) since the 1970's. For Suntech America, the New Mexico facility was their first manufacturing plant in the U.S. The company hired a few key American managers for its New Mexico manufacturing plant who had significant manufacturing experience. These manufacturing managers at Suntech were frustrated with their lack of autonomy in everyday decision making in the manufacturing processes. Although corporate control by headquarters was especially noticeable in the manufacturing area, this seemed to annoy both the Japanese and American managers. An American administration manager even told me that he could not authorize any check exceeding the amount of 500 dollars. He was required to ask his boss at headquarters in New York to authorize any check that exceeded that amount. In my interviews with American managers, they tended to reveal their frustration with these aspects of the corporate structure of the company. Moreover, as I describe in chapter three (case study chapter), these American managers were frustrated with the Japanese engineers who had demonstrated significantly different work attitudes at the workplace. The Japanese engineers tended to work longer hours than American managers. In addition, when problems come up, these Japanese engineers also tended to report to and ask advice from the parent company in Japan. In the repair (refurbishing) area, many American workers were frustrated with their Japanese department manager who exerted extremely tight cooperate control that they did not clearly understand. Thus, it seemed at least true that there was a covert (if not overt) antagonistic sentiment between American and Japanese employees at Suntech when I entered the company and started my research. The skeptical attitudes of some American managers at the initial stage of the research, however, did not last long once they knew the purpose of my research and understood that I really was a student and not a corporate man.

At the beginning of every interview I gave each employee a copy of the interview sheet that outlined all the questions. I also presented an interview consent form establishing privacy and confidentiality. In addition, I strongly assured them that I was a graduate student, thus, not representing the parent company in Japan, or corporate headquarters in New York. After explaining the nature of the interview, one American manager told me, "I was keeping an eye on you since you came to our company . . . but now you seem to be okay, I think." Throughout the interview he stated repeatedly his ongoing frustrations with management practices.

Another research instrument I employed during the case study was participant observation. I did participant observation at the case study company although the opportunity to do this was severely limited, because I was not officially employed by the company, and also because industrial organizations are usually closed to outsiders. I could enter the production area and talk to employees only when I was accompanied by another employee. Usually managers escorted me around the whole plant and answered my questions. I was able to take extensive notes whenever possible during the plant visits. Besides these formal aspects of data collection, I had access to employees during lunch hours and breaks, thus gaining much insight and information in a less formal situation. I also participated in several company sponsored activities; for example, I attended a company picnic.

At the beginning of my research in this company, I was strictly prohibited from entering the production area by the top manager. As time went by and as many employees became more familiar with me, it gradually became easier for me to informally enter the production area because some of the employees from the previous interviews were able to accompany me into the area.

I usually tried to arrive at the company 40-60 minutes earlier than the time scheduled for the interviews so that I could sit around the lobby area. While I was waiting in the lobby I talked with the receptionist. Since many employees were passing through this area while at work, I could talk with employees whom I had already interviewed and catch up on recent events with them. When the interview was through I often stayed in the office area and chatted with some employees. They were usually American middle-level managers or Japanese staff. Employees in the production area (non-exempt employees) usually had left the company by the time the interviews were over. The head of the company had told me that I should not disturb employees' work especially in the production area. Therefore, it was usually two or three o'clock in the afternoon when I could schedule interviews with employees. On the average I conducted interviews three times a week at the company. My interviews usually lasted 60 to 90 minutes with non-exempt employees, and 90-120 minutes with managers. Some of the longest interviews with managers lasted from 4 to 6 hours over several different interview sessions. I spent 3 to 4 hours at the company in each visit.

Finally, I have to note some difficulties I encountered regarding the confidentiality of the interviews. It became a difficulty when the top manager who initially introduced me to the company people wanted to know how the interviews were going. Although I was feeling partially responsible for reporting to him what I was doing at the company, I had difficulty in dealing with the situation when he wanted to talk (informally) with me right after an interview was over. After each visit at the company, I ordinarily said good bye to him in his office; most often after six o'clock I would knock on his office door as I was leaving. At this time, when most non-exempt employees were gone and official work hours were over, the managers would begin to relax a bit, and the top manager liked to chat with me. He frequently stopped me and invited me to his office. He was interested in knowing how the interviews went and typically asked me, for instance, "How was today's interview with Polly (pseudonym)?" I usually answered that I could not reveal what was said in the interview because of the confidentiality agreement. However, it happened sometimes that I felt compelled to explain some of my general impressions of an interview with some particular employee. Some American employees (managers and sometimes secretaries) were often there around the office area when this manager invited me into his office. Though this did not cause any particular problem for the confidentiality of the interviewee in his/her everyday worklife, it contributed to my image at the company as being directly connected to the top manager. Although I was concerned with the possibility that this perception of me might limit the gathering of in-depth information, especially from American employees, basically everyone seemed very frank about telling me their problems in their everyday worklife, if there were any. The size of the company was small enough (108 employees at the time of study) that everyone knew one another fairly well. Once employees became familiar with who I was and what I was doing in the company, they became less afraid of what they addressed in my interviews. This was probably one of the reasons why the processes of data collection went relatively smoothly.

Another difficulty which relates to the issue of confidentiality surrounds the information from the interviews with higher-level managers. During the fieldwork, my interviews with top-level managers were very successful in eliciting in-depth information. They were especially successful with Japanese managers in eliciting *"honne"* (true feelings) about their everyday interaction with American employees. The difficulty, however, was that most of "interesting" information for a field researcher is very sensitive in nature, and, therefore, the interviewees requested that they remain strictly confidential. They disclosed such information on the condition that I would never reveal its source in any future reports or publication. By disguising names and the locations of companies I tried to reassure them as much as possible that the information would never jeopardize an interviewee's career or everyday worklife. The following is a typical example of a situation where a manager asked me not to put information on the record.

Shibata:(pseudonym) By the way, please don't put that in your writing . . . about what I said that [xxx]. I just told you only here, okay?

Sumi [myself]: Oh, really?

Shibata: That's not really good. Please don't write that, for sure, okay?

Sumi: So, I can put it in my record, can't I ?

Shibata: Well . . .

Sumi: Well, about this . . . this is excellent information, but, of course, I wouldn't include this if you don't want me to do.

Shibata: I don't want you to include this, no matter what.

Sumi: I just leave this on paper as a record.

Shibata: Please don't include this. Can you promise?

Sumi: [show embarrassment]

Shibata: I just can't say this kind of thing, no matter what.

Sumi: Yes, I understand this. This is your 'honne,' isn't it?

Shibata: People don't work with 'honne,' you know.

Sumi: Well, you can't run a company with 'honne', I guess.

In spite of all the problems and difficulties that I encountered at the case study company, this part of the fieldwork was relatively easier and quite enjoyable at times. Everyone was relatively accessible, friendly, and cooperative.

FIELDWORK IN THE MIDWEST AND IN CALIFORNIA

It was a coincidence that the University of New Mexico had just established the Center for the Study of Japanese Industry and Technology Management (the US-Japan Center) in the fall of 1992, when I was struggling through financing the second part of my fieldwork. Fortunately I was able to obtain financial support for the research project in the Midwest and California from the Center. Because of this financial support I could move on to the next stage of my fieldwork. In addition, having the Center's name supporting my research represented greater legitimacy in conducting research in business organizations.

Although I was fortunate to have the US-Japan Center's support, the second part of the fieldwork turned out to be substantially more difficult than the case study. Again, the first difficulty was the problem of gaining access, especially to American-owned companies in the

Midwest and California. During my fieldwork at the case study company, Suntech in New Mexico, I attended meetings of APICS (American Production and Inventory Control Society) and through an introduction by one of the Suntech employees, and I was able to develop a network thereby gaining access to various companies. Another American manager at the company was helpful in introducing me to other managers in companies he had previously worked for in California.

I was also acquainted with one human factors consultant from the US-Japan Center at the University who put me in touch with some American companies in the Midwest. I was able to study two Japanese transplants in the Midwest through the center. I was also introduced to a research group of the School of Labor and Industrial Relations at Michigan State University, where I was able to share my research experience and information. Through a member of this research group, I was able to communicate with a few individuals from American auto industries. Further, through a referral from a representative from JETRO (Japan External Trade Organization) in New Mexico, I gained access to a few Japanese companies in California. I was also able to study one American-owned company in the Chicago area through the efforts of some colleagues in the field of anthropology in Chicago who were conducting similar studies. I also knew one anthropologist who was working for a Japanese-owned company in California at that time, and thus gained entry into two Japanese-owned companies through her. In addition, one Japanese manager whom I knew from my preliminary fieldwork in Kentucky introduced me to some other Japanese companies in the region. Finally, at the time when I was carrying out the second phase of fieldwork, I got to know a group of Japanese and American managers from one Japanese-owned company in the U.S. who were considering building a plant in Albuquerque. Through this personal connection I was able to visit two of their subsidiaries—one in California, the other in the Midwest.

This part of the fieldwork was, I should say, more like a field trip rather than fieldwork, where a researcher spends a prolonged period of time at one particular site. Besides the difficulties I had in accessing companies and gathering the information, I had to spend considerable amounts of time and effort in locating these plants on the map in unfamiliar and sometimes obscure industrial areas. Since my schedule was basically determined by the informants' (employees') schedule, I had to move according to the availability of employees for the interviews. For instance, I had to be in the Detroit area on Monday and had to drive down to Cincinnati in Ohio for Wednesday's appointment, and had to come back again to Michigan on Friday. In the following week, I had to be in Kentucky again. I usually got directions to find a particular plant by phone, and then had to locate the plant on the map. It was usually the case that manufacturing plants were located around the outskirts of large cities, in areas that are difficult to find on maps. In addition, I had to take traffic conditions into consideration so that I could arrive at the company on time. If I missed an appointment, the opportunity was gone forever. It was extremely strenuous to coordinate the interviews and gather information extensively on business organizations in unfamiliar areas.

SUMMARY

As I have described the fieldwork process in this chapter, it was very different from the majority of other anthropological studies. This is mainly because business organizations constitute very closed social groups, and because business organizations have more decision-making power over any outside researcher. Generally speaking, my Japanese nationality helped me to gather the in-depth information from both American and Japanese employees in the Japanese transplants, while I had more difficulties in gathering information in American-owned firms. This indicates the existence of structural factors, such as the national level industrial competition between Japan and the U.S., and the corporate or management control in the Japanese transplants that influences individuals' behavior in organizations. In addition, the wide gaps between Japanese and American perceptions of each other, including stereotypes, create a unique social context at the workplace, where employees perceive the reality through the distinction of "Japanese" versus "American" as a frame of reference. In the following chapters, therefore, I must frequently refer to these distinctions.

In Chapter One I mentioned eight elements that are generally perceived as the salient characteristics of the Japanese organizational forms and production systems. In the following chapter I will examine these eight characteristics among five (5) Japanese automotive-related transplants in the Midwestern area. I will also examine the significance of these eight characteristics among three (3) Japanese high-tech transplants, and a corporate headquarters of a Japanese automotive manufacturer in California in Chapter Four. In Chapter Five I will examine the significance of the same characteristics more closely in the case study company, Suntech America in New Mexico.

NOTES

1. Ruth Milkman also used the name "Suntech" as a pseudonym for one of the companies in her study (Milkman 1991). There is absolutely no relationship between the company in her study and my case study company. This was simply a coincidence.

2. I do not intend to say here that employees in American-owned companies were less cooperative. As a Japanese I certainly had more difficulties in American companies making myself familiar to many Americans who do not know very much about Japan. For those reasons that I mentioned in the main text, it was certainly more difficult for me to make myself familiar to American employees who were afraid of revealing what they do to a stranger. This is, of course, subject to many individual factors. Some of the American employees whom I interviewed were actually very informative and were willing to tell me about themselves. I want to note, however, that I met more protective attitudes against me from American managers in American-owned companies than from American and Japanese managers in Japanese transplants. I also have to note that I did not have many opportunities to interview shopfloor level workers in American-owned companies.

3. The phrase in Japanese "*domo*" has a very vague meaning. It is frequently used with other phrases like, "*domo arigatou*" (thank you), or "*domo yoroshiku*" (I humbly would like to ask your care and guidance). When "*domo*" is used by itself, the word implies various meaning depending on its context. For example, "*domo*" can mean "How do you do?," "Thank you very much," " yes," or "no." In this case, "*domo, domo*" means "How are you? Please excuse me for being a little late."

4. "*Sempai*" means an experienced senior or predecessor. He was in fact a graduate from the same school as I graduated. Therefore, he considered himself as my "*sempai*" in the context of this conversation.

5. In Japan general assistance jobs, such as translating, are usually considered "women's work." For example, Japanese mangers at my case study company preferred hiring a female for a translator's position. There was one native Japanese woman, Tomoko, at the case study company who worked as a

liaison between the New Mexico facility and the parent company in Tokyo. Tomoko was not a student but a legal resident in the U.S., and therefore, was able to officially work in this country. Although several American men who were proficient in the Japanese language had applied for the position, the company hired Tomoko (pseudonym). Don Grace, an American employee at the company, thought that Tomoko's English lacked the necessary proficiency for the job, and explained how he perceived the situation. He stated:

> [Those Americans who applied] spoke, wrote and read [Japanese]. But they were turned down and she was hired. And I have to ask myself why. And when I went to Japan I think I got part of my answer. It is that a woman is always used as kind of a servant to a high-level manager . . . But it is very—it's a very negative thing for this business, and for Americans. I don't think that people find it difficult to work with Tomoko, it's simply because her skills are not up to what they require. But, she makes a great cup of tea, you know. There's not very much respect for her—her position. And that's not fair to her . . . it's not fair to the company, and it's—it's another one of—it's a characteristic of a Japanese company.

6. The case study company had a classification of "non-exempt" and "exempt" employees. "Exempt" refers to the status of an employee who get a monthly salary. "Non-exempt" refers to those employees who get paid by hour. Non-exempt employees are required to punch in and out on time cards. At this company exempt employees do not get overtime pay, whereas non-exempt employees get 1.5 times the regular amount of pay when they work overtime. Exempt status applies to the positions above supervisors level. Below supervisors basically all employees are non-exempt. This distinction somewhat varied among the companies I visited.

7. By "voluntarily basis," the company meant that it is basically up to employees whether to cooperate or not cooperate with the interviews. The management had no power to encourage or force employees to cooperate with my research. After I was introduced to managers in every department by the top manager, I had a meeting with personnel administrator. She provided me a copy of the employee roster of the facility at the first meeting. At the time of the research I basically did not know anybody on the roster, and I randomly selected employees from the list according to the position, gender, and ethnicity of employees. Once I showed her a list of employees with whom I was interested in conducting the interview, she could connect me to the employee. I could then arrange the time and date of the interview. As mentioned, the length of the interviews with non-exempt employees was

strictly limited to a maximum of one hour. However, as my interviews with employees proceeded, it became more frequent that the interview exceeded more than one hour. The top manager, though unwillingly, eventually consented that I could exceed one hour if the employee wanted to keep going on.

8. When I began the research at the case study company, the company had a legal problem because one American employee has filed a complaint with EEOC (Equal Employment Opportunity Commission). Although the fact was being kept strictly confidential among the management staff, most of employees at the company basically knew about what was going on. The top manager again told me that I should not be dealing with this matter in my research. Though the topic came up several times during the interviews, especially with the management-level employees, I tried not to deal with the problem per se in the research. Because of this circumstance, some employees at the beginning wondered if I was from EEOC or the Department of Labor for the purpose of investigating this problem.

9. Part of conversation at the end of the interview shows this aspect of the research.

> *Sumi* (myself): Well, thanks a lot for all of this, you know.
> *Karen* (pseudonym): I spilled my guts—I feel like I've been in a therapy session, or something.
> *Sumi*: Did you feel like that?
> *Karen*: I should say, "Well, doctor, thank you."
> *Sumi*: Well . . .
> *Karen*: Charge people.

10. This was, of course, not directly elicited by employees. No employees actually said that they were not going to tell me their negative perceptions because they were afraid that their managers might discover them. In fact most American employees were quite frank in telling me problems when they existed. This was especially the case with lower-level employees. On the other hand, some American managers were very cautious because I was Japanese and because I was introduced by the top manager. Being in a small size company with about 110 employees, it was only a matter of time until I had a more valid picture of an employee after talking with several other employees who were working closely with the person.

11. Corporate control by headquarters over the new facility is not special to the case study company. See Yoshino (1976) , also Richard Johnson (1977).

CHAPTER 3

Organizational Practices Transferred to the U.S.—the Midwest

In Chapter One, eight significant characteristics of the Japanese organization of production were outlined by Murakami and Rohlen (Murakami and Rohlen 1992). The transferability of the organizational practices of Japanese firms to their U.S. subsidiaries entails examining these eight characteristics of Japanese organizational practices among transplants in the United States. This chapter will examine the significance of these eight characteristics among Japanese transplants in the Midwest. They are (1) Lifetime employment (or long tenure of employment); (2) Seniority-based wage and promotion systems; (3) Elaborate welfare, bonus, and other benefits systems; (4) Company-based labor unions; (5) Considerable inter-job mobility within a firm and emphasis on internal promotion; (6) Small group activities on the shop floor level; (7) Intensive training and socialization of new employees by the management; (8) Attention to developing a corporate culture and management philosophy.

I had access to five (5) Japanese-owned and two (2) American-owned companies. I interviewed 19 individuals, of which 6 were Japanese managers, 10 were American managers and 3 were American non-managerial employees. Four (4) of the Japanese-owned and one (1) of the American-owned companies were in automobile-related industries. One (1) Japanese-owned company and one (1) American-owned company were in computer-related high-tech industries. In terms of the company size, four (4) Japanese-owned companies fell into the category of medium-large (100-999 employees), and one (1) was a large company (more than 1000 employees). On the other hand, the two (2) American-owned companies had more than 1000 employees. Generally speaking, Japanese transplants in the U.S. tended to be smaller in size than their American counterparts.

Before proceeding to the discussion of these eight elements, it is important to look at the general characteristics of industrial environment of the Midwest.

Table 1. List of Companies and Interviewees in the Midwest.

Company Name	No. of Employees	Products
Japanese Transplants		
Midwest Silicon	500	Silicon Wafers
Oyama America	440	Automotive Body Stamping
Yamadadenso	1254	Automotive Radiators
Y.K. Manufacturing	152	Automotive Rubber
United GM Glass	491	Automotive Windshield
(A Joint-Venture)		Glass
American Companies		
Michigan Automotive		
Components Group	500	Automobile Manufacturing
Futuretech	4300	Cellular phone

Interviewee	Title	Company
Norbert Estes	Human Resources Manager	United GM Glass
Masaya Sato	Cost Analyst	United GM Glass
Yasuo Takizawa	Marketing Manager	United GM Glass
Tetsuo Sakamoto	Vice-President, Engineering	Y.K. Manufacturing
Harry Stewart	Quality Control Manager	Y.K. Manufacturing
George Donald	Executive Manufacturing Manager	Oyama America
Dan Dooley	Vice-President, Human Resources	Yamadadenso
Masao Nagato	Coordinator, Corporate Services	Yamadadenso
Laura Lotovski	Senior Specialist, Human Resources	Yamadadenso
Karen Gutman	Director of Planning	Michigan Automotive Components Group

Note: Only interviewees whose names appeared in this chapter are listed.

CHARACTERISTICS OF AUTOMOBILE INDUSTRIES IN THE MIDWEST

Traditionally, industries in the Midwestern states were structured around automobile manufacturing and related steel industries. Those industries have employed the traditional Fordist organization of production (cf. chapter one) with a heavily unionized labor force. Urban centers, such as Detroit and Cleveland have developed in the course of industrial expansion of automobile and steel manufacturing. Although automobile and steel manufacturing have formed a basic infrastructure of the industrial activities in the Midwestern area, since the 1960's new semi-conductor industries have evolved in relation to auto manufacturers.

Another significant characteristic of the industries in the Midwest is the Japanese entry to the traditionally American-owned automobile and steel industries. Beginning in the 1960's and certainly by the 1970's, some of the Japanese automobile manufacturers had started the US manufacturing of the Japanese automobiles. In addition, especially after Nissan and Toyota started their American production in the early 1980's, hundreds of Japanese auto suppliers including those of the rubber and electric industries started their overseas production in the US. As Kenney and Florida pointed out, the Japanese entry to the auto industries in the Midwest has resulted in forming a transplant complex in this region (Kenney and Florida 1993). Moreover, in contrast to the traditional American-owned industries that are mainly concentrated in urban areas, the Japanese transplants showed a tendency to locate in rural "greenfield" areas. I will discuss in detail the process of site selection of the Japanese transplants that I visited during my fieldwork.

What is the most salient characteristic of the Japanese entry into the automobile industry in this region is their effort to implement a radically different organizational form of production with the American labor force. What is often coined as "innovation-mediated production" (Kenney and Florida 1993), or "lean production" (Womack, et al. 1990) characterizes the team-based organization of production in Japanese factories in Japan. The consequences of the introduction of the Japanese organization of production in transplants are quite complex as I examine in this chapter.

Finally, racial and ethnic composition of the local labor force shows a unique characteristic in the Midwest. As I mentioned in Chapter One the percentage of minorities in managerial positions and the immigrant professional is very small. In areas where the Japanese transplants prefer to locate themselves, the local population is usually very homogeneous. In rural areas of Michigan, Ohio, Illinois, and Indiana, for example, whites comprise more than 90 percent of the local population. The local labor force, therefore, reflects this racial and ethnic composition. Minorities are usually concentrated in the production area, whereas most of managerial positions are held by whites and the Japanese. In Japanese transplants the percentage of African-American is often two to three percent of the total work force.

Regarding five (5) Japanese-owned companies in the Midwest, two (2) of them are located in small towns in Michigan, and three (3) others are located further south from southern Ohio to Kentucky. Three of them cited as one of the important factors for site selection that they wanted to avoid large urban centers such as Detroit or Cleveland, and that they chose the location mainly because of the proximity to the Japanese automobile manufacturers, such as Toyota in Kentucky, Honda in Ohio, and Nissan in Tennessee. All of these five Japanese-owned firms that I visited started their operations between 1985 and 1989 (cf. Toyota started its operation in 1983). Only one rubber manufacturing company in Kentucky and a semiconductor company in Cincinnati mentioned that it was simply a coincidence that they selected their location because they purchased pre-existing facilities from American companies. Two Japanese-owned auto parts suppliers in Michigan mentioned that their central location to the American automobile manufacturers in the Detroit area as well as Japanese automobile plants was the main reason for the site selection.

The popular press frequently reported that Japanese-owned companies in the U.S. tended to avoid locating in big cities because they were reluctant to deal with a large number of ethnic minorities. Cole and Deskins pointed out that Japanese automobile transplants in the U.S. showed the tendency of excluding African-Americans and other ethnic minorities in their hiring (Cole and Deskins 1988). Kenney and Florida also agreed that there was the tendency, but stated that "there is significant variation in minority hiring by company" (Kenney and Florida 1993).

During my fieldwork I sometimes tried to discuss this issue when interviewing the Japanese managers. No direct information came up in my formal interviews regarding Japanese transplants' bias against hiring certain racial and ethnic minorities. In my informal interactions with Japanese managers, however, some of them showed their concern with the "work attitudes" among African Americans. Some of them asked me, "What is the work attitudes of black Americans as compared to white Americans?" Racial stereotyping always exists more or less in any social group. Some Japanese managers, especially those who had just come to the United States, held the notion that black Americans tend to be very confrontational and difficult to work with. The concern with the racial and ethnic issue seemed to be a certain point of discussion in the site selection process of the Japanese transplants.

Mr. Sato, a Japanese manager of United GM Glass in Kentucky, referred to the site selection process of the company, and explained that at first the southern mentality of the workers of the state appealed to the Japanese. When he came to Kentucky Sato felt comfortable with non-confrontational and obedient attitudes of local workers. He later concluded, however, that local workers in general tended to take advantage of the personal days or the sick leaves and tried to work as little as possible.

> Another reason for choosing Kentucky was that it was different from the Detroit area. Its people are innocent. Indeed I guess, it's a little better than Detroit, but I stopped having the image of Kentucky workers as simple, innocent, and easy to deal with. It's totally different.

It goes without saying that there are many other factors involved in site selection of companies, such as the incentive packages (industrial bonds) from local governments and an infrastructure that accommodates the presence of the Japanese in local communities (Japanese grocery stores and restaurants, educational facilities, etc.). From the data that my interviews provided, financial incentives, such as the price of the land and industrial bonds, and the proximity to customers were more important than all other factors, including the issue of race and minorities.

I interviewed one American manager at the corporate headquarters of Nippon North America in California. Carolyn Monroe referred to the site selection process of their Smyrna factory in Tennessee.

> [T]hat, of course, reflects some other issues. Part of it is the price of land because factories are big, and no one could afford them [in California]. Our factory in Smyrna, Tennessee is enormous. It's the biggest automotive assembly operation under one roof in North America. I mean, there are corridors where you're in there, and you're walking, like, more than a quarter mile . . . land prices and wages were high out here [California], I mean, 'cause for a regular factory worker to afford a house out here would be almost impossible. But in Tennessee, people can have a pretty good life on what we can pay factory workers. Also, that area had an over-supply of labor. There had been a military base that had closed in Smyrna. So, that particular community was very anxious to attract investment and attract a manufacturing plant. They had the people already there. And, of course, the states here in the U.S. compete with each other to attract manufacturers. In fact, Tennessee changed its law on tax loss carry-forwards to match—the federal law is fifteen years. The state law in Tennessee would only be seven years. They changed it to fifteen to match the federal, primarily to attract Nissan, because that meant—you know, 'cause you usually have losses on a plant the first few years, and you want to be able to use those losses against your earnings in later years.

She also mentioned the importance of business issues, such as competition with other manufacturers and the close proximity to the pre-existing suppliers and automotive market.

> [A]lready some of the other companies had some suppliers there in that same general region, you know—Ohio Valley and on down. So, those were the big ones. And I think there was one or two—I think Alabama was also very close in the running, the northern part of Alabama was also under consideration. And, of course, there's getting to be more there. It looks like Mercedes will locate their plant in North Carolina. And, of course, BMW's plant will now be in South Carolina—so, that whole region. There's also good transportation infrastructure there . . . especially for automobiles. Good confluence of interstate highways and railroads. So, 'cause

Nashville—which is, of course, where Smyrna is—is very good that way, and good proximity to most of our market. For us, locating all the way up in Detroit probably wouldn't have been quite as good. Partly, costs would have been a little higher. It would've been tougher to be so close, I think, to the Big Three. But, you know, a cold-weather state like that is not good for transportation. It's more costly to live there. Energy costs are high.

In addition, the R & D facility of Nippon North America was located in the Detroit area. Monroe referred to the importance of the quality of labor issue and explained why her company located its R & D facility in Michigan, not in California.

Partly because that's a good place to hire automotive engineers. The University of Michigan and some of the other schools that have automotive engineering specialties. So it's easier to hire new graduate engineers in that area than almost anywhere else in the U.S. Of course, it's easier to steal them from the Big Three. So, it was better for us to locate [Nippon] (pseudonym) R & D there where there were good suppliers and a good labor supply of engineering talent there than out here [California].

The Japanese transplants' concern with the characteristics of the local labor force certainly involved their questions of turnover rate, absenteeism, attendance, and the general work attitudes of the racial and ethnic minorities. Moreover, the Japanese managers from Japan were not very well informed about the social and cultural diversity of American society. Here, what Kenney and Florida mention comes to be of particular importance.

Generally speaking, the hiring practices of transplant manufacturers have been shaped by their initial acceptance of the long history of discrimination, segregation, and outright racism in American labor markets in particular and American society in general. However, it does seem likely that the transplants will respond to public and legal pressure on this issue and work to overcome discrimination in hiring (Kenney and Florida 1993: 283).

Finally, the existence of American labor unions in the automobile industries in the U.S. was also a substantial factor in the site selection process of the Japanese transplants. I will examine this issue in the section on "company-based labor unions."

1. Lifetime employment (or long tenure of employment)

The practice of lifetime employment in Japan has been limited to regular, male full-time employees in large Japanese companies. To examine the significance of lifetime employment practices among the Japanese transplants in the Midwest, I will look at Japanese managers' expectations regarding length of employment of American employees at the company.

The practice of lifetime employment was basically nonexistent among five Japanese transplants in the Midwestern area. However, all of the Japanese transplants I visited clearly expressed their commitment to preventing layoffs. As compared to the American-owned companies I studied, five Japanese transplants did not have a long history in the U.S. In addition, four of them were smaller in size, and had been constantly expanding their workforces. The Japanese concept of lifetime employment was expressed in the Japanese transplants in the U.S. as their commitment to prevent layoffs. Mr. Sato, a Japanese middle manager in United GM in Kentucky, said they would even pay overtime in order to avoid layoffs.

> The way we have dealt with the situation was . . . because we don't want to layoff workers . . . we usually carry a little less workforce than what we actually need. For example, say, we need 500 workers, there are actually 490 workers in the plant. We make up for the rest of 10 workers by doing overtime.

When talking about how his company reconciled this commitment with periodic economic downturns, Mr. Sakamoto, a Japanese manager at another Japanese transplant in Kentucky, commented:

> Economically it's the same as in Japan. We try to cut any kind of expense as much as possible. We also try to keep costs down. You can't survive in this country if you can't do this. Cutting the workforce is the last resort . . . at least we don't have this idea in our

management policies.

He was well aware that American employees would not remain with the firm as long as most of workers of large firms in Japan. He was ambivalent about how long he expected employees to stay, but he also showed his true feelings—"*honne*," and revealed his desire for American workers remain with his company until they retire.

> Personally, to be frank, here in America, this is a culture in which you will move when you get a better offer. So I can't complain if you find some other place where you feel more comfortable and get better treatment. But I dare to say something about how long. I want to create a company where workers feel that they want to stay forever.

In my study Japanese managers in transplants expressed that the stability of American workers was a critical concern. Mr. Nagato, a Japanese coordinator in another Japanese transplant in Michigan, commented as follows:

> My biggest, probably many Japanese have the same concern, but my biggest concern is that a person will stay long here.

Mr. Estes, an American human resources manager in United GM, a joint-venture company in Kentucky, also mentioned that he wanted workers to stay with the company for a long time because it was a loss to the company when an employee left after the company had invested in his/her training.

> I mean, you know, I hate to see an employee come in, we train that employee, that employee's a good employee, and then they get another job. That means we have to do the same cycle all over again. So, I like to see them come in and stay until they retire. That's my expectation.

All in all, the practice of lifetime employment was virtually non-existent among five Japanese transplants that I visited in my study. Although there was a certain expectation among both American and Japanese managers that workers would stay for a long time with the company, the actual employment practice tended to conform more to the traditional American pattern, where workers changed jobs frequently.

2. Seniority-based wage and promotion systems

The seniority system, by definition, refers to the organizational practice that a company determines wages and promotions of employees according to the length of service in the company. Most of companies in Japan now utilize a combination of seniority and merit criteria. Although there were minor variations, all of the Japanese transplants that I visited in my study also used a combination of both seniority and merit criteria in evaluating employees' wages and promotions. If anything, the Japanese transplants tended to rely more heavily on seniority criteria especially when deciding employees' wages. When compared to their American counterparts, Japanese transplants showed heavier reliance on seniority criteria in deciding both wages and promotions.

Generally speaking, wages and salaries in the transplants were not higher than those of the American-owned companies. In addition, in three of these transplants American white-collar employees tended to get frustrated by the company's slow promotion pace and wage increase. As I show in the section on internal promotion, Japanese transplants tended to lose their qualified young white-collar employees, especially engineers, who were not satisfied with their salary level and promotion experiences. For the Japanese managers, however, seniority was one of the fairest way of treating employees. On the other hand, seniority was a major element that the American white-collar employees perceived as a rigid and inflexible corporate structure.

I should note here that there appeared to be some regional differences to the extent which seniority appealed to the American employees. In my study, it was mostly in the five transplants in Michigan where the American white-collars voiced their frustration. On the other hand, Mr. Sato, a manager in Kentucky, complained about the company's heavy reliance on seniority because the system basically assured workers a steady pay increase without the pressure of improving job performance. At this company, American workers took advantage of the security that the seniority system offered to them, which resulted in lowering the morale at the workplace, exemplified by high absenteeism among American workers.

In contrast, the seniority system was not appreciated in one American-owned company in the Detroit area. Karen Gutman, a director of planning at the company, referred to the seniority system as a "backward" practice. She believed that the overall performance of an organization was greatly enhanced by the merit system, where workers were rewarded through pay increase and promotions for their job performance, thus increasing motivation to do a good job.

3. Elaborate welfare, bonus, and other benefits systems

Many researchers have documented the highly elaborated benefits systems of many large companies in Japan; allowances for housing, family expenses ("*kazoku teate*"),[1] commuting expenses, and bonuses for all employees. Dore saw this elaborated benefits structure of Japanese companies as a significant part of "welfare corporatism," in which a company was involved with the total well-being of their employees (Dore 1974). All of the Japanese transplants in my study offered their employees a benefits package that was somewhat different from both the traditional American and the traditional Japanese systems. Unlike firms in Japan, none of the transplants offered American employees extensive allowances such as housing and family allowances. Instead, most transplants offered the benefits package that typically consisted of several insurance programs, such as medical and dental, and insurance programs for retirement, such as 401K plan. In this sense, the benefits packages of Japanese transplants resembled those of American firms.

There was a significant difference, however, in bonus structures between the Japanese transplants and American firms. Although there were minor variations in terms of the number of sick days and/or personal leave time that employees could receive, the bonus in Japanese transplants tended to be distributed more evenly among managers and workers when compared to the bonus structure of American firms, which tended to favor the upper-level management. Dan Dooley, an American human resources manager at an automotive radiator transplant in Michigan, said that his company did not rely on the traditional American benefit structures to keep certain employees.

We don't have the golden handcuffs that you'd find in Dresser, for

example, where you put together a system that says, 'Boy, if you stay
for so many years, you get certain bonus levels' that makes it almost
impossible to leave. We don't do any of that kind of stuff. So, we
don't take any steps that are going to keep anybody. But we want to
encourage them.

The benefits structures of transplants differed from the systems of
companies in Japan in the sense that most transplants did not offer their
American employees as extensive benefits as firms in Japan. At the
same time, transplants also significantly differed in their bonus
structure from American firms. All in all, the benefits packages of
transplants were unique when compared to their counter-parts in Japan
and in the U.S.

4. Company-based labor unions

Company-based unions in Japan evolved in the post World War II era
as a response to a growing militant labor movement that threatened
established industries. American Occupational Forces were also
concerned that the labor movement in Japan could be a spring board
for communist infiltration into the culture at large. In order to reduce
the threat of strong independent unions, leaders of the Occupational
Forces along with established industry leaders created company unions
to reduce the effect of and eventually eliminate militant forces that
were seeking to establish strong independent unions.

In the midwest, the company union was virtually non-existent
among five Japanese transplants. None of these transplants were
unionized, nor was one American-owned company. Only one
American-owned company in the Detroit area in my study was
unionized. Managers in the above six non-union firms preferred that
plants remain non-union. This attitude was especially strong among
auto-related Japanese transplants. Unions were a crucial factor in site
selection for the Japanese transplants. Mr. Sato of United GM, a
manufacturer of automotive windshield glass in Kentucky, summarized
his company's policy as follows:

We thought that if we go into the Detroit area, we would be
unionized sooner or later. Although Kentucky is not a union state,
there are many unions here, too. Their influence is relatively smaller

than in other states. However, in reality, there are very aggressive approaches from unions here. There are representatives from Detroit, and they have offices here. They are very aggressive. Their true intention is to unionize Toyota. But Toyota is too protected to be unionized, so they try to unionize the Japanese suppliers here first. That's their strategy . . . which is very aggressive. It's also partly our mistake, too. There are some workers in our plant who are influenced by unions.

The company had a union drive by the UAW in the fall of 1992, and the management was particularly nervous about the union influence. One manager told me that not having a previous union membership was one of the most important factors when hiring new workers. The company had just recently hired a new human resources manager who has a long history of fighting against unions. Mr. Estes, a human resources manager at the company, clearly addressed his anti-union attitude in the following remark.

I've worked in my career keeping unions out of our plants. And the plant I was at before was a union plant. And personal satisfaction being in a union-free plant is the main thing. The most challenging thing in my job is keeping this plant union-free. Well, it—I have to make sure everything is running smoothly. If it's not, then the employees will ask the union to come in and interfere. And so, it's very challenging on a day-to-day basis to just make sure that what we're doing is right—right for the company and right for the employees. So, it's very challenging. I have to make sure the policies are set properly. I have to make sure they're administered properly. I have to make sure that we're fair with what we're doing.

Sato at United GM also said the UAW were making steady efforts to unionize the plant. It was always during September and October when the management dealt with pay raises. They started seeing workers with union T-shirts walking around the production area. The company hired professional lawyers and discussed issues on union influence with the human resources staff. They even made a special manual for managers and supervisors regarding how to handle the union-influenced employees in the company. When noticing any union-related activities on the shopfloor, managers and supervisors were advised to not to take any immediate actions that would violate the laws. Sato said he would not do or say anything because he was not directly supervising anyone. As a Japanese manager Sato recognized that the Japanese in the U.S. should be more aware of the legal framework that concerns union activities. Sato, however, thought that locally hired managers and supervisors tended to be ignorant of the union activities in general.

> Not only for Japanese but also for American managers. It's not only Japanese managers but also American managers who don't have a lot of knowledge on this. This is especially true of locally hired young supervisors. We [Japanese] are also in danger, but it is American supervisors who are in more danger. We talk about such things as how to handle the situation when you find union meetings in the production area. We have a series of manuals and specific guidelines for this.

Obviously my visit to this company coincided with a time when the management was very nervous about the local union activities. In general, the management's concern with staying out of the unions was very strong among the Japanese automobile related transplants in the Midwest. Harry Stewart, a quality control manager at the automotive rubber manufacturing plant, also discussed the Japanese transplants' concern to control the American labor unions' influence.

> [A]s companies are relocated to places like Kentucky, Tennessee . . . away from the Detroit area, they tend to be able to stay non-union . . . [A]nd part of that [is that] managers understand things that they have to do for workers. I think the Japanese are very interested in doing that.

In America, unionism has had its own bloody history. The fear of communism in America was also high in the post WW II era and into the 1950's, the decade of the now infamous "McCarthy Era." The strength of unions, therefore, declined significantly in subsequent decades and by the 1990's had diminished to an even greater degree. American management in general has never been allied with labor unions. As I have shown here, both American and Japanese managers in the Japanese transplants in my study clearly expressed their interest in remaining non-union. Although parent companies in Japan are mostly unionized, Japanese unions are often described as "company unions" and are less militant than their American counterparts. On the other hand, the idea of company unions is very uncommon in the U.S. and, therefore, difficult for American employees to understand. It is not likely then that the Japanese transplants will institute company unions.

5. Considerable inter-job mobility within a firm and emphasis on internal promotion

The management of five Japanese transplants in my study generally encouraged promoting employees internally. Though there was an emphasis on internal promotion, four of the transplants, especially small-sized transplants, did not have any systematic company policies and procedures that supported this emphasis. All of these Japanese transplants also hired many workers on a temporary basis, not only as a buffer against fluctuating labor needs but also for the purpose of hiring full-time employees. One Japanese manager told me that he preferred to hire permanent workers from the temporaries already hired when there was an opening in the production area, because he knows the applicants personally by the time they apply for the position. All of transplants I studied were using the temporaries for a short term because of a sudden increase in customer demands. In this case, companies usually carry temporary workers for a three to six month period before they can be hired on a permanent basis.

Though Japanese managers in transplants emphasized internal promotion, the high turnover rates among the American white collar employees often impeded a steady internal promotion processes. At Yamadadenso manufacturing in Michigan, Laura, a human resources specialist, mentioned that white-collar workers had more opportunities nation wide while factory workers had opportunities only in this area. Because of this situation, in Yamadadenso, there were high turnover rates among the white-collar staff. This was the case especially among American engineers. The turnover rates of the white-collar staff probably was equal to the rate of the blue-collars. For example, according to Laura, engineers received excellent technical training from Yamadadenso then they become very valuable to other American companies. These trained engineers were sometimes "headhunted" by American companies with higher salaries, and they left the company. Laura said that this happened frequently. She found the white-collar staff in general at Yamadadenso tended to get frustrated with the company's slow rate of promotion, rigid rules, and lower pay. She explained the company's condition as follows.

> So, usually people who are like birds who fly to different companies have different career goals. The main complaint that I hear from white-collar staff leaving company are the rules are too strict for white-collar staff. So, they feel that because of their college education—they should have, for example, flex time. They also complain that salary for white-collar people is a little bit less at Japanese companies . . . compared to many American companies. That's another big complaint. And the third thing is slow promotion. Those are the three biggest complaints, generally, that I hear.

Although transplants were interested in keeping employees through internal promotion, their own policies undermine the process particularly in an economic climate where firms compete for professionals, such as engineers. Two transplants in Michigan lost some of their very important American managers and engineers, in whom the company had invested time and money for their training. In addition, there were few avenues for blue-collar workers to move up through the process of internal promotion and become white-collar employees. There were a few supervisor-level employees who had been promoted from the level of line workers. However, they represented very rare cases in my study.

6. Small group activities on the shopfloor level

All of five transplant companies had a positive attitude toward implementing QC activities and team concepts in the production area. Coupled with the fact that many Japanese-owned companies in the U.S. were relatively new, QC's and teams did not have a long history in the plants. In reality, the process of implementing team-oriented activities had been a continuous struggle. Although American managers in Japanese-owned companies that I talked with generally felt that they were successful in implementing them, many Japanese managers told me that these programs were by no means the same as they were in Japan. Mr. Sakamoto, an engineering manager at Y.K. Manufacturing, an automotive rubber manufacturing plant in Kentucky, commented as follows.

> There are small group activities . . . what we call in Japan QC circles. We have teams in every production area. But, actually, these are Kaizen suggestion teams in Japan. They can't function up to the same extent as QC circles in Japan. The way employees are trained here is different from Japan. In Japan we teach workers how to take responsibilities, to think, to be creative . . . and to act autonomously at the plant. Here, there is no atmosphere like that for Americans or Japanese. So, if anything, Japanese [must] ask Americans to suggest their problems. At any rate, Americans can't do the job autonomously because they have not been trained in this manner . . . they can't improve things unless they rely on somebody else's direction. They have to ask, for example, technicians or manufacturing engineers to do it for them. To have Kaizen suggestion teams seems good enough right now here. I am not sure if they will be more like QC's in Japan in the near future.

Mr. Sato at United GM also talked about how difficult it is to realize worker participation.

> We simply recognized that it [QC's] would be impossible. At this stage this is just a dream . . . because of so called 'low morale' . . . because workers are not trained at all about how to think at work. In the traditional American environment, workers think of themselves as being exploited, and top management thinks that they should just use workers to make a greater profit for themselves, although it is a little better now. There is no way of realizing worker participation. In addition, American managers don't have the 'feel' of what it is like to run QC circles in the workplace. It is not good when you understand only from books, but you have to have understanding based on your real experience. On the other hand, we, Japanese, don't know what it is like to implement QC circles in the U.S., so, it is almost impossible to realize this because both of us don't know how.

George Donald was an executive manufacturing manager at Oyama America, the automotive stamping plant in Michigan. He came to this company from a major American automobile manufacturer, where he tried to implement several small group activities in the production area. He was very cautious concerning ways to realize worker participation. He said that small group activities could be misused as a tool for management control, partially because of the American managers' lack of experience of successfully implementing QC's on the shopfloor level.

> I think it's a great idea. I really do. Number one I have to admit that I don't have much experience in this. I've read a lot about it. I've seen other companies, and gone to seminars. I had some experience at Chrysler, which I thought was not well done. So I came here lacking in experience, but with a lot of knowledge I picked up from reading . . . but without having successful experience it's difficult to start . . . So I don't want to move too quickly. It would be very easy for me, or any company, to dictate: 'We will have these activities. Form groups, start having meetings.' That's very easy to do, but they lose their meaning when it's done that way. You must cultivate the philosophy and the intentions of the meetings. They're for the personal involvement for the employees. They have a purpose. They have to be involved, and it's for their own job enrichment and fulfillment. So you must approach these things very cautiously, especially in America. Americans are skeptical, they're very freedom-minded. When you start sitting down and talking about more efficiency, and getting them involved in things like that, it's like an anti-union activity . . . from American standpoint. But I think it has great value, and I think it can be very successful and rewarding. They have to feel good about doing it. So you have to— in order to get employees involved in that sort of thing, and then have them be successful—you have to approach that very carefully. Because if you rush into things and do it incorrectly and have failures, you're going to create bad feelings and bad attitudes. Then that will create more problems than it will solve.

In addition, the consensus decision making that is inherent in the idea of the shopfloor-level team activities turned out to be an obstacle

in the context of the American workplaces. Dan Dooley, an American
human resources manager at Yamadadenso in Michigan, talked about
the conditions at his company.

> Probably the most challenging is when you get into decision making.
> I think the concept of consensus decision making is very
> intellectual—all companies talk about, you know, 'this is the way to
> go.' But to actually do that is very difficult, because consensus
> decision making is great when I'm making a decision about your
> department, or someone else's department. But decision making's a
> big burden when I'm allowing you to make a decision in my area.
> And this has been—this has probably been one of the most difficult
> things to really implement in an American company. So, we see
> ourselves as experts. Our whole career has been in that area. And
> now, to allow some accountant to come in and make a human
> resource decision, or even to have to listen to him, is kind of a
> burden. So, it's been much more difficult to implement than frankly I
> expected. We hired people that we felt agreed with the concept and
> ideal of consensus decision making. So, we at least had that basis of
> everybody saying, 'Yeah, yeah, yeah, this is what we want to do,'
> but we found it very, very difficult to implement. Most of the
> American management teams are very territorial—'This is my area
> and I will make all the decisions in this area. And if you interfere, it's
> interference.' So, that's probably been one of the most difficult
> aspects of Japanese system.

When talking about the workforces in America and Japan, Mr.
Sakamoto at the automotive rubber manufacturing plant in Kentucky
perceived a lack of initiative coming from workers.

> In the production area, whether or not you ask questions is the
> difference. Workers in Japan have questions about what they are
> told, what they are instructed to do, and what they do. But in
> America, there are no questions coming from the workers. They just
> do what they are told, and don't question if what they do is right or
> wrong. This is generally true of the workforce in America. Therefore,
> the people who tell what workers do have to have responsibilities.
> Unless you prepare really well, products won't improve at all.

As shown in comments by both American and Japanese managers, QC's and team activities cannot be isolated from other factors, such as the difficulties of consensus decision making and the territorial nature of the American workplace. In reality, implementing QC's and team activities with American workers requires significant changes in the culture of the company. Mr. Sato saw difficulties as follows:

> [A]s a direction of the management, we want workers to think more and suggest more even if they are subordinates. They know what they do the best, and all I do is to sign, or give permission. We want this kind of environment. This is very much emphasized by many companies like Toyota, but it is difficult because we have to change the culture of the company. When we try to change, first of all, the subordinates get lost. They were used to following their bosses. And now they are expected to come up with their own ideas, which they can't because they are not trained to do so. Bosses, on the other hand, think that their 'territory' is violated, and feel like they have been demoted.

In my study, both American and Japanese managers addressed the difficulties in implementing QC's and team activities on the shopfloor. Some of those activities were actually successful in some transplants. The Japanese managers, however, pointed to the fact that even those successful QC's and teams were by no means the same as QC's and teams in Japan. Small group activities in these five Japanese transplants had turned out to be different from those of firms in Japan and American firms in their attempt to overcome social and cultural differences between Japanese and American workers. Some managers, like Mr. Sato, indeed saw the need of changing the whole culture of organizations if they were to succeed at all.

7. Intensive training and socialization of new employees by the management

Only two of the Japanese-owned companies I visited had structured training programs—one with more than 1000 employees, and another with about 500 employees. These two companies had their own full-time training facilitators. The other three transplants were small/medium-sized with employees ranging from 100 to 500. In these companies, training—especially technical training for production workers—was carried out on an OJT (on-the-job training) basis. Training structure was left up to team leaders, facilitators, or supervisors. There were no company-wide systematic training programs for managers and workers.

Non-technical training typically involved orientation programs for new employees, basic SPC (statistical process control) training, and basic safety training. Other management seminars and classes involved human resource issues and company morale, such as "How To Get Along With People," or *seiri-seiton* (Keeping the workplace clean and in order). When employees attended training sessions, seminars, or classes outside of the company, they were often paid by the company depending on the relevance of the classes to the job.

The training programs among five Japanese-owned companies in the U.S. appeared to be very different from training programs in Japan. This was especially true when compared to training programs in Japanese parent companies, and for several reasons. Mr. Nagato had been sent to Yamadadenso Manufacturing in central Michigan in 1990 from the parent company in Japan. At this U.S. facility he was responsible for coordinating the American and the Japanese employees, and for structuring the training programs for managers. He referred to the general differences of the training curriculum between Japan the U.S., and stated that the training programs in Japan were more general, whereas the training in the US focus on the development of specific skills.

> [C]omparing it with Japan and the U.S., we have more training courses here. As far as the management training is concerned, we have eighteen courses—just courses for team leaders and above. And a lot of training courses are more based on focusing on the skill, management skill, like teaching subordinates, or dealing with a complaint, or helping with performance improvement kind of thing. But the Japanese management training is more focusing on the general concept or general behavior, not a specific skill. But that's a very different point.

He further characterized the differences as follows:

Mainly I am involved in management training, therefore, let me talk about the differences in management training. Training style is very different between Japan and the United States. One of the biggest different points is in Japan, the training or education is more lecture-oriented style. The teacher provides some knowledge or skills to the attendants. And sometimes, the teacher scolds and shouts at the class. Therefore, training or education in Japan is a more teacher- or lecture-oriented style. But meanwhile, in the United States, the training or education is more participant-oriented. Actually, not the—no—the participant is not as passive. They are not waiting for the information or skill the teacher provides—more participative type of training, here in the U.S. Therefore, management training in Japan, for example, is a very quiet classroom itself—very quiet—and the teacher tries to give the lecture.

At United GM in Kentucky, Mr. Sato referred to the general differences of the training programs between Japan and the U.S. and mentioned that the training programs in the home plant in Japan were more holistic in nature.

[O]ver there nobody feels that they need training. So what they have been doing is . . . that every year, they hire people fresh from high schools and colleges . . . the production area, too. For example, our factory has 500 workers only for the production area . . . they hire, say . . . 10-20 workers every year, then they put those workers in functional departments, such as manufacturing. Over there we have a lot of *'sempai'* (seniors or veterans) who have 10 to 20 years of experience. So what we have been doing in Japan is to leave those new workers to them, asking them to make sure to train those new workers. So all we do is to throw them into each department. That's all . . . it's easy. Then those veterans teach and train new workers about how to work, how to greet, how to write reports . . . indeed everything on the job in everyday worklife . . . not only technical matters. Then they will become veterans in 10 years who can train the next set of incoming workers. Therefore, we don't need any management-made training manuals. It's easier. In contrast, our company here built a plant five years ago and all of a sudden hired 500 workers. So when it came to training, there was nobody who knew how to do it ... everybody was a layman. It's different from Japan. In this case, we are supposed to have management-made training manuals, or an intentionally-made textbook that tells workers how to do the job step by step ... describing all the processes involved.

As Mr. Sato described in the above quote, the existence of veteran workers (*sempai*) in the home plant in Japan makes a significant difference from the training processes at the transplant. Transplants, especially smaller ones, did not have any choice other than going through a process of trial and error in their training of American workers because they did not have much accumulated knowledge and experience on implementing the training programs with American workers.

Furthermore, the training involved some form of rotation practices. There were some significant differences in the ways job rotation was realized in the Japanese transplants compared to those practices in Japan. Job rotation in Japan is more general than in most of the Japanese transplants. At United GM in Kentucky, Mr. Sato said that there was basically no rotation practice for the training purpose. When they rotated jobs, they only did it only on an ad hoc basis in the production area.

On the ad hoc basis, when Japanese managers thought they needed to, it sometimes happened that we moved a maintenance manager to a production manager, or moved a production engineer to the quality department. But this is not practiced as a system at all. It only happens sometimes. When dealing with personnel matters, we sometimes move a person in maintenance to production because we think he will be better off, or he better learn some mechanical aspects in stead of dealing with maintenance all the time. In this way we Japanese here, put some of our influence on the process. But as a system, we don't have any. If you get hired as maintenance, you will be maintenance all the way, finance will be in finance all the way. Even in finance, if you are a clerk, you will be a clerk all the way. We don't have rotation for the purpose of training a clerk to be a manager in the future.

At Y.K. Manufacturing, a manufacturer of automotive rubber in Kentucky, they allowed some job rotation for training purposes, but their curricula were differently structured from those of the parent company in Japan. Mr. Sakamoto said that rotation processes in the U.S. were based on job responsibilities, while rotation processes in Japan were based on the number of years of work experience on the job.

> For example, we put some workers in a QC circle for a certain period of time. This is because we want workers to have basic knowledge, like, to do a certain kind of job, you need sales experience, or to attend some QC's. The way we organize the curriculum, however, is very different from Japan, where the curriculum is structured according to the first year, the second year worker, and the like. The first year worker would do a year job, and the second year workers do the second year job. Here, if anything, the curriculum is based on job responsibilities. So, a manager when hiring a worker, makes a curriculum and asks a prospective department. Then, each other department responds to us. We have this procedure for the office area.

In addition, Japanese managers in transplants and American managers in American-owned firms had different opinions about employees' education. Japanese managers were skeptical about supporting employees' efforts to further advance their university education. For example, in the manufacturing environment, Japanese managers did not see MBA degrees as special or useful. Rather, some of them told me that Americans with professional degrees are harder to work with. Instead, they seemed to appreciate employees who had a lot of on-the-job experience and a long work history. In general, they were skeptical about the training in a school environment. One Japanese employee told me that employees should pay for a long-term education themselves, since the company already gives bonuses. He said that this would be a fairer system than selecting a few employees who would be able to get additional education.

On a general level, educational allowances may relate to the size of the company. As I mentioned, most of the Japanese transplants in the U.S. tended to be smaller in size and more recently established than their U.S. owned counterparts. When the company is new and small, many organizational policies and processes tend to go through a period of trial and error. This was especially the case with three Japanese transplants in my study, where both the Japanese and American managers and workers did not have a lot of experience in implementing new organizational policies and processes. Mainly because of smaller size and short history, these three transplants did not yet have a systematic company policies and practices within professional departments. Instead, both managers' and workers' job functions tended to be more multiple and less specialized. The boundaries of workers' jobs on the shopfloor, therefore, were more diffused. Under these circumstances, managers did not even need an employee who was a specialist with a professional degree.

On the other hand, managers in American-owned companies were proud of their structured training and education programs. The two American companies I visited were large, had longer company histories and thus, had very thorough and highly structured programs for employees. In contrast to Japanese managers, all the middle to upper-level managers with whom I talked appreciated professional degrees. In fact, some of them had already achieved graduate degrees, such as an MBA or Ph.D. in industrial engineering or design. They also completed those programs with the support from the company. Ms. Gutman mentioned her company's education support programs.

> Other benefits we have are educational programs where you can—depending on it being related to your job—you can get your tuition reimbursed, if you're going to night school. Or we do have [MAC] (pseudonym) fellowship programs. If your unit sponsors you and if you're one of the top candidates, then you can go on for your master's or doctorate . . . and that's what I did for my master's and doctorate—went on a [MAC] fellowship program for that.

Socialization of employees in firms in Japan typically involves the process, where newly hired employees are socialized into company's norms and values through several group-oriented activities, such as intensive training sessions and teams at the workplace. Among five transplants, socialization of new employees to the work culture was non-existent. As I previously mentioned, all transplants in this study were recently established in the U.S., thus, had not been able to form any established organizational culture into which new employees were socialized. On the other hand, managers of transplants considered social interaction among employees, especially interactions between Japanese and American employees, an important element in forming a corporate culture unique to the company.

In this sense, there was a great deal of emphasis on the socializing of new employees by both the Japanese and American managers in transplants. For the Japanese managers in transplants, however, the reality was that they could not afford to pay company-level attention to the implementation of any systematic programs that promote social interactions among locally-hired new employees, especially between the Japanese and American employees. All transplants except for one company had only been able to implement some company-sponsored activities, such as picnics and Christmas parties.

Though four of the small to medium sized transplants in the midwest generally conformed to the picture that I described in the above, I visited one large sized Japanese transplant in central Michigan, Yamadadenso Manufacturing. This transplant had been so successful that the management was very open with me about their accomplishments. In this case, the company recognized the importance of the social interaction between the Japanese and American employees, and had been able to put considerable amount of management-level effort to implement several social programs. Dan Dooley recognized the importance of social interaction between Japanese and American employees. However, referring to other Japanese transplants' struggles to integrate the Japanese and American workforce, he pointed to their mistakes of selecting qualified American managers.

You know, we have twelve Japanese plants here in [Central Creek] (pseudonym), and some of them are better managed than others. And the biggest thing that I've seen is the talent that they bring into the organization. And in my mind sometimes I wonder if the Japanese parent company intentionally tried to hire weak American managers, because, you know, in that organization, you look at it and the staff that they have just doesn't have the talent to run the organization. And so, in my mind it's like 'Why would they hire such a group of people?' I mean, 'Do they intentionally, you know, have these people here?' They're not even very good figureheads. And I think that's probably the biggest failing of some of the Japanese plants, is some of the talent, that they just weren't real capable of selecting some of the people. In other companies that are more successful, they've put together a good team of people.

Dooley emphasized the importance of having strong teams that consist of the Japanese staff and qualified American staff. He further stated that the company had to make a conscious effort to integrate Japanese and American employees.

The other thing is you continually have to work at that element. The socialization is very, very important. For example, in our cafeteria, if you go down there at lunch, you'll find American and Japanese at the same table. Now, in the beginning, it was very easy for all the Japanese to stay at one table and all the Americans at a different table. And the reason is it's so tough to speak in limited English for a four-hour period and then go to lunch with somebody and still continue in limited English—and it's natural to sit down at that at that table with your own group of people so they can speak Japanese and we can speak whole English. So, from the beginning, we cannot allow that to happen, because that will create a schism between the Americans and the Japanese. So, we struggle with the language during lunch. We made up the golf teams—Americans and Japanese as a golf team—not all Japanese teams and all American teams.

For Dooley, the key was to make a management-level effort to mix the American and Japanese groups when the company started its operation.

We emphasize that, like for my human resource manager, I told him, 'Kim, you have a Japanese friend. I don't care who—select someone. I want him to come to your house. I want you to go to his house. I want you to understand as much as you can the Japanese system and his mind, and socialize together.' So, I really believe that's probably one of the key things, when we started our company. We really spent a lot of time with the two groups. We have a meeting once a year.

We go off-site for three days and two nights, and we have a business meeting. We also have golf, and we go out drinking together, and we play darts, and we, you know, try to get some quality time to try to understand the two groups. That was, I think, important.

In addition to the importance of social interaction during working hours, he also pointed to the importance of the after-work social contact between the Japanese and American employees.

The other thing is I encourage after-work socialization—going out and having a few beers together, or go to someone's home. Last night, the vice-president of engineering, [Mike Yamada], brought his family to my house. And we went out and taught his children to water-ski. And so, they were probably, maybe five hours at my home last night. And he's new to the United States. He came in January. So, it gives his wife and his children an opportunity to kind of meet my wife and my children, and they see a different lifestyle and the homes. And I think that's important. To help develop a level of trust, you've got to know each other—both on the job and off the job.

Dooley said that it was very difficult for the Japanese managers to understand why they had to make such a company-level conscious effort to blend the Japanese and American workforce. When transplants were going through the start-up phase, everyone, both workers and managers, tended to be overwhelmed by the amount of work required to catch up with the original schedule. Even in that case, according to Dooley, it was critical to spend quality time and lay the ground work so that future relationships could develop. Dooley recalled how difficult it was when the company was starting.

And that was very difficult for the Japanese to understand at first. If you remember ... I said this plant started in June of 1986. In February of 1986, in the wintertime, I started talking about having a golf tournament, a golf league. We play golf every week. And one of the Japanese executives, he said, 'Oh, we cannot do.' And I said, 'Why?' He said—at that time, we had a hundred Japanese technicians installing equipment. And we all worked really long hours, you know. It was not unusual to be here at ten o'clock at night. They said, 'How can we, on Wednesday night at five o'clock, leave the plant and go play golf, and they're still working?' Very valid point. I said, 'That's true. But more important is we're going to work together for the next five years or four years. That relationship needs to get started very early. And so, it's more important than the management team.' And I don't mean just management team, because we had supervisors and we had some production associates. 'It's more important that we start working together and socializing together right now with the beginning of the company, because we'll never have time in the future.' And he had a very difficult time on Wednesday night. I'd say, 'Okay, Gene, it's five o'clock. It's time for the golf league.' For him to leave that plant and leave the technicians still installing machines was very difficult. But I think it was very critical to the start of the organization—it was just a minor piece, but a critical piece.

Speaking of cultural differences, Dooley said that these differences were not something that were addressed in everyday worklife. For him, cultural differences were not something that hindered the development of the working relationship between the Japanese and American employees when the company made an conscious effort at its early stages.

As a general [rule], I don't think that there's that much difference. You know, here we spend a lot less time writing lengthy reports because it gives the Japanese headaches if they have to read it. So we don't write lengthy reports or try to summarize things, so . . . I don't like to write, so that makes it easier for me. But I don't think there's anything really that pronounced. I think if you talk to a company and they start talking about, 'Gee, we have this big cultural barrier.' I really think they don't know what the hell they're talking about. I really don't think that they worked at it, you know. When we started this company, we really worked at developing relationships.

Mr. Nagato, a coordinator at the same company, also recognized the need to develop a cross-cultural training course for the newly assigned Japanese personnel.

The purpose is that, as I explained, American associates have lots of opportunity to attend management training here. They are learning a lot of things. On the other hand, Japanese people here don't have opportunity to learn, actually. So—and in this type of company, we have lots of, you know, conflict between Japanese and management which sometimes creates a problem. That's because of the lack of understanding of American business environment or culture and the way of thinking of American people. Therefore, the president consented that a course be developed for Japanese. And actually, we are conducting some cross-cultural training in Japan before they come to the U.S. The basic content is—it consists of three or four items. One is interpersonal communication. It involves confrontation skills, or constructive criticism method, or praise and recognition, which Japanese are not good at that kind of skill. And also, we teach the human resources system, which is very different from Japan—[and] like recruiting, you know, performance appraisal, and—discipline, salary structure, or sexual harassment, or equal employment opportunity, or such kind of things.

Yamadadenso was the only Japanese transplant in my study that was able to organize a management-level effort to emphasize the importance of social interaction between the Japanese and American employees. For the rest of four Japanese transplants in my study, however, the reality was that even though they could not afford to make a management-level effort, the individual managers, both Americans and Japanese, recognized this importance.

Among five Japanese transplants in this study, socialization of new employees by the management by no means paralleled the socialization processes of companies in Japan, where new employees were intensively inculcated in the company's norms and values by the management. These transplants have not been able to form any established company's norms and values mainly because of their short history in the U.S. Instead, managers at transplants emphasized the importance of social interaction between Japanese and American employees in their effort to create a company's unique corporate culture. The discussion of socialization processes in the Japanese transplants, therefore, necessitates examining the issue of corporate culture of the transplants. I will look at the processes in which the

Japanese transplants try to develop their unique organizational (corporate) culture in the next section.

8. Attention to developing a corporate culture and management philosophy

In my interviews, managers in the Japanese transplants frequently talked about their unique corporate culture. Most of this "uniqueness" was focused on how they tried to integrate the Japanese and American workforce. As in the case of social interaction of employees, Japanese managers in my study tended to emphasize the importance of having strong managerial philosophies and policies. All of these transplants made a certain effort on the shopfloor level and created suggestion groups and work teams with American and Japanese staff. However, the reality was that both managers and workers were going through a process of trial and error, and did not yet see a clear direction, mainly because of their lack of experience.

Regarding social interaction of the Japanese and American employees, all transplants in the Midwest also demonstrated a similar pattern. The worker interactions at the workplace between Japanese and American employees often involved a great amount of dissatisfaction that was mainly derived from the differences in perceptions (and expectations) about how work should be done and how work tasks should be accomplished. This dissatisfaction was often voiced by both the Japanese and the American employees. In addition to the dissatisfaction which was mainly due to cultural differences, the American employees' frustration was also directed at the organization's managerial structures, such as their slow promotion track, the glass ceiling, and few female employees in higher-level management.

The process of interaction at the workplace also involves the issue of workforce diversity. All Japanese transplants that I visited in the Midwest were located in the area where the proportion of racial and ethnic minorities to the total local population was very small. One Japanese automotive stamping transplant in Michigan, though they were close to the Detroit area, was located in a county where the percentage of ethnic minorities were 3-4 percent of the total local population. Yamadadenso in Michigan was located in an area where there was a 10 percent minority representation in the local population.

Midwest Silicon, a silicon wafer manufacturing plant in southern Ohio, was located in a region where African-Americans were 2 percent and Asians were 2 percent of the local population. Two companies in Kentucky, United GM and Y.K. Manufacturing, were also located in an area where the percentage of ethnic minorities comprised only 1-2 percent of the total local population. Most of managers that I interviewed, both Japanese and American, almost unanimously mentioned that it was not difficult for the company to abide by the EEOC federal guidelines because of the small percentage of racial and ethnic minorities in the local population.

Interviews with some non-management level employees, however, showed that some problems existed in everyday worklife at the workplace, if not on the management policy level. Laura worked as a human resources specialist at Yamadadenso Manufacturing. She thought that there were certain limits on how far women and minorities could be promoted. Laura did not really see that being an American in the Japanese transplant hindered her professional growth. However, it made a significant difference to be a male or a female, especially in the production area. Men generally had more opportunities for promotion than women. Men tended to get promoted more quickly than women. In addition, Laura thought that it was very difficult for Japanese managers to accept a female team leader. She characterized the situation as follows.

> I think Japanese managers have been taught that in America you must respect female workers, and so they make that important. But many American managers don't make that very important. But in general, I mean, it's very good. I mean, I haven't had any really bad experiences here. I don't feel discriminated against because I'm American working for a Japanese company. I don't know. That's a really difficult question for me to answer. There's no special attempts made to promote good working women, only pretty much white men . . . [M]aybe because in the office, the managers are at a much higher level, and so therefore have more exposure to qualified women professionals. But in production, they have very little exposure to qualified females, professionals.

According to Laura, women's promotion usually stopped at the sub-leader's position. At the time of my visit to the company, Yamadadenso had 75-80 team leaders, of which only four (4) were female.

> [I]f you talk non-management, I mean, just associates in general, it's pretty standard. I mean, it's very cut-and-dried—'If you meet these criteria, you will be promoted. If you don't, you don't.' So it's very objective. Moving from advanced associate to sub-leader or team leader, in my opinion, is very unfair. There's very few women in management positions, like sub-leader or team leader.

Laura's case was not unique to Yamadadenso. Many female workers in the production area at other transplants in the Midwest, California, and the case study company in New Mexico tended to express their opinion that being an woman mattered more than being an American in the Japanese transplants.

In the previous section of the socialization, I quoted Dan Dooley's comments on the importance of selecting qualified American managers, and the social interaction between the Japanese and American employees. Yamadadenso was the only transplant where the company was able to put considerable amount of a management-level effort into programs that promoted social contact between Japanese and American employees. However, as Dooley suggested, many transplants actually had employed American managers who were quite frustrated with the ongoing management practices and with the ways they were treated by other Japanese managers.

Kenney and Florida refer to the "unreconstructed American managers" in the Japanese transplants who are immobilized in the corporate structure and, therefore, quite frustrated with working under the influence of the Japanese production system.

> The U.S. corporate world is organized in a caste system of salaried managers and blue-collar workers who toil on the factory floor. The clear distinction between white-collar and blue-collar workers is codified in a legal system that separates employees by categories such as exempt and nonexempt. The hallmarks of American management are centralization and a command system of authority. American managers who have been trained to protect their own

power and authority have trouble understanding the Japanese system, which operates on the basis of securing workers' participation—not the unilateral exercise of managerial power. Under this system, workers have a great deal of discretion and even authority. In Japan, shop-floor workers often move into lower management tasks. More importantly, their 'stake' in the firm is similar to that of the managers. American mangers find it difficult—and sometimes impossible—to manage in the Japanese production system. They are used to taking orders from superiors and telling their subordinates what to do (Kenney and Florida 1993: 287).

For Dan Dooley, these "unreconstructed American managers" were the result of the weak American management teams. He thought this was a failure that many Japanese transplants had made in the process of hiring American managers.

I guess the other thing is in some cases the Japanese have not been very successful in hiring people in many companies. And as a consequence they have a very weak American manager in that company. It's true, the Americans don't make any decisions, because they have a weak management team. And I have very little sympathy for those American managers, huh? So, in my opinion, it's how you made it. But I don't think there's a—I don't believe that there's some big plot that was born in [Yamadadenso] Japan that they introduced into an American plant.

In his case, Dooley did not see that being an American has hindered his professional growth in his company. When the company was new, he needed to ask for consent from the Japanese president to make important decisions. Now, as he described below, the company was leaning more toward consensus decision making. Although his comments below also indicate that the decision making power eventually belonged more to the Japanese, Dan Dooley exemplifies a case where an American manager has earned the trust of the Japanese management.

I've been in three other companies in my life. And when I was in Dresser, Dresser is a Texas company . . . And we used to complain in

Wisconsin that the people in Texas didn't understand us. It's the same. But my point is that, you know, any time you have a corporate office in another location, you have differences. And I don't think the fact that a person's Japanese or American is any different. There's cultural things that, you know, you have to be aware of. The reason I have a personnel guy from Japan is I asked for him. And the reason is it's very difficult for us to sell concepts to the Japanese and the staff, because none of us had any experience really in doing that. And so that more often—you know, when the Japanese put it down, they put it on a one-page document, and they have a lot of little boxes and arrows pointing to things. And typically, Americans don't sell their concepts using little boxes and arrows. And so, when Jay— a friend of mine—he's able to take our ideas and show us how to make—to present these to the Japanese staff so that they're comfortable. And the first five years of the company, it was easy because everybody was very, very busy. And so, basically, we'd go in and say, 'We need to do this.' And the Japanese president would say, 'Is this important?' And I would say, 'Yes.' And he'd say, 'Okay, do it.' But that operating fashion isn't as acceptable today as we look for consensus decision making as the company's matured. So, he's real important to us for that reason. So, I asked that they send him from Japan to help teach us how to make presentations. And so, we're much more polished on how we present ideas now to the Japanese executive staff.

In contrast, George Donald represented a typical case of the "unreconstructed American managers." As I referred to him earlier, George was an executive manufacturing manager of Oyama America Corporation, a Japanese-owned automotive stamping plant located in a small town in Michigan. Compared to many other Japanese transplants in this study that belonged to Keiretsu[2] groups in Japan, Oyama America was family-owned, and did not belong to any Keiretsu groups in Japan. As a family-owned company, Oyama America had strong top-down corporate control by the Japanese management. Although Oyama America may be unique in this, the following remark by George illustrates the general perception of the Japanese and American relations in the workplace.

I know people that worked for Toyota, for Honda. I talked to American people there, and wherever you go, the story is very similar. There are always some differences, but fundamentally the problems are the same. That is, the impatience on the part of Americans, the differences in how people look at jobs and how they should be done, management styles, the glass ceilings, and there is a basic problems of their disrespect for Americans coming from the Japanese. The Japanese don't think much of American auto people. I, as a highest ranking American here, I know that even though I am executive manager, [the Japanese president of the company] he places more value, on the least lowest ranking Japanese person here. Tells him, rather than me. I know this happens time and time again.

As illustrated in George's case, he represented one of the unreconstructed American managers in the Japanese transplants, who perceived that Japanese staff members thought of themselves as superior to Americans. Speaking of a new manager from Japan, George showed his frustration.

They bring another manager here, and this new guy, he doesn't understand me, he doesn't know me, has not much respect for me, he's Japanese. Automatically he comes here thinking he's superior to everybody, and unfortunately that's the case, not in every case, but unfortunately in too many, too often, it's the case. They come with a superior attitude too often.

What was significant about Americans' perception of Japanese managers' feelings of superiority was that this was often communicated in very subtle ways.

[I]t's very difficult to sit down and accept that I will be treated as an inferior human being for the rest of my life working right here. Not that there is any day-to-day conflict, or friction. That's not what it's all about. It's about subtleties.

What George pointed out about the managers' subtle sense of superiority was by no means limited to Oyama America corporation. As Dan Dooley illustrated before, Yamadadenso was the only transplant in this study that consciously emphasized the integration of the Japanese and American workforce. However, even at Yamadadenso, Mr. Nagato suggested that the Japanese management was better than the American management, though he tried to be open to the ideas coming from the American workers.

> Probably this sounds very arrogant, but I think—you know, somebody said Japanese style of management and U.S. style of management, there are lots of differences. I don't think—yeah, we have lots of differences, but I think there are no pure American or Japanese ways in management. A lot of things should be one. I mean, Japanese management has a lot of things we learned from the United States. I mean, lots of management philosophy which was established in the United States. And Japanese learned a lot of things from Americans. And for some reason, the United States did not follow quite well such good philosophy which was established in the past. But the Japanese—we tried to digest lots of management philosophy—good philosophy—which was created in United States. So, therefore, I think, as far as management concerned, there are lots of good points in the so-called 'Japanese management.' So, I am not pushing that Japanese style. I am just pushing what is good. For some reason—a lot of things have come from my background, which is a lot I learned in Japan. So, some of the American associates alarm me—fear that, you know, 'Mike is pushing the, you know, [YDJ]'s [Yamadadenso Japan] way or Japanese way.' But, you know, if the American associates bring up some better idea, better than, you know, so-called 'Japanese way,' I will be ready to accept. But in many cases, you know, he did not bring me a better idea. Therefore, if so, let's do this. Is my fear—this sounds Japanese way, but I think at this moment, this is the best way, as far as we know. But in the American style, there are, you know, a lot of good things too. For example, training field—training method or training technique, or— is very, very advanced. Like, you know, we have lots of good training courses and training material, participant work—that's very, very standardized. In that sense, that's much better than the [YDJ]. In that field, we can learn a lot from the United States. That's my impression.

Among the Japanese transplants in my study, most of the frustrations of both the Japanese and American employees were derived from the differences in perceptions regarding company policies and processes, and worklife in general. Most of them concerned cultural differences at the workplace. Mr. Estes, a human resources manager at United GM, talked about the cultural differences as follows.

> I notice it, but I don't know how to explain to you how I notice it. It's not—it's not something that I pay attention to, because I treat— you know, I work with you as a Japanese, I'll work with you the same as I'll work with any American that comes in. So, I don't try to make a distinction. But I think there is a cultural thing, and the cultural issues are something that I'm not familiar with because I'm not as familiar with the Japanese culture. But I have to be cognizant of that and make sure that I recognize—you know, recognize that difference. Just like lay-offs, when we talk about lay-offs, I realize there's a difference there. And I realize that a Japanese worker— based on my knowledge of what the Japanese tell me here—you know, they say, 'Well, we don't understand why you have to do this'—whatever it is—'because in Japan' . . . Let me talk about promotion for one thing. We were talking about making a supervisor our team leader. And in Japan, the Japanese were telling me, 'We just go out and find the person, and we say that's your job.' Here, we look around and we talk to different people—'Are you interested?'— and give them the opportunity to move up to that job. Whereas in Japan, from what I understand, in [Musashi Sheet Glass] (pseudonym) they look at a person and say, 'I want you to do that job tomorrow.' So, that's a difference that I've noticed.

Mr. Nagato, a coordinator at Yamadadenso, also saw cultural differences at the workplace.

> I think the sense of values is different. For Japanese, the worklife is sometimes more important than private life—and they're very dedicated to the job for the company. And therefore, we have such background, so, we sometimes—we Japanese—expect same things of American people here. Generally speaking, Japanese people tend to have such expectation of American associates, yes. But once we

come to the United States, everybody's sense of value or—how you say?—work ethic, is completely different. Private life is more important than life in the company. And so, sometimes Japanese peoples' expectations are totally destroyed until some point. But we should understand that the society itself very different. So, it's—we should not expect as Japanese. So, sometimes, of course, I learn from American people that I should more—I should think much of the family, or private life, or my own time.

As Mr. Nagato pointed out, the difference in worklife style between the U.S. and Japan was perceived as the most obvious and visible difference at the workplace. Needless to say the difference in working hours—the overtime work—was the most conspicuous among many other differences. Laura at Yamadadenso recognized that the Japanese staff at the company worked much longer hours than the American staff.

Working hours—Japanese work much more overtime than U.S. associates. That's a big one . . . Oh, yeah. Much longer.

At Y.K Manufacturing in Kentucky, Sakamoto emphasized the "work comes first" attitude. In his company, the overtime work was an informal contract with American workers upon the time of employment.

Our understanding is that when we hire on the condition that they (exempt) agree to do about 20 hours of overtime a month, although this is not written. Here, work comes first. If you don't get through the work, you simply stay longer to complete. So, sometimes you see some Americans working most of the time, sometimes on Saturday. Engineers often do this. But if you work hard we reward you through a raise.

As I mentioned before in the section on the lifetime employment, United GM in Kentucky relied on overtime work so that the company could keep the minimum numbers of production workers and could avoid laying-off those workers when the company faces an economic downturn. Moreover, Sato mentioned that the overtime work at his company was used for making up for the absenteeism of the workers. This was posing a problem for the company.

> [B]ecause now we have a problem of having too much overtime. Overtime here is different from Japan. In Japan, we do overtime to do additional work. Whereas here, it is basically for making up for absenteeism . . . about 90% . . . including absenteeism and personal vacations. The reality is that there is always some workers who are absent from the line . . . and we keep production going through the overtime work of other workers from other shifts. This is very costly, one of the big factors for reducing the profit for the company. So, there is a problem: how not to increase overtime when we implement QC's.

In addition to the difference of the working hours of the Japanese and American employees, Mr. Nagato of Yamadadenso pointed to the difference in the processes by which the Japanese and American made certain decisions. In my study, many American as well as Japanese employees mentioned this point.

> American people tend to decide something very quickly. But Japanese are not comfortable to decide quickly without lots of information, or what other companies do, or what professional analysis of that issue. How about us? How about the increase of other companies, or other industry, or the Kellogg Institute? It is very hard to make decisions without such—lots of information. American style—this might be a kind of stereotype—Americans tend to decide very quickly. And if it's not good, later change. Japanese are not comfortable with that. Get a lot of information as much possible very beginning, and spend a lot of time to analyze and decide. And once they decide, they don't want to change a lot.

Laura, an American human recourses specialist at Yamadadenso, made the same point as Mr. Nagato.

> Problem solving is also different—because we don't spend as much time searching for a cause of the problem before we solve it, so the solution may not be best, whereas the Japanese spend more time

looking for a cause of the problem, which is part of decision making,
I guess—kind of linked to decision making.

Dan Dooley also pointed out the Japanese's inflexibility in decision
making in the American workplace, where most American managers
were used to "fire-fighting" when solving problems.

> One of the funny things when they first started the company was we
> found that actually that the Japanese were not very good at quick
> decisions, or what we call fire-fighting. When the plan goes to hell,
> and then we need a quick decision, it becomes very comical when
> you're watching a Japanese manager who can't cope with that very
> well. And, as a matter of fact, we've told them—one time we said,
> you know, when there's an emergency situation, we will revert to
> American-style decision making, because frankly, the Americans are
> very good at it—because we spend all of our lives fighting fires.
> Now, there's—in this statement, there's bad news. The bad news is,
> as a manager, I'm very ashamed to think that all of my life I have
> managed through crisis-by-crisis. But we're very good at managing
> crises because we have a lot of experience. The Japanese have almost
> no experience in crisis management because they do such a good job
> of planning. So, that's kind of an area that is a concern.

In addition to the differences of "styles" in worklife and decision
making processes, there usually is an employee in the Japanese
organizations who acts as an information agent and mediating
influence in the midst of the organizational hierarchy. Mr.Sakamoto
referred to the "fukukan" [3] as a crucial difference of the organizations
of control between the Japanese and the American organizations.
"Fukukan" originally referred to the name of the position in the
Japanese navy during World War II, who served directly under the
captain and supported him. In Japanese organizations some managers
use this metaphor to point out the effectiveness of leadership style and
the importance of "human relations" in everyday worklife in the
company. Sakamoto remarked as follows:

> They do say a lot freely for their boss. In Japan, there is a kind of
> person created by its organizational culture who can listen to his

boss's or company's shortcomings and good points as well as to the workers' concern, called *fukukan* . . . and this keeps the company going. They are also the ones who have a good grasp on what's going on among workers. Here, however, you don't see this system.

All these differences that were pointed out by the interviewees (both the Japanese and American) in my study eventually lead to the question of how the transplants can integrate the Japanese and American workforces and create a unique corporate culture. In the context of the Japanese transplants in my study, this posed a question of how the Japanese managers could transplant what they perceived as positive elements in the American industrial environment. Mr. Sato talked about corporate culture as follows:

[I]t is how to change the corporate culture of this company. I am not talking about changing the culture of the U.S. but changing the 'culture' of the company. The majority of workers here are Americans. So, we cannot expect that they change totally in and out . . . they are Americans and we are Japanese. So, the question is how we can transplant here what we consider good parts of Japanese corporate culture, ways of doing things, or ways of thinking, within the range that is applicable to the American context. How much we can introduce these parts to Americans, and how well can Americans adopt them and practice them in their own terms. So, our task is to throw a ball in their court tactically. Concretely speaking, as I said, for example, concerning training, Americans tend to just follow what they are told. What we have to do, then, is to make the system of training, to create the idea of what is training about, and to change the relationships between boss and subordinates culturally. The problem is how to change the system so that the boss can train and 'rear' subordinates until they can take over his position . . . then he also can be recognized, too. In so doing, he also can be further promoted. So, this is only one of many examples. I want to create this kind of culture. Also the same is true of QC circles and small group activities. This idea was born originally in the U.S. and grew up in Japan. And I think this way actually works out the best. But we don't know how. So, we have to create a culture in which this practice really takes root, for not only on the worker-side, but also on the management-side. This is really the most challenging thing.

Harry Stewart, a quality control manager at Y.K. Manufacturing, mentioned that the Japanese managers at his company had made more effort to pay attention to the issue of corporate culture than the American employees.

> I think the Japanese here at the company have made a very conscious effort, probably much more so than Americans have, to adopt an American culture, or at least an understanding of American culture. I think they have done more than we have tried to understand the Japanese culture. That's the way I personally feel. Because I know my boss is very concerned about what Americans think. I think our Japanese have spent awful lot of time considering [this] issue. They think about that a lot. All of our Japanese [managers] have made a very good effort to understand American culture.

Considering that the Japanese managers actually live in the U.S., it may be reasonable to say that the Japanese managers in the U.S. have made relatively more effort to understand the American culture than vise versa. However, as shown below in Mr. Sato's comment, the question is whether the company can afford to pay a management-level attention to the issue of corporate culture.

Eventually, the issue of corporate culture poses a significant challenge, not only to the American managers and workers, but also to the Japanese managers in the U.S. For Mr. Sato, this was the area that many Japanese transplants had neglected, while some of the well-established, successful Japanese transplants in the U.S., such as Toyota Motor Manufacturing, had made a management-level conscious effort to overcome cultural differences and create a unique corporate culture of the company. The issue of corporate culture had long been set aside among transplants because of the urgent everyday business issues. This was particularly the case among smaller-scale transplants, whose parent companies in Japan did not have much accumulated knowledge and experience on production in foreign countries. As Dan Dooley noted, many Japanese transplants had made mistakes in the personnel areas. It is quite paradoxical to note that Mr. Sato also argued that the Japanese transplants had not been able to select well-qualified American managers as well as Japanese staff for their overseas production, despite the stereotypical images on the Japanese management in the West that the Japanese systems value human resources. After the interview, Mr.Sato reflected on what he thinks the Japanese transplants need to do in order to succeed in the U.S.

> This is something I felt for the first time after I came here. For Japanese companies like us, before we teach Americans about our management practices, we should come here after reviewing our own culture, and what we have been doing in Japan. For instance, in our glass manufacturing environment, what training is all about, what items we should be training, from the manufacturing techniques about glass making, to how you should deal with people in the production area, including human skills. There are certain points that we should cover in order to manufacture high quality glass. In Japan, we know somehow . . . vaguely. When we are asked to write it down, we just can't. This is true for not only myself but also many others, too. We haven't thought through our procedures clearly enough to be able to write them down and show to others. It is probably the same in other companies. But Toyota-san has probably done this. But the second-rate companies [like United GM] have not yet been able to organize this. This is because there is historically accumulated knowledge even though there are no systematic training programs. For example, there are many persons who are like walking dictionaries in each workplace, not only in the production area but also in the office area. We really don't have to organize the knowledge as long as those people are there, and when a new worker comes in through rotation practices, he will learn the know-how in 10-20 years and grow with it. So, we don't have to do particularly anything for him. However, when we come to places like here, we intentionally have to prepare manuals for training. Nothing starts if we just throw workers into the production area. So, before we talk about such-and-such about American culture, we have to review what we have to do to manufacture high quality glass and how we have been going about it, like, itemize everything, and then, talk about. For example, this is too unique to bring to the U.S., or this is a wonderful way that can be transplanted not only to the U.S. but also to Europe. We have to select these aspects. Things don't work unless

we come here after understanding this. I guess most of the companies except Toyota or Nissan came to the U.S. without going through this process. So, it's always the same. You come here and start complaining about everything in the U.S., this is not good, that's not good in the U.S. . . . until you reach certain level. You now say, 'Wait a minute, now I understand that America is not good, but what about Japan?' Then, you find out that you don't know how to write manuals. You find that you were not doing work really systematically. (*'Tekitou ni yatteta'*) [4] This is not the way things work in the U.S. And this is not something that can be accomplished only by Japanese employees dispatched here. There are nine altogether. I think there should be some settings where we can do this in Japan. Companies like Sony, and Matsushita which now produce the same quality goods or even higher with low cost in Brazil or Malaysia. I think they have already got this . . . in some form or another. We don't have this yet. And the parent company side, if they have the attitude, like 'Let Americans think about everything because we're in America,' we will never succeed. I think this takes us several generations to do this. But when looking at those trading companies that went to overseas right after World War II, there were dispatched employees who stayed here long time ago and went home, and got promoted to high levels in Japan. They have had an accumulated exchange of Japanese personnel between Japan and the U.S. So, they have an accumulated knowledge of what is American culture, and what is our own culture, as well as what are transferable and what are not. That's why they don't face a lot of troubles when opening an office overseas all of a sudden. For example, when deciding whom they have to select, they don't have a lot of difficulties. Whereas we have been making a lot of mistakes in judgment.

Thus, the process of creating a unique corporate culture necessarily involved the process of localizing the management of the company. Moreover, localization, or hiring American managers for important positions, was a matter of restructuring the pre-existing corporate-level control and management control at the workplace.

United GM was a joint venture company between GOM (Gregory-Owens Motor) and MSG (Musashi Sheet Glass). Norbert Estes, a human resources manager, mentioned as follows regarding the relations of corporate-level control between the two parent companies.

[GOM] controls a lot of the policies that we do—because it's American, and we're dealing with American workers. So, the policies are more geared towards the American culture than [they are towards] the Japanese culture. So, [GOM] sort of focuses that way. [MSG] gets involved in the finances and the technical [areas].

Like this joint-venture company, there was a tendency for the Japanese transplants in my study to have more American control in personnel matters, while preserving stronger corporate control from Japan on financial matters and on the actual production processes on the shop-floor. At Y.K. Manufacturing, Mr.Sakamoto talked about localizing the company and how he wanted the company to be.

I want this company to be run by Americans, although I am not sure if this can be realized or not. So, this will never happen if Japanese employees keep doing crucial jobs. So, even if your answer is no, you let Americans do it and wait patiently. This is the style. In this sense, things take time. In truth, if we Japanese do everything by ourselves, it would be the fastest. This is because, here, we have moved our business from Japan. So, the Japanese have knowledge, and experience. It's quicker if we Japanese do it. But if we keep doing this, we will always be a Japanese company, and never be able to be an American company. So, now, every Japanese company here in America is doing the same thing, letting Americans do it instead of doing it by ourselves and showing them. I constantly say this to Japanese employees here. It may look like we are holding back. But that's better, I think. From Japanese standard, they say, 'why don't you guys just do it.' But here I think this is the best way and I haven't changed this in any situation. I, for one, want to shift more to the coordinator system. Otherwise, this company will never be American. Then, the customers should be American, too. So, for the time being, it's the best for our company to keep the present condition, the same mixed-management, the same number of Japanese coordinators. But eventually I want this company to be managed by all Americans. Considering problems we have now, I think that we shouldn't change our system so rapidly.

Regarding the "mix" of Japanese and American elements in the organizations of production of the company, Sakamoto further stated as follows:

> I guess we have a mix of both. It is that Japanese basically are in charge of business side, because we can 'read' customers. But, in practice, it is Americans who do the job in our company. So, Americans are in charge of the matters inside the company. So, it is a mix, I think. If you talk to any Americans, nobody says Japanese did it. They say we did it. Of course, we made lots of mistakes. But looking back now, that was an investment. We [Japanese] couldn't foresee, and the Americans have learned from that, too. But in terms of the necessary functions as a company, especially in terms of customer services, I think it's more Japanese. Americans do very well, but they are still at the stage where they can't decide by themselves. This has a lot to do with customers. Regarding customers, Japanese actually decide which customer we should be dealing with. So, it is Japanese here, too, who can deal with Japanese customers. This is something I shouldn't say in public. We, of course, use 'omote' and 'ura' ['front' and 'back' distinction] with one another. So, sometimes it's difficult because of this. All in all, we have a mix. But it is Americans who actually run the company. And it is Japanese who make subtle decisions and watch over and make sure that things are going okay.

The above statement by Sakamoto showed the subtleties of corporate control in the process of localization in the Japanese transplants. Five Japanese transplants in the Midwest allocated corporate control to the American managers in some areas, such as personnel, where it was more practical for the Japanese to allow American managers to exercise control. When the company had to deal with American customers, the Japanese managers preferred to place Americans in the position of control. When the company dealt with Japanese customers, they preferred to have the Japanese staff in the position of control. However, as shown in Sakamoto's remark, there were always Japanese advisors behind the scene, usually under the title of "coordinator," who actually supervised the American managers and workers in the workplace. Mr. Takizawa, a marketing manager at United GM, said that there were Japanese coordinators who, though perhaps not overtly, supervised American workers.

> In practice, everybody is American. I have some Japanese employees who act as coordinators. But, in reality, they are just like supervisors behind the scene.

CONCLUSION

Organizational practices among the five Japanese transplants in the Midwest were different from those of firms in Japan and American-owned firms in the U.S. For example, training programs and small group activities on the shopfloor have resulted in different practices because of the social and cultural differences of the work environments between the U.S. and Japan. Although the Japanese managers at these transplants recognized the need to be more systematic in their approaches to implementing training programs and small group activities, they have not been able to realize this mainly because of their short history of U.S. operations and their lack of experience. Likewise, all of the transplants except Yamadadenso could not afford to make any conscious, management-level effort to promote social interaction between American and Japanese employees.

Both American and Japanese managers emphasized the importance of developing a unique corporate culture within the company. The issue of corporate culture among Japanese transplants always concerned ways and means of integrating American and Japanese workers, and creating a hybrid corporate culture. In reality, however, transplants could not attend to these issues on the management level, in part because management did not recognize the importance of doing so in the initial start up phase, partly because they did not have the experience and accumulated knowledge, and partially because of the Japanese management's inability to hire qualified American employees.

Except for Yamadadenso, a large transplant in my study that was successful in integrating both American and Japanese workforces, four medium/small-sized transplants still employed so-called "unreconstructed American managers" who were virtually immobilized in the corporate structure because of the social and cultural differences. Indeed, many transplants had not succeeded in hiring qualified American managers and workers who were able to adapt to such a unique environment. The issue of corporate culture thus has posed a significant challenge to both American and Japanese employees at transplants.

On the other hand, Yamadadenso, was succeeding in overcoming cultural differences at the workplace and creating a hybrid corporate culture unique to the company. As Dan Dooley noted, the management at Yamadadenso started making conscious corporate-level effort to promote social interaction between American and Japanese employees when the company started. For him, it was critical that the management took the initiative to mix American and Japanese employees, not only during normal work hours but also after work hours. It was also important for the company to have strong American management teams so that they could earn the trust of the Japanese management teams from the parent company in Japan.

The company was preparing to implement cross-cultural training courses for their Japanese employees. As Nagato noted, this curriculum involved some critical issues for newly assigned Japanese employees dispatched to the U.S. Courses and seminars in such critical areas as interpersonal communication, confrontation skills, constructive criticism methods, praise and recognition, performance appraisal, sexual harassment, and equal employment opportunity were to be offered. In my study, many of these skills were notably lacking among most of the Japanese employees according to American employees I interviewed in the Midwest, California, and in the case study company in New Mexico. Again, in my study sample, only one transplant, Yamadadenso, was able to successfully attend to these social and cultural aspects of everyday worklife at the company, while among the remaining four transplants, both American and Japanese managers were lacking in the ability to systematically approach these issues.

There were individual managers like Mr. Sato, who had begun to realize what could be done to create a hybrid culture at the transplant. For example, Sato realized the importance of preparing training manuals for American workers which would instruct workers systematically in all the necessary work procedures. He realized that a first-rate company ("*ichiryu kigyo*") like Toyota could prepare training manuals for American workers, but he was not certain that his company could do so. Because there was a lack of accumulated knowledge and experience at the corporate level to deal with cross-cultural issues, he felt that his company would be unable to produce such manuals.

It is clear that among the Midwest transplants unique organizational practices have emerged, different from both their counterparts in Japan and the U.S. Although not all of the eight elements have been transferred, at least some components of each have been utilized to create hybrid cultures in the transplants. Cultural awareness at the highest levels of management was demonstrably successful in creating a unique corporate culture as evidenced at Yamadadenso. Next I will examine these same aspects of organizational practices among high-tech transplants in California.

NOTES

1. *"Kazoku Teate"* in the benefits packages in Japan typically provide an employee the expenses for child rearing. For example, the company provides a certain percentage of education expense per child in an employee's family.

2. The *"keiretsu"* are industrial groupings in Japan, where large manufacturers, trading companies, large banks and insurance companies are closely linked through providing for their members reliable sources of borrowed capital as well as a stable core of shareholders. *"Keiretsu"* generally involves the firms and industries from former *"zaibatsu,"* such as Mitsubishi, Mitsui and Sumitomo, that historically dominated the Japanese economy before and during World War II. They also organize suppliers and distribution outlets hierarchically under large manufacturers. It is very common for the large banks and other financial institutions to exert corporate control over trading companies and manufacturing companies, as well as these manufacturers exerting corporate control over suppliers.

3. As Sakamoto mentions, *"fukukan"* is certainly a product of the Japanese corporate culture. Fukukan is usually a male Japanese employee who is in the middle level of the managerial hierarchy. He usually functions as fukukan because he has earned enough trust from his bosses in everyday work, because he is extremely talented in human skills, because he is politically very skillful, and because he is very loyal to his boss and the company. He is quick in noticing the strengths and weaknesses of his boss and those of the organization to which he belongs. Moreover, he can make up for the

shortcomings and pitfalls of his boss's conduct, as well as go back and forth between workers and higher-level managers. This process is often referred to as *"nemawashi,"* which is an important part of consensus decision making.

4. A Japanese phrase, *"tekitouni yatteta"* literally translates to English, "We have been doing things without any systematic considerations." When he used this phrase, Sato referred to the difference in a work environment between Japan and the U.S. In Japan, managers and workers have been able to speak Japanese and to convey messages without systematically elaborating as much as they have to do in the U.S. when dealing with American workers. Because of the relatively homogeneous social and cultural environment of Japan, the organization's structure and culture had not needed to go through the process, in which things had to be explained to outsiders. For example, Sato referred to the training manuals. Companies in Japan did not need to make systematic training manuals because there were *"sempai"* on the shop-floor who could teach and train new employees on the basis of shared cultural tradition. However, the Japanese are now facing the situation where they have to explain the concepts to American workers from scratch. Sato said that most Japanese managers were not prepared for implementing such systematic training instruction for American workers.

CHAPTER 4

Organizational Practices
Transferred to the U.S.—California

My fieldwork in California provided me with access to four (4) Japanese-owned and two (2) foreign-owned companies. I interviewed 13 individuals, of which two (2) were Japanese managers, and eleven (11) were American managers. One (1) Japanese-owned company was the corporate headquarters of an automobile manufacturer, and the remaining three (3) Japanese-owned and two (2) foreign-owned companies were in high-tech industries. In terms of the company size, all the high-tech firms I studied, and one (1) headquarters of an automobile manufacturer were medium-large sized. As in the previous chapter on the Midwest, in this chapter, I will examine the eight elements among these four (4) Japanese-owned companies in California.

Considering the enormous number of high-tech factories in California, the study of high-tech transplants in California for this chapter was difficult because of the relative small sample size in this study. I attempted to present the situations and circumstances of particular managers at the three transplants and one corporate headquarters solely as a case study. Before I proceed to the discussion of the eight elements, I will look at the general characteristics of high-tech industries in California.

Table 2. List of Companies and Interviewees in California.

Company Name	No. of Employees	Products
Japanese-Owned Firms		
Micro Scientific Instruments	240	Clinical, Analytical Instruments
Suntech America, RC (Repair Center)	115	Medical Instruments
California Silicon	123	Silicon Wafers
Nippon North America (Corporate Headquarters)	150	(Automobiles)
Non-Japanese firms		
Elmer Corporation (British-owned)	200	Uninterrupted Power Supply Equipment
Caltech (Swedish-owned)	178	Computer Circuit Boards

Interviewee	Title	Company
Carolyn Monroe	Corporate Manager, Product & Market Strategy	Nippon North America
Bob Mosser	President	California Silicon
Lam Fong	Controller	California Silicon
Freddy Marquez	Repair Center Manager	Suntech America, RC
Satoshi Tomioka	Vice-President	Micro Scientific Instruments
Roberto Montoya	Director, Administration and Corporate Secretary	Micro Scientific Instruments

Note: Only interviewees whose names appeared in this chapter are listed.

CHARACTERISTICS OF HIGH-TECH INDUSTRIES IN CALIFORNIA

The auto-related Japanese transplants in the Midwest were typically located in areas where only 2-3 percent of total local population was comprised of ethnic minorities. In these transplants almost all American managers and professionals, such as engineers, were Caucasian. Racial and ethnic minorities (mostly African-Americans) were found primarily among the production workers on the shopfloor. Although the sizes of the transplants were not as large as those of their American counterparts, the nature of automotive parts production required significant numbers of blue-collar workers who operated heavy machinery.

In contrast, the situations of four Japanese-owned companies in California were very different. Among four companies, three companies were high-tech related firms in Northern California, and one company was corporate headquarters of an automobile manufacturer in Southern California. The workforce of the three companies in Northern California reflected the racial and ethnic composition of the local population, where more than 70-80% of the population was composed of ethnic minorities.

When compared to the industrial environment in the Midwest, not only the large proportion of racial and ethnic minorities in the workforce, but the presence of the immigrant managers and professionals in the workforce also formed a significant characteristic of the high-tech industrial environment in California. Many of these immigrant populations, such as Chinese from Hong Kong, Taiwan, and Southeast Asia, belong to the "middle class," and are found in white-collar jobs or professional positions (Lamphere, ed. 1992). In my study, two successful upper-level managers that I talked with were minorities. One was an administration manager at Micro Scientific Instruments, and he was an Hispanic American. The other was the manager of the repair facility of Suntech America, and he was an immigrant from Central America. A controller at California Silicon in Fremont whom I interviewed was a Chinese-American. One engineer was also an immigrant from India, who worked full time for the company and went to college part-time. One Japanese manager told me that he had experienced more problems with Caucasian managers than with those from other ethnic groups. A Japanese vice president of another company expressed a sense of appreciation toward a group of Vietnamese engineers because of their loyalty to the company and their highly disciplined work ethic. He told me that they were like "jewels" in the company.

Another significant characteristic of the high-tech industries is the large presence of female workers on the shopfloor. In contrast to the automotive-related manufacturing plants, where the production processes require the operation of heavy machinery and equipment, the actual work processes of computer-related products demand more dexterity rather than intense manual labor. Milkman's study also shows that there was a significant presence of female workers in the total number of employees among Japanese-owned firms in California (Milkman 1991: 51).

Finally, the existence of an established infrastructure in the industrial environment in California, such as the presence of the related manufacturers, attracted high-tech manufacturers in spite of the high cost of real estate property. Lam Fong, a controller at California Silicon, a silicon wafer manufacturer, explained as follows:

> In Fremont there aren't—from a financial point—there are not many [advantages for being in California]. From a practical point there are some. There's a good infrastructure here, meaning our equipment manufacturers are here. Of the three types we have, two of them are located within ten miles. The other thing is a lot of equipment manufacturers—that for measurements, many technical people, when we have problems—we get advice from. They're all around this area. So, there is a good operational infrastructure in the area.

In addition to the existence of a good operational infrastructure, he suggested that there is a good pool of manufacturing labor, mainly cheap immigrant labor, in California. He mentioned that employing the immigrant labor force helped the company keep its labor costs down.

> It is costly to do business in this area and in the state of California. But we have overcome that with some of the infrastructure, and our direct labor is not very high, you know. There's a good pool of manufacturing labor here and that we can support. Because of so

many immigrants that come into this area, it has allowed us to keep our direct labor costs in a good area.

In addition to the large presence of high-tech firms in California, there exist some corporate headquarters of the Japanese automobile manufacturers and their design facilities in Southern California. There are good reasons for the headquarters and design facilities to be located in California. Carolyn Monroe, a corporate manager at the headquarters of a Japanese auto manufacturer, explained that the local supply of competent automotive design engineers and the established infrastructure able to accommodate the Japanese presence in the region were attractive to them.

> Although some of our other things—design centers for these automobiles are mostly out here in California. Toyota has its design center. And ours is down near La Jolla, in San Diego County, [Nippon] Design International (pseudonym)—which does car designs. Now, please remember once again, just like the University of Michigan produces automotive engineers, out here you have things like the Pasadena School of Design, which probably is the best automotive design school in the U.S., and very famous. So, there's a local supply of designers here. There's a place where they come from. But also, there are other reasons, I think, that we're out here. Part of it is this is historically one of the Japanese-American communities. There was already infrastructure. It made it a little easier for Japanese executives to come here and find, you know, printers who could make business cards in both languages, or other sorts of office suppliers . . . [R]eal estate agents. I mean, you can't locate a building like this or locate housing for ex-patriate executives if you can't talk to the agent. So, these sort of things are also some of the reasons.

As expressed in the above quotes, the abundant presence of cheap immigrant labor force for manufacturing as well as immigrant managers and professionals, the presence of good automobile design engineers, and the pre-existing infrastructure for the Japanese presence, all formed significant characteristics of the industrial environment in California.

In the next section, following the same structure as in the previous chapter on the Midwest, I will examine the significance of the eight elements among four Japanese-owned companies in California.

1. Lifetime employment (or long tenure of employment)

As previously stated regarding the Midwest, the practice of lifetime employment was nonexistent among the Japanese transplants in California, though both American and Japanese managers expressed that lifetime employment of workers was the company's ideal. Lam Fong, a controller at California Silicon in Fremont, talked about his ideal picture of employment, where workers would stay with the company for decades.

> [A]nywhere from fifteen to twenty years. And I would suspect, and expect, that many employees will spend a lifetime here.

Bob Mosser, the American president of the company, also expressed that he did not want to lose employees.

> Our objective is to keep employees here as long as they are progressing along their own career paths, as long as they are, you know, producing satisfactorily for the company. When I got here in 1986, the turnover rate was 35 percent per year. Our present turnover rate is less than 1.5 percent per year. You know, after you spend three or four years working with an employee, training him, getting him into your system so that he understands how to function effectively in your system, you don't want to lose him.

In addition, he clearly expressed his commitment to preventing worker lay-offs in an economic downturn. He said that the company tried to retain workers and put them in the training programs instead of resorting to layoffs. Regarding the layoff of workers, he commented as follows:

> We don't do it. We don't hire any more people than we need, and we don't lay people off. You know, if you spend four years training a person to get him to the place where he can do your job—we don't need to trim employees. There are other ways to save money. What

> you do, you see, if you're really in a bind, you send them to school,
> you train them more because the downturn's not going to last
> forever. So, you put them in a training program.

Mr. Mosser stated that the company was motivated to absorb
training costs because such training would eventually prove more cost
effective than losing a worker and later hiring another whom the
company would have to train from the initial stage.

> You have to have a certain staffing level in order to run a business. If
> you can't support that staffing level, then get the hell out of the
> business. We do whatever—you know. And I also clean the
> restrooms if I have to. Whatever it takes to run the business is what
> we do.

Most Japanese managers in Japanese transplants also aspired to
retain workers for a long period of time. The rationale for this
expectation was that the companies did not want to lose employees in
whom they had invested so much time and cost in training. Mr.
Tomioka was a Japanese vice-president of Micro Scientific
Instruments. His following remarks echoed many other Japanese
managers whom I interviewed in California.

> If possible, I want them to stay here for good . . . and if they can't, I
> want them to stay here at least five years. You can't be efficient after
> spending one year here, or at least for six months, when you are still
> learning the basics of everyday work. In the case of R&D, it usually
> takes from one to two years at least to learn the basics . . . so, the
> worst case is when employees leave right after this. Then, we don't
> get anything in return.

As a scientific instrument manufacturer, Micro focused on its R &
D activities, where engineers' knowledge of the job and work
experience were important assets for the company. Tomioka also
mentioned that some American employees had taken advantage of the
work training and experience they had acquired in Japanese-owned
companies, thus enhancing their career opportunities.

Speaking of shortcomings... some of the precious workers are sometimes recruited by much larger companies. From the viewpoint of the person who is leaving, the name [Micro] (pseudonym) looks great on his resume. And having work experience in Micro can spur on their careers. So some of our workers were recruited with unbelievable salaries by American companies. This happens frequently, even now.

Considering the emphasis on training of employees, it has been a significant loss to the company if employees leave after such training. Moreover, despite the expectation of this long-term employment that was shared among both American and the Japanese managers, the Japanese managers tended to take it personally when American employees suddenly left the company. On the other hand, American managers had a more instrumental attitude toward their workers changing companies. Roberto Montoya, a director of administration and corporate secretary, observed the difference as follows:

> [I]t seems the managers here, especially the Japanese managers, seem to be hurt more if we lose an employee than American managers are. They just—they take it personally—'What went wrong? What happened?' They take it badly. And the Americans are like, 'Well, that happens sometimes.' They go out and they go, 'We'll hire another one.'

Like Mr. Tomioka, Montoya mentioned that because the company invests in employees through various training programs, the company expected employees to remain with the same company for a greater length of time, although this expectation was more significant among the Japanese managers than American managers. Montoya referred to the benefits that the company receives from employees' stability.

> In this regard, I think that, you know, I'm very—the Japanese issues, that we like our people to stay a long time, because I do view the employees as an asset to the company, and that if they leave the company, then that's training that is gone. And I try to impress upon them that the longer they stay, the more we the managers know about their abilities, and we're able to put them in the best position. And as

an employee, that they know better about the company and what they can expect from the company, whereas if you're changing jobs all the time, that familiarity on both sides doesn't exist as well. So, as I mentioned, you know, we try to hire people with the idea that it's going to be controlled growth. We would like to maintain our core people. And it concerns me when we have people that leave. Our expectations are that the employees will stay.

All in all, both American and Japanese managers in the transplants held expectations that employees would remain with the company for longer periods, though the practice of lifetime employment was still virtually non-existent. They also perceived the layoff of workers as a last resort in solving the company's economic problems. The primary reason was that it was a significant loss to a company when employees left because management had invested time and capital in the training of employees. In addition, some American managers viewed the Japanese managers as more emotionally attached to their employees, while American managers were more instrumental and impersonal about their workers leaving for other companies.

2. Seniority-based wage and promotion systems

Among the three Japanese transplants in California that I visited, the significance of the element of seniority in deciding employee's wage and promotion varied somewhat. One transplant, California Silicon in Fremont, relied almost totally on merit criteria. Mr. Mosser, the president of the company, told me that the company did not value seniority criteria because the company was an American company, not Japanese. On the other hand, two other transplants utilized a combination of both the seniority and merit criteria, though, if anything, these companies, especially the Japanese managers, valued seniority more than merit criteria.

In the previous chapter on the Midwest, Laura, a human resources specialist at Yamadadenso, pointed out the slow promotion and rigid corporate structure of the company, which had often frustrated some white-collar American employees, especially middle-level managers and engineers. The seniority system was a significant factor for slow promotion and the rigid structure that was a point of dissatisfaction among some American employees in Japanese transplants.

Carolyn Monroe was a corporate manager at the headquarters of a Japanese automobile manufacturer, Nippon North America, and was also trained as an anthropologist. She did her dissertation research in Japan, and had extensive knowledge and experience in dealing with the Japanese organizations. Referring to her own promotion at Nippon corporate headquarters, Carolyn Monroe was also concerned with the issue of time regarding the slow promotion track of the company.

I'm someone who's open to either moving up here or changing. I mean, I'm not quite like most Japanese employees. I don't necessarily think I have to retire from here. But I—I don't think my career is stalled here. I think I could move up. Probably mostly for me, it's a little bit of time, because I'm considered very young to be a corporate manager, and, you know, a grade 47. Getting to grade 48 probably wouldn't be that hard. For making the jump from corporate manager to director requires both a good track record and probably a few gray hairs. So, there's a time issue there. And, in fact, if I were to leave [Nippon North America], it would be because I judged that time to be longer than I wanted to wait, not that I didn't think it would happen. You know, it'd be that kind of an issue.

The extent to which seniority criteria has been utilized in the transplants appeared to depend more upon each company's unique characteristics, which were created and established by the top management of the company. For instance, in case of California Silicon, the American president, Bob Mosser, strongly opposed having Japanese staff from Japan. He emphasized the rendering of the company as predominantly American by resisting cooperate control from the parent company in Japan. In addition, as an American businessman who had developed his career in the high-tech industrial environment, he had little faith in seniority systems. On the other hand, the Japanese managers, even in high-tech industrial environment, generally valued the seniority system. For example, Micro in Japan is famous for its traditional Japanese corporate policies. In this sense, Mr. Tomioka, a vice-president of Micro Scientific Instruments, was a typical "Micro man" who valued the ethic of hard work, the seniority system, and workers' loyalty to the company.

3. Elaborate welfare, bonus, and other benefits systems

Although benefits structures among the four Japanese-owned companies varied somewhat, they were different from either the typical systems of Japanese firms in Japan or those of American-owned firms. For example, at Micro, Roberto Montoya mentioned that the company offered benefits that were fairly conservative and basic. He explained how the company's health benefits structure was different from that of American companies.

> With respect to the health benefits, we tend to be very conservative. I think Japanese companies tend to be conservative. We have what we call an indemnity program, although we're exploring the PPO. Right now, the company pays all of the benefits. Okay, the employee doesn't pay. So, we're very different from the American company in that regard.

Montoya viewed Micro's benefits structure as more paternalistic than those of American companies. He remarked as follows:

> We may be a little bit more conservative in our approach toward implementing those [benefits policies]. We may be a little bit more paternalistic, in the sense that this is why we have the indemnity program as opposed to the PPO.

Unlike many other American-owned firms, none of the Japanese transplants in California offered benefits packages that particularly favored higher-level managers by offering exceptionally high bonuses. In addition, none of the Japanese transplants introduced benefits packages as extensive and elaborated as those in Japanese firms in Japan, which typically included various forms of housing and family allowances.

4. Company-based labor unions

No Japanese-owned firms that I visited were unionized, though their parent companies in Japan had company-based labor unions. As in most transplants in the Midwest, both the Japanese and American managers in transplants in California tended to express strong anti-union attitudes. Labor unions, such as the machinists' union, had a relatively stronger influence in the northern areas of California than in the southern areas. Managers at the two non-Japanese firms in the southern California also demonstrated strong anti-union attitudes.

5. Considerable inter-job mobility within a firm and emphasis on internal promotion

Both the Japanese and American managers in the transplants generally emphasized internal promotion of employees. Mr. Fong, a controller at California Silicon in Fremont, described the process of internal promotion for the production workers as follows:

> [W]e try to promote and encourage learning. After six months, an operator goes through extensive training. And he will go through certification. He must pass the certification, and if he does, he goes to the next level and gets promoted. We pay after six months. And then, six months later, he will get an annual review on his performance. Half-a-year thereafter, when he's been in the company a year-and-a-half, he's been at his current level for one year, and we will certify him again if he is qualified. After a year-and-a-half, he's called an 'advanced material processor.' So, he has had three pay increases at that point. After that, he had to wait another year, which means he has two-and-a-half years. And if he qualifies, he'll be certified and his new title will be a 'senior material processor.' And after that, people will get promoted to a lead material processor.

As in the transplants in the Midwest, some Japanese managers in California pointed out that internal promotion was emphasized more for the production workers, and less so for management-level employees. Most American managers in transplants came from other American companies where they already had managerial-level experience. In my study in California, there was only one manager who had been promoted internally from a level of line technician to a manager. Although this was, I believe, a very rare case, I would like to illustrate the case of Freddy Marquez of Suntech's repair center in San Jose. Marquez had immigrated to the U.S. from Central America, and had been working for Suntech America for almost 20 years. He exemplified the Japanese managers' ideal image of an American manager in Japanese transplants, who is a loyal, diligent, and dedicated worker, and who understands traditional Japanese culture. Since he immigrated to the U.S., he had many opportunities in working with Japanese employees. He felt comfortable working with the Japanese. Marquez explained how his beliefs in management were similar to those of the Japanese managers.

> I have worked almost 19 years in this company, in [Suntech in San Jose]. And I never forget how Japanese management treated me. When I was a technician . . . Okay? They hired me when I could not speak the language very well. They helped me out. So, they trusted me. I don't forget that. And also my way of thinking—traditional way of thinking—I think is very similar. And not so unique to Japanese. I think a lot of people everywhere, all over the world. To me, I like to invest myself in what I do. I don't want to just say, 'Do it,' and walk away. You have to invest yourself in what you do. And it's more rewarding to me. To manage business that way is more exciting, more productive, and less stressful than if I try to do the other way. Because how could I? I can't conceive of doing it any other way. I can't.

Although Marquez represented a rare case among the managers in Japanese transplants, his above comment reflects and illustrates the Japanese companies' expectations towards American employees. In actuality, those expectations were not easily realized among American employees particularly because they were not accustomed to the patience and time that were often required to develop careers in Japanese-owned companies.

6. Small group activities on the shopfloor level

Generally speaking, most of the Japanese and American managers in the transplants also emphasized several forms of small group activities on the shopfloor-level, such as QC's. Compared to the Japanese transplants in the Midwest, where managers lacked confidence in implementing such activities, managers in the transplants in California showed more confidence in realizing them on the shop-floor level. However, these teams were mostly informal, ad hoc teams, reflecting the small size of production at the transplant, as compared to Japanese transplants in the Midwest. California Silicon in Fremont utilized problem solving oriented teams on the shopfloor-level. Bob Mosser, the president of the company, characterized the company's small group activities as follows:

> [W]hat I'm saying is that, you know, each production shift functions more or less as a team. But we do form special teams for certain requirements throughout the production and quality area, but they're multi-disciplinary teams. We may have a guy from Finance, a guy from Quality, a guy or two guys from Manufacturing, somebody from Maintenance, you name it—whatever, depending on what the problem is that we're currently working on. We have, you know, I think that our group embraces the total quality management concepts pretty much. But, you know, we're also a small enough organization that we don't have to get really formal about all of the crap that has to go on, you know. We talk continuously.

At California Silicon, Mr. Mosser emphasized worker participation. Through several forms of worker participation, such as suggestion programs and company sponsored after-hours activities, Mosser commented that his company was trying to raise the morale and to reduce the worker turnover.

> We have suggestion programs. We have quarterly meetings, employee meetings which, you know—unfortunately, I talk too much—but it's a mutual interchange of information. We have, you know, basically open-door policies where people can—can come and talk to any level of management anytime about problems, or about concerns, or about things that they think need to be done. You know, we have the opportunity to use the team approach when people say, you know, 'Here's a problem that needs to be resolved.' We'll let them propose a solution to the thing and then basically support them. Management will support them in taking care of it. So, we use—we use all kinds of—of methods to get people involved in the company. You know, we have company parties. We have Christmas parties. We have picnics every time we reach what we call 'million dollar milestones,' where the company produces, you know, goes from one million to two million in production per month, or two to three, or

three to four, or what have you. We have—we have a big party. And the parties are, you know, for everybody, management and production levels. And we—you know, it kind of cements relationships, brings people closer together so that people not only work together but they play together, and they communicate. And all of this goes into, I think, building morale and reducing turnover and stabilizing your work force.

In the case of California Silicon, I should note that there were no Japanese managers or engineers at the company. Mosser strongly opposed the parent company in Japan that was insisting on sending some Japanese managers to his company. Therefore, the company did not have any problems, at least at the workplace level, in dealing with cultural differences.

7. Intensive training and socialization of new employees by the management

On a general level, the majority of Japanese and American managers in transplants emphasized the importance of the training of employees. As in transplants in the Midwest, the training focused on the development of specific job skills. There were no intensive training processes such as those in Japanese firms, where newly hired employees are socialized into company's norms and values. Not only was this "socialization," in the Japanese sense, virtually nonexistent among high-tech transplants, the managers' emphasis on social interactions among employees, especially interactions between the Japanese and American employees, was less obvious than in the auto-related transplants in the Midwest.

There was some variation among the transplants regarding the kinds of training on the shopfloor. For instance, Mr. Tomioka at Micro Scientific Instruments recognized the need that their training be more systematic. On the other hand, Mr. Mosser at California Silicon was proud of the company's structured training programs. This variation among the Japanese high-tech transplants was to a large extent due to the nature of the production processes of the company and the company-specific emphasis on training by the top managers. As I described before, Mr. Mosser was the American president of California Silicon, which manufactured silicon wafers for other computer manufacturers. He exhibited strong resistance to corporate control from the parent company in Japan, and was trying to make the company as "American" as possible. However, his attitudes toward employees differed from the traditional "American" attitudes concerning the treatment of workers.

> I think the important thing is that we treat people like human beings, okay? An awful lot of companies, you know, think that when their employees come to work, they immediately become robots with no brains. We believe that people are people, whether they happen to be at work or whether they're at home. We treat people with, you know, with respect. We treat them as though they're all smart, intelligent individuals. And we let them participate in what's happening in the company.

At California Silicon, like most of the companies that I visited, there was no direct relationship between training and promotion. Going through the training program and getting a certification did not automatically guarantee an employee's future promotion, though this at least made an employee more qualified for more advanced and higher-level positions in the company.

> But you'll probably not get promoted without it. I mean, you know, if you—if you can't pass our training—well, it's very simple. If you're not involved in our training programs, you don't work here.

As in the auto-related transplants in the Midwest, most of the Japanese managers in my study recognized the need for more systematic training programs for their U.S. operations. Nonetheless, investing as much attention on worker training as they did in Japan struck Japanese managers in the U.S. as unrealistic because of the differences that they perceived in Japanese and American worker training environments. Mr. Tomioka mentioned that the training in Japan was more holistic as compared to the training programs in transplants which focus only on technical matters. He explained these differences:

> In addition, the way the company invests in the education of workers is totally different in Japan and the U.S. In Japan we spend far more

money on education. Like everywhere else, we have a training period for about a year for new workers. You will experience several jobs in different departments in this period, like, if you are a production worker, your boss may say, 'Why don't you go to sales department and learn what customers really want.' This kind of thing is just out of question here, just like a dream for a company like us. Moreover, it will be a disaster if workers leave after the company invests that much in their education.

The above quote also shows that job rotation practices in Japanese transplants were not the same as they were in Japan. What I observed in some Japanese transplants was rotation in a technical sense, that is, job rotations within the production area. It was more like the cross-training practice. Regarding the differences in Japanese transplant rotation practices from those in Japan, Tomioka remarked as follows:

[I]t happens often in Japan that an inspector becomes a production manager, or a worker who is responsible for engineering goes to sales department and becomes a sales manager. But this rarely happens here. In America, I guess this would be more or less the same everywhere. It never happens here that workers go around several functional departments in [this company].

Compared to the training programs at Micro, the training at California Silicon was more tied to their structured certification program. Mr. Fong, the controller at California Silicon, remarked that workers had to go through job rotations when going through the company's certification program.

[I]n the production area, yes. I'm not sure how often they do it, but there's—there is—people will rotate their jobs. And they—at least in their first four years here, they all need to get—go through certification programs. And they will get promoted each time they pass. In fact, you cannot go to the next level unless you get certified.

Mr. Mosser mentioned that the main purpose of the company's relatively structured training programs was to have a flexible and versatile workforce that could deal with multiple work tasks. He described the company's training process.

> Well, he or she can start by doing what everybody in this organization does. The first thing they do is go through our three-week introductory training program. They enter as a trainee. They have three months of training programs and on-the-job training to develop their skill levels and see if they can really survive here. If they survive, we—they're promoted from a trainee status to the lowest level of operator. And if they don't survive, within ninety days they're fired. After they become an operator, we have basically on-the-job training, and we also have classroom training to train the people in every job in the organization. It's our objective that every—every manufacturing person will be able to do every job in the company. And currently, about 70 percent of them are cross-trained to the place where that's almost possible.

California Silicon was a manufacturer of computer silicon wafers, whereas Micro was manufacturer of the scientific instruments for the medical environment. In this case Micro resembled Suntech, the case study company in New Mexico. Compared to California Silicon, Micro did not have extensive and automated production lines on the shopfloor. Instead, the production area resembled an R & D laboratory with several short-batch processing lines. Under these circumstances, most of the training was carried out through a man-to-man, on-the-job process. In comparison, California Silicon had to equip various kinds of machinery that were necessary for the production of silicon wafers. California Silicon had more structured training programs particularly because the actual silicon wafer manufacturing processes required such structured training programs for workers at the shopfloor level.

8. Attention to developing a unique corporate culture and management philosophy

As in the automobile-related transplants in the Midwest, in the Japanese high-tech transplants in California, the issue of developing a unique corporate culture was frequently focused on how the company could integrate the Japanese and American workforce. In this context, social interaction between Japanese and American employees became an important issue, though managers' emphasis on this issue was not as significant as those in the auto-related transplants in the Midwest. Except for one corporate headquarters, the three Japanese high-tech transplants that I visited were small-to-medium in size. As in the cases of the Japanese auto-related transplants in the Midwest, these transplants could not provide the management-level attention to issues of social interaction among employees, except for some company-sponsored after-hour activities, such as picnics and parties.

In contrast to the auto-related transplants in the Midwest, the issue of workforce diversity became an important element to consider when discussing the corporate cultures of the transplants in California. Basically all of the managers in the Japanese transplants in California told me that they did not have any problem with workforce diversity on the shopfloor level. However, as in many other auto transplants, it was more difficult for women to move up the corporate ladder. Mr. Mosser, the American president of California Silicon, boasted that his company's workforce was very diverse. Although the comment below involved some management cliché's, it illustrated that the workforce at California Silicon reflected the racially and ethnically diverse local population in the northern California. In addition, a large presence of female workers in the production area was one of significant characteristics of the high-tech related industries, especially when compared to the auto related industries.

Sure! Take a look around. We have women in management. We have—we have women in production. We—you know, we have women in supervision. We have—you know, there probably aren't more than a dozen what you would call 'Americans'—that's not true, but, you know, what people consider to be 'American'—white, Anglo-Saxon Protestant, right? There are probably ten of us in the whole damn company. We have people here from—from the Philippines, and from Mexico, and from China, and from Taipei. We have people from Portugal. We have people from Yugoslavia. We have people from Ireland. We have people from—you know, you name it. And—and it doesn't make any difference, you know— Thais, Koreans. We have all nationalities. We have both male and female. 50 percent of our production people are female. They all get the same—they all get the same attention, and they all have the same opportunity for promotion. There are no second-class citizens in this company.

No matter how often upper-level managers emphasize women's progress in the company, in reality, there is always the proverbial "glass ceiling" where women's progress is hindered in corporate hierarchies. This related more to the way manufacturing environments have traditionally been dominated by male workers, rather than whether the company was Japanese or American. As previously mentioned, Carolyn Monroe was a corporate manager at the headquarters of a Japanese automobile manufacturer, Nippon North America. She received her doctoral degree in anthropology, and had done her research in Japan, thus gaining extensive knowledge and experience in dealing with the Japanese organizations. She described the reality of women's career progress in the company, and said that a woman's progress stops when she becomes a manager.

> Though I see many minority employees go up higher in the management in companies that I visited in California, they are usually male employees. It is not easy for women to move up. There just aren't very many female managers, although it's a lot easier to get to be a female manager than corporate manager here. Like I say, a corporate manager is just very rare, still. Like I said, legally, it's possible. Human Resources, we have somebody who's been with the company a long, long, long time. And—it's easier for women to get promoted in Human Resources . . . [I]n terms of how fast people get promoted, males versus females, I think probably [at] the early levels there's no difference, you know, the lower ranks. I think the problem is right about at manager level the women get frozen. You don't move up.

In reality, there were not many differences between the Japanese and American companies. The manufacturing environment has been traditionally quite male dominated. Carolyn mentioned that the setting is particularly difficult for women with children.

> I think it's the sort of thing you see—and, you know, of course this is no different between American companies and Japanese companies—people tend to promote people they feel comfortable

with—and that usually means people that are like them—or people that are like the last one who had the job. So, if the last one was a guy, it's sometimes hard for the manager to feel comfortable putting a woman there, or he just envisions a different sort of person in that place. And it makes it very hard for the women to move up. Also, like I say, there's an issue about women who have children . . . If they leave early, that's often, you know, a black mark on their record.

Longer working hours were also a significant factor in keeping women from moving up. Although workers were expected to work longer hours in manufacturing industries in general, the Japanese emphasis on working long hours was also closely tied to the traditional cultural value of the Japanese work ethic. In the male-dominated environment of the manufacturing, working long hours is sometimes difficult for female employees with families. Monroe continued:

But because in general people work longer—and so far it's always been female staff—if someone leaves here at five o'clock consistently to take care of their kids, some of the—particularly some of the male bosses here don't like it. They see that as not pulling their weight, or not being loyal to the company. And, in fact, Jane had an argument with one of our superiors over this issue. He felt that her leaving at five showed a lack of company loyalty. It damaged her feeling about the company when he did that. But it still is an issue. I mean, the car industry is traditionally very male, and traditionally has long hours—at least, for white-collar workers. And, you know, a lot of people resent it if someone leaves at five o'clock. And so, it's sometimes difficult for our female employees that have families, because usually—you know, sex roles are what they are—it's usually the women who go home. And, in fact, we lost one employee. She still works for us, but only part-time, as a contract worker, like three days a week. And she had been in the car industry a long time. She'd been at J. D. Power, she'd been at Toyota, she'd been at Hyundai. And she came here—excellent worker. Real smart. But she has two small children and she went home at five. And she felt—even though no one actually ever said anything to her—she felt everybody noticed when she left and didn't think well of her because she left at that time. So, it was more like social pressure. And she finally decided she'd be more comfortable working part-time contract instead of, you know—I think she would have been happy to work full-time if she hadn't felt disapproval.

Monroe also said that it was much easier for her to take advantage of the formal nature of the corporate structure in the Japanese organizations. She thought that once she earned a certain status and position in an organization, the Japanese managers started treating her with more respect. In this sense, it became much easier in a Japanese company for her than in American companies, where employees tended to see a woman in higher position as a "token."

It's the individual things that happen to individual people. And all I can say is I think I've been treated pretty well, at least as well as I've been treated at American companies. And there are even some areas in which I think Japanese companies are a little bit better on that . . . [I]t seems to me that in Japan generally, people give a lot of credit and status to the position. They tend to take it for granted that you were good enough to get there, that you earned it, you know, at some point. I feel like if an American sees a woman at, say, my level or higher, sometimes what they're thinking is, 'Oh, well, she's just there because her company had to put a woman in that spot or needed to promote a minority,' or whatever it is, you know, that they pick on. They're a token. They didn't really earn their spot. And I feel like I get less of that from Japanese people than Americans. And also, I think for a lot of—and this is sort of the other side of that—for a lot of Japanese managers, it's so weird to work with, you know, '*gaijin*' [a foreigner] anyway, that there's not much difference between female and male gaijin, that the big difference is the cultural difference, and that sex difference, you know, doesn't change— doesn't move you very far along that dimension.

Carolyn acknowledged that some mistreatment by the Japanese managers was due to cultural differences. For her, these cultural differences at the workplace level were possible to overcome in the transplants.

So, in that sense, you know, I mean, you hear stories about—I think there are certainly individual incidents of prejudice or discrimination that happen to women because they're women at Japanese firms. But I don't think I've personally experienced very much of that. And I can only have a problem with discrimination I can see or experience. I mean, I can't assume people are going to mistreat me. I can only deal with it if I think they have. And, like I say, we have had once or twice—we had, once again, an incident where actually a visitor from Japan sort of, during a business event, kind of treated one of our professional female staff kind of the way he might treat an office lady in Japan, and caused a problem. She was pretty upset, but she was able to make her complaint to one of the Japanese upper managers, and he said, 'I'll take care of it.' And he did. The guy who had been rude in that particular way apologized individually to that employee, and also did a similar apology in front of the whole work group. He said he was sorry, and he was very convincing. I think he was very sincere. It was a mistake, you know, one of those cultural things that happen. And, you know, I don't think he had meant to treat her poorly. And I don't think you wanted any better response in an American company with a similar incident.

Carolyn felt her best opportunity was to work for the Japanese company because she could make the best of her experience in Japan. She said that she had known what to expect from her Japanese bosses when she came to Nippon North America because of her experience in Japan. She talked about the differences that she perceived when she dealt with Japanese and American bosses.

They certainly are very different sorts of relationships. I'd say that— that the foundation, I think, of American employee relations is always the contract. Some written set of rules, specifications, 'This is good,' 'That's not good,' 'If you do this you're a good person,' 'If you do that you're a bad person,' and very explicit.

In contrast, she pointed to the group dynamics among the Japanese, in which the power relations within the company are perceived through groups and cliques.

You know, they're [relationships] more taken for granted. And there's certainly also a sense of groups. I mean, even as an American, you can see when you're here some of the various sort of Japanese cliques or groups. That is—and sometimes they go up and down in power in the company. And even here we can experience that when there's changes in Japan. For example, at times the group that is sort of our sister office in Japan—it's called—we refer to it as 'Tokyo Zoo' because it's divisional designation is set to '00.'

In addition, one of the biggest differences for her was that Japanese relations were more ambiguous and "fuzzy" from an American's point of view. She pointed out the highly personal nature of Japanese relationships, which were supported by the high frequency of interpersonal interactions. On the other hand, the American employee relationships were more contractual in nature.

> Probably the biggest difference is that, to me, the Japanese boss-employee relationship was much more—much more of a personal relationship, and a lot less of a contract-type relationship. That is, you know, the American styles have very defined [positions and roles]. And then, at the end of the year, we're going to have an evaluation. 'Did you meet these goals? Do we agree on the measurements? How'd you do?' and in many cases, actually written, and very explicit, very detailed that way. The Japanese style was much more soft and fuzzy in a way, just ongoing contact and ongoing dialogue. Sometimes that can be a little bit of a problem because there wouldn't be much guidance. You know, well, yeah, he sort of vaguely told me what he wants me to do, but I kind of have to figure it out. And most of the time that would work. But once in a while, we would have a miscommunication or misunderstanding about that. On the other hand, I always felt with the—because it had that high frequency of interaction, you know, and casual discussion, and things like that, you always knew how you were doing or, you know, whether the boss is in a good or bad mood that day, or how you were looking in his eyes—very—you knew how you were doing.

These differences in the Japanese and American styles of

interaction were often difficult for American employees to cope with. She gave an example of an American manager who could not deal with the Japanese staff in the company very well. Here, again, the issue of developing a unique corporate culture is closely linked to the question of how the company can integrate the Japanese and American workforces.

[O]ne American I mentioned I didn't think was a very good boss, he also had a lot or trouble with his Japanese boss because he, you know, was reporting on up—there's a Japanese above him. And I think the main reason he is no longer here as a director was that he could not learn to get along with the Japanese. He was so much of an American and so insensitive to the differences. Well, he was almost a stereotype of the American car guy, you know. He was from the Midwest originally. He also was a Wiwaf^I long, long ago, but not recently. He had been to Ford, and then to Toyota, and then to Hyundai, and then here. So, he'd been all over the car industry. And I understand why he had not stayed at Toyota and why he had not stayed at Hyundai, because he had problems with the Koreans, as well. It wasn't just with Japanese managers, but he was very much the 'I know it's right. I have a gut-level, instinctive feeling for what's going to work on a car.' You know, 'I can look at a design and tell you whether it's going to be a market success. I can—you know, just let me do it and I'll do it right.' He didn't want people looking over his shoulder on his decisions. And he wasn't willing to do any of that sort of cultural bridge kinds of things. I mean, here's a man who had been at three Asian companies and had never taken, for example, even a conversational Japanese class. In other words, he had never tried to take that step. He had never even learned much about the cultures of either Japan or Korea, even though he worked in those companies. I mean, he made dozens of visits over to the home offices. In other words, if it's, you know, happy hour and people are going out to have a drink, he would never, you know, say, walk to Mr. Saito's office and say, 'Hey, several of us are going out for a drink. Would you like to come?' You know, for him his little invitation didn't even usually include all the Americans. It kind of included his favorites in the office. So, he never developed a larger network, and his network never integrated into the Japanese network.

Because I think a lot of it does have to do with just how open-minded someone is to working with someone from a different culture, or what they expect from that. In my case, I expect Japanese to be Japanese. I lived there. I, you know, have some experience in the study of the culture, study of the language, all that. And I'm not surprised very often. But I think Americans who haven't had that background or aren't open to that kind of experience find a lot of things—are surprised with the Japanese manager. You know, they're surprised about, the vague performance review or the inexact description of tasks. They're surprised about the bureaucracy of a big Japanese company. They think they have authority to do something, like 'We'll all just make this decision and go.' Well, it's not that easy. There's a lot of people whose input and agreement, the nemawashi[2] type stuff. And, you know, some Americans just aren't able to, or willing to adapt to that. I think there are also, of course, some Japanese managers who have trouble adapting towards North Americans.

As a corporate manager Carolyn was in fairly high rank at Nippon North America and, as she mentioned before, she received a certain respect and sense of acknowledgment from the Japanese employees for being in that position. Speaking of cultural differences at the workplace, she felt a "barrier" when she tried to socialize in an all-Japanese context. I mentioned before that it was difficult for women to be in the manufacturing environment, in both Japanese and American organizations. On the other hand, the social cultural differences in the work environments of the U.S. and Japan certainly created a barrier in everyday interactions. She pointed to the subtlety of this separation between the Japanese and American employees, which usually worked against the American employees in the Japanese organization. I asked Monroe whether she experienced greater difficulty based upon her gender or her nationality. She responded:

More probably for being an American in the company [than being a woman]. Because there are—there are some decisions and things like this that tend to happen in, you know, casual, after-hours settings. And, of course, that's very traditional in Japan. Sometimes those casual, after-hour settings won't include Americans. And it's not that it's a deliberate exclusion. So, you know, people will go out for a drink or a bite after work, or we even joke about if you're a non-smoker it's a different problem. Most of the Americans don't smoke. Most of the Japanese do. So, they stand around out—this is a non-smoking building—so they have to stand outside and smoke. Well, there's conversations and things that happen. Sometimes they're very important because some of the highest-ranking people smoke. So, you know, a young Japanese coordinator may get a chance, standing out there smoking, to talk to the vice-president or the president. Most of the Americans can't participate in that. Well, because they can't take it, they can't stand the smoke. But simply because they're not part of that social group. And so, sometimes things happen, like I say, usually in these casual settings—decisions get made or ideas get bounced around, and then, the Americans weren't participating in that. And they're either behind the decision, or they disagree with it. They think it was a wrong decision. There's more problems over that than male-female. And like I say, smoker/non-smoker turns out to be an element of that. It's an element that divides Americans and Japanese. I bet it happens at other companies, too.

Carolyn Monroe was in the white-collar, office environment in the corporate headquarters. However, on the everyday work level, these social and cultural "barriers" were often a problem for many managers in my interviews, and were common in the production areas of the Japanese transplants in both California and in the Midwest. It is important, however, that the issue of corporate culture was not only limited to the production area and everyday interactions. This was also an important issue on the corporate structural level as long as corporate control was exerted by the parent companies in Japan. It has been a crucial issue whether or not the parent companies in Japan have dominant influence on their U.S. subsidiaries.

Here, I want to go back to the case of California Silicon in Fremont, a silicon wafer manufacturer, that was a wholly-owned subsidiary of Daido California Silicon in Japan. As I mentioned, at California Silicon, the American president, Bob Mosser tried hard to maintain the facility's autonomy from the influence of parent company in Japan. Because of his effort, there was virtually no presence of the Japanese in the company. The California Silicon case clearly exemplified that the issue of corporate culture mattered even in the corporate structural level relations, such as the one between the parent company in Japan and its U.S. subsidiary. Lam Fong, a controller, mentioned that there were few interactions with the Japanese in everyday work situations, but that there were some in higher-level management.

> Again, we have not had much interaction with the Japanese, that they have left us alone. When it comes to larger decisions, I think there's a mutual respect of each other's opinion, especially the higher managers, the senior managers. There's good respect there and they listen to each other.

According to Fong, the financial aspects of the company had been controlled by the parent company, but were no longer.

> I believe what happened here when [Daido] (pseudonym) purchased our company—however, they had told us that we will be independent. And the only restriction they would have is their chief financial—they will have a chief financial officer. After about one or one-and-a-half years of operation, they moved the chief financial officer off our division and moved him to a new division.

He thought that it was important for the parent company to allow a wide margin of autonomy to its subsidiaries. It was frequently the case that control from the parent company tended to increase when there were problems at the U.S. subsidiaries. In case of California Silicon, however, the parent company in Japan allowed the U.S. plant such autonomy and did not interfere in their business, even when the U.S. subsidiary in Fremont was not doing very well.

> [I]f you look up and down the businesses that were bought by other businesses, many times it doesn't work because the philosophies are different, and there's a conflict of that. It's very difficult to work with, and many businesses fail. I'm not sure how the Japanese businesses have done when they've bought other businesses, but you need to—you know, [if] they do what [Daido] does where they give you a level of confidence and they give you a level of freedom, it can

prosper . . . [O]ne of our competitors got bought out by a Japanese company, Kawasaki. And they, I'm not exactly sure what happened, but all the managers got either fired or left. So, there was a problem. And I thought—I understand Japanese are long-term-oriented and very patient. But we were not doing so well our first year and the Japanese management left us alone and tried to let us do our business. And we've been very grateful and very successful thereafter. They do not pose much interference. And, you know, I think that has allowed our management to be more creative and more open.

Bob Mosser mentioned the relations of California Silicon in Fremont with the parent company in Japan as follows:

Well, you know, most of the—most of the people that know me, and they know how old I am, look at me and say, you know, 'What are you doing working for the Japs?,' you know, in which case—in which case I tell them, you know, it's better than going hungry. I have no problem working for the Japanese. And it turns out that their business philosophy is probably closer to mine than the business philosophy of some of the American companies that I've worked for. And probably that's the reason that—that, number one, we don't have any Japanese managers over here, and number two, we're as successful as we are. The general questions are, I mean, there are a lot of people that have known me for a long time and they say, 'How in the hell can you put up with all of the regimentation and everything that is typical of Japanese companies?' I say that they don't bother me. And they don't. And, the Japanese have never found it necessary to send any managers over here to try and run our business because we run it very effectively ourselves.

Bob Mosser was a somewhat aggressive manager when compared to many other American managers. In addition, he was not afraid of confrontation, which certainly posed a lot of difficulties for the Japanese management at the parent company. Though, as I mentioned before, Mosser emphasized the participatory management practices at his company, he demonstrated his strong top-down management control, which resembled the hierarchical control that I will analyze in

Chapter Six. His attitude is clearly reflected in the following statement:

> A Marine Corps captain that can get people out of a safe, little
> foxhole and send them over the top into machine gun fire is a leader.
> Okay? And that's the same kind of guy you need running a business.

Mosser also said he had to make great efforts to earn the trust of
the Japanese management at the parent company. Once he earned that
trust, he thought they started giving him a lot of autonomy, though he
was aware that the Japanese managers in Japan had difficulty with his
confrontational management style.

> I have no problem dealing with them. I deal—I deal with—with
> Sumitomo at a fairly high level, and all of the people that I deal with
> are gentlemen. We certainly have differences of opinion. It was long,
> it took two or three years for me to establish the credibility that I
> needed with them to be very effective at—not here in the United
> States—but at a corporate level. Now, I feel that—I have as much
> credibility as any manager in Japan. And quite frankly, there are
> times when I have reversed decisions that have been made in Japan.
> And so, I don't have any problem working with them. I think they
> have a problem working with me. Because I don't have any problem
> with confrontation management. I don't have any con—I have no
> problem with telling somebody that they're crazy, from a technical
> standpoint—not personal. There's nothing personal, okay? Japanese
> have a very difficult time, you know, relating to that kind of an
> environment. And so, sometimes, you know, I think they have
> problems with that, okay? The only problem I have with the Japanese
> is getting them to tell the truth. They're habitual liars, you know.
> They refuse to admit failure, or they refuse to admit that anything's
> wrong.

Mosser's derogatory statement clearly illustrated his irritation with
the Japanese for what he perceived as rigid and inflexible decision
making processes. As Mr. Dooley of Yamadadenso described in
chapter three, Japanese management in Japan tended to take more time
in making decisions, and they did not easily change a decision once it
is made. Mosser showed his frustration in the following comment.

How can you fix it if you don't admit that you have a problem? Okay, now, if I have a personal problem, that's it. You know, they have—there are problems in Japan that I could fix. But they won't admit that they have the problem. And yet, we see it continuously in the results of their operations. So, I guess there's a certain amount of frustration that comes from that. And on the other hand, I'm sure that they're frustrated in working with, or trying to work with me in the methods that we use, where we are—again, you know, we can be confrontational, but it's not personal.

In addition, Mosser mentioned the difficulties based upon the cultural differences in the communication processes between the parent company and its U.S. subsidiary. For him, these problems were not something that he had to worry about everyday, but a significant matter of concern on the level of corporate communication.

Communication between the United States and Japan is an extremely difficult problem. You know, it always has been and it always—I think it always will be. Now, maybe not always. But for my generation and for the generation of people that I work with, it's a difficult problem because even though they speak the American language, they don't understand it. They don't understand the inflections in the voice. They don't understand, you know, they don't understand when you ask a rhetorical question.

Well—but, you know, it's not something that I worry about, okay? Well, I do worry about it because I want to be sure when I present a mid-term strategy to them that they understand exactly what I'm saying, okay? I mean, they can understand the numbers, but they have to understand the philosophy of how this was developed and why it was developed, and everything else. And—and I'm concerned many times that—that they don't get the full understanding of that. And, I owe them that. You know, if I'm working for this company and I'm running this business, whether we're successful or not—and we are successful—but I have to be sure that my superiors understand what we're doing. They need to have that understanding. They need—and there are many times when they don't get the complete understanding, okay? And that concerns me, you know. I don't lose any sleep over it, or anything. But, I want to be as thorough with them as I can be. And I think—they have the same problem. They make decisions sometimes that, by our standards, are completely irrational—you know, stupid. But, you know—and many times, unfortunately in the past—once they made a decision they would not reverse it.

Generally, the issue of corporate culture in the transplants I studied in California was closely linked to the question of how management could integrate Japanese and American workforces at the workplace. On the corporate structural level, however, when I examined the relationship between the parent company and its U.S. subsidiary, it was evident that changes in the culture of the parent company in Japan, not only in the U.S. subsidiaries were necessary. As Mosser described, this involved the exchange of personnel between the U.S. transplants and their parent companies in Japan. He talked about the case of one Japanese employee who could not fit in the parent company after spending years in the U.S.

And—smart guy, you know, a very good guy, fits in well with our organization. He'll probably spend five years here, and he'll go back to Japan and they'll refuse to talk to him or to use him, because now he's an outsider. And this really bothers me. And, again, I think that this is related to the culture of the older generation, which hopefully will soon go away. But, you know, I knew that was going to happen. And I—I even—before we sent the first engineer back to Japan, I negotiated to get him a specific job so that he would have some authority, and so that he could use the talents that he had learned here. And they assured me that he would be given the position, and that he would be used effectively. And they did give him the position. But basically, he's not—they've made him very ineffective. He can't—he can't do the things that he should be doing. He's—he is very frustrated. He's too—he's too Americanized. He does things— he does things the way we do them here in the United States. And— we do things much differently than they do in Japan. And so, he's having a tough time readjusting. And the unfortunate thing is that we now have another person here. He'll be here for five years. And I'm sure he'll face the same problems when he goes back.

When California Silicon's management exchanged employees between the U.S. transplant in Fremont and the parent company in Japan, the result was not impressive. Mosser said that the management in the parent company did not want to work with the American managers, though the relationships improved later.

[B]cause none of our people speak Japanese very fluently, we have not sent anybody over there for longer than two weeks—three weeks, three weeks. We've had some people over there for about three weeks. It was an interesting experiment. But, you know, after all of the tours were over, basically the Japanese did not want to work with our managers. They didn't want them on the production floor watching what was going on. And it became a very difficult issue. It was not addressed properly. We've learned from that, you know, we in the United States learned from it. The Japanese have learned from it. Things are working better now. They do work better now. But, you know, it's very difficult getting, you know, the two countries [together].

Although Mosser thought that the more flexible interchange of personnel between the U.S. and Japan might be possible in the future, at this moment, the social and cultural differences are too great. For him, it might take several generations of effort.

Maybe over three or four generations. You know, thirty years from now, it's even conceivable that—that the person who is in my job could be on the board of directors in Japan. That possibility right now is non-existent. They would not accept me on the board of directors. And I realize that. And, you know, a lot of Americans would be frustrated and would feel that they were not reaching their full potential, and that they were being discriminated against, or something. I don't feel that way at all. You know—they're not discriminating against me. But their culture is not yet ready to have an outsider on their board of directors, okay?

Considering the significant difference in the corporate structure and business practices of the parent company and its U.S. subsidiary, he did not think it was possible for an American president of the subsidiary to have significant control over the parent company in Japan. For the time being, it was acceptable, he said, as long as Japanese management did not interfere with the way in which he functioned on the everyday work level.

> I understand—I understand the situation, and I think I understand why the situation exists. And it doesn't bother me. You know, it does not impact the way I have to do my job, okay? And I do not have to be a senior managing director of [Daido California Silicon in Japan] to be a success, okay? I can be the executive vice-president or the president of the American company and, we can be just as successful as if I were a senior managing director on the board. And I would not fit into their method of consensus management and—I would not fit into their—you know, they've spent lifetimes developing relationships in their company. And, you know, I don't speak the language, and—I've not been an associate of theirs for forty years. So, I don't fit into that pattern, and I never will. And I should not try to force myself into that pattern. That's when you become frustrated—when you try to force yourself into a situation where you don't belong. And I don't belong there. And—that doesn't bother me, and it does not—it does not have any impact on the way that I can do my job for this company. So, why should I care about it? They have to accept me as I am, and I have to accept them as they are, okay? And fortunately, I think, we both do that.

As shown in the case of California Silicon in Fremont, corporate control has taken a significant role in developing a unique corporate culture within the company. The importance of maintaining good corporate level relationships between the parent company in Japan and its U.S. subsidiary was also voiced by Freddy Marquez of Suntech's repair center in San Jose. Marquez perceived that one of the significant challenges for him in working with the Japanese was to develop more frequent interaction between Suntech Japan and its U.S. subsidiary–Suntech America. He described the need for more continuous interaction between the Japanese staff and local employees.

> We need to interact with each other more. For example, when I go there [Suntech Japan], they treat us very well. That's good. But, after

we come back from Japan, there are no follow-ups. When the Japanese staff come here, they usually stay for five years and return to Japan. Again, there are basically no follow-ups of the relationships that we developed while they were here. Then, another staff comes here from Japan . . . and we have to create a totally new relationship all over from scratch again. There has to be more frequent interaction. And we need to follow up these relationships even after Japanese staff return to Japan. The most challenging thing working with Japanese . . . if you asked me 10 years ago, probably it was 'communication.' But, now, [it is] to interact more between the Japanese office and here.

Both Mosser and Marquez suggested the importance of corporate structural level attention to issues at the workplace, namely, creating a unique corporate culture for the U.S. facilities. At the high-tech Japanese transplants in California, the issue of corporate culture concerned the increased interaction of the Japanese and American workforce. Nonetheless, the corporate cultures of their parent companies in Japan also became a crucial matter of concern in the larger picture.

CONCLUSION

As in the Japanese auto transplants in the Midwest, the transplants that I studied in California generally exhibited different organizational practices from those of Japanese firms in Japan and American-owned firms. There were some variations among the three transplants, especially in the area of training practices. These variations were, however, mainly due to the different requirements derived from the different nature of production processes at each transplant. Compared to the auto-related transplants in the Midwest, small group activities on the shopfloor were more ad hoc in nature, reflecting the smaller scale of production. Managers' emphases on social interaction between the Japanese and American employees were not as obvious as in the Midwest transplants, though this was always a focal issue in the discussions concerning the creation of a unique corporate culture for the plant. Instead, a few managers pointed out the significance of corporate structural level efforts to successfully create a unique "Third culture" (Fuccini and Fuccini 1990) by integrating the Japanese and

American workforces. At the time of my study, however, the social and cultural differences of the work environments between the U.S. and Japan were so significant that managers at the three transplants I studied could only hope for the improvement of their relationships with the parent companies in Japan in the future.

NOTES

1. The term "wiwaf" is an acronym for the phrase, "When I was at Ford." The phrase was used by former Ford employees. Because sometimes they started conversations or ideas, "Well, when I was at Ford, we did it this way," employees at Nippon North America (NNA) called them "Wiwafs." Sometimes there was some friction between Wiwafs and people from other backgrounds. Ford had a particular corporate culture, and Wiwafs often reflected that culture. Sometimes that conflicted with the work processes at NNA.

2. The term "*nemawashi*" refers to the informal process of negotiation preceding the formal decision-making process. A member of a social group tries to informally negotiate, persuade, or even counsel people whom he thinks might oppose his opinion at the time of formal decision-making. The process of *nemawashi* usually takes place during non-business hours, such as around the lunchtime table, at the bar or restaurant after work hours, or might even take the form of a private telephone call during work or after work hours. The process of consensus decision-making in Japanese organizations is often accompanied by *nemawashi*.

CHAPTER 5

Organizational Practices Transferred to the U.S.—The Case Study Company, Suntech America

In this chapter I will examine the significance of Murakami and Rohlen's eight characteristics of Japanese organizational practices at my case study company, Suntech America. As I mentioned in chapter two, the process of data collection in the Midwest and California was based almost solely upon interviews with Japanese and American managers, but not with production workers. My visits of transplants in the Midwest and in California were most often for only one day. Therefore, I needed to examine in depth one particular company. At Suntech, I collected information through extensive interviews and on-going conversation with both managers and production workers for a period of four months.

Japanese managers at Suntech America recognized that they could not implement all aspects of organizational practices used at plants in Japan. Although they had expectations that such practices at Suntech remain as close as possible to those of the home plants, they understood that American workers had assumptions and expectations about their worklives that were significantly different from those of workers in Japan. Because of social and cultural differences in industrial environments of the U.S. and Japan, they had, in reality, selectively adjusted Japanese practices to American social and cultural conditions.

Before examining the eight elements at the case study company, Suntech America, I will look at the surrounding industrial environment of the state of New Mexico. It is important to look at the political and economic characteristics of New Mexico in relation to the reasons for the site selection of the company.

CHARACTERISTICS OF INDUSTRIAL ENVIRONMENT OF NEW MEXICO

A major characteristic of New Mexico's political economy since World War II has been the state's heavy reliance on defense-related production, and the low level of industrialization in the private manufacturing sector. Traditionally, New Mexico has been primarily an agricultural state with the city of Albuquerque as its main service and commercial center. Although this has been a significant characteristic of New Mexico to this day, the existence of national laboratories such as Los Alamos and Sandia, and Kirtland Air Force Base has substantially changed the state's political economy since the end of World War II, and has made New Mexico a center for research and development (R & D) of nuclear and defense-related activities.

Manufacturing in the private sector has been based on traditional industries, such as food processing, lumber, furniture making, arts and crafts, and building supplies. Along with this defense/nuclear environment, the lack of presence of heavy industries with a highly-paid, unionized workforce is also a characteristic of New Mexico. As Evans mentions, when compared to Arizona or Texas, New Mexico has not traditionally been attractive to new industries because there was neither a pool of skilled workers, nor a mass of unskilled, low-paid workers that could lead to cost reductions for potential employers (Lamphere, Zavella, Gonzales, and Evans 1993: 36).

New Mexico's geographical isolation from the Northeastern frostbelt cities would also mean extra transportation costs for manufacturers in heavy industries such as steel and automotive. Among those industries that have been established in New Mexico, therefore, are newer industries such as electronics, or less high-tech but more labor-intensive industries. For these businesses the cost of receiving raw materials and shipping finished products was not a primary consideration (Lamphere et al. 1993: 36-37). In addition, some of the newer high-tech companies in New Mexico are actually spin-offs from Sandia and Los Alamos labs, reflecting the federal initiative of cutting down its defense production since the Cold War era. New Mexico thus has developed its infrastructure and a local labor force "with a bit of industrial experience but a labor market that is still loose, dominated principally by low-paying service jobs rather than by other industrial employers" (Lamphere et al. 1993: 39). In terms of its political and economic environment New Mexico has become attractive to the spillover industries from other sunbelt cities, if not to heavy industries from the frostbelt.

The case study plant, Suntech America, is one of the manufacturers that was attracted to New Mexico because of this political and economic climate. Suntech America is a wholly owned subsidiary of a large-sized Japanese parent company, Suntech Corporation (pseudonym). Suntech America, headquartered in New York, was established in the late 1960's to facilitate the sales of medical instruments from the parent company to the U.S. market. The New Mexico plant is Suntech America's first manufacturing facility in the United States, and has been engaged in manufacturing and repair of medical instruments and related products in the United States since 1989.

Like many other manufacturing companies in Japan during the 1980's, Suntech Corporation saw an opportunity to enhance U.S. sales capabilities by locating manufacturing facilities in the United States. The decision was made by a search committee from Suntech Corporation and Suntech America to select the site for their first manufacturing facility. The principal issue in site selection was labor. The present location in New Mexico was selected for several reasons. First of all, the state has strong engineering and technical labor resources. Second, local references revealed a large number of trainable, unskilled laborers available for industry. Third, the local government was aggressive in terms of attracting new industries to New Mexico through issuance of industrial bonds to new industries. Finally and most importantly, the relatively lower cost of living in New Mexico was attractive to the company.

Suntech America has its repair (re-assembly) facility in San Jose, California. One of the important reasons the company located its first manufacturing facility in New Mexico was to avoid crowding and the highly competitive labor market in northern California. For Suntech America, issues relating to quality of life in New Mexico were a central concern, and were as crucial as the relative low wage level of the state.

Coupled with the basically nonunion political climate of New Mexico, the affordable living standards of the region have provided the company a relative advantage in recruiting competitive professionals from the national labor market. In addition, the turnover rate of the local workforce was also a major concern for Suntech America. Since the Suntech San Jose facility had a problem of high turnover in the past, the company was looking for an area where the inter-firm mobility of the local labor market was not very high.

When Suntech America came to New Mexico in 1989, the State's defense-related industries had begun down-sizing and laying off considerable numbers of employees, both assembly line workers and middle-level managers. These circumstances, i.e., the low turnover rate of the local labor market, actually represented for workers a lack of job choice. Referring to this point, one of the managers at Suntech said, "Albuquerque is a trap . . . there aren't many jobs. The overall factor for anybody who has a job in Albuquerque . . . to be truthful, is where are you going to go if you quit?" In fact, for Suntech America, many employees (both workers and managers) came from American-owned manufacturing companies that used to rely heavily on defense-related contracts, and thus, in the process of down-sizing many employees lost their jobs.

THE SETTING

There were only about 40 employees when Suntech America started its New Mexico production facility in 1989. The company had steadily continued to expand its workforce since then, and the facility had 110 employees at the time of this study in 1992.[1] There were four departments in Suntech: (a) administration, (b) research and development (R & D), (c) manufacturing, and (d) repair. Administration and R & D were relatively small in size compared to the manufacturing and repair departments. The R & D department had only seven employees compared to the repair department which had 49 employees. At the time of the study there were 11 Japanese employees at the facility. Mr. Shibata, a top manager of the plant, was originally from Japan, and had been living in the U.S. for almost 20 years, working for Suntech's corporate headquarters in New York. While working at the headquarters, he became an employee of Suntech America, though he had initially been sent to the U.S. by the parent company, Suntech Corporation in Japan. Similarly, Mr. Nogi, the repair department manager, was also from Japan but was an employee of Suntech America. On the other hand, one (1) manager of the R & D department, three (3) engineers in the manufacturing department, and two (2) managers of the repair department were dispatched employees from the parent company, Suntech Corporation in Japan. Unlike Mr. Shibata and Mr. Nogi who were part of the pay system of Suntech America, these dispatched employees were paid by Suntech Corporation in Japan. In addition, there were three (3) Japanese women at the facility. They were American citizens and, therefore, paid by Suntech America. There were, of course, several American managers. Like many other foreign-owned firms in the United States, Suntech America had an American human resources manager. The manufacturing department manager was an American as were the operations manager of the manufacturing department and the assistant manager of the repair department. In addition, there was one American female manager who served as a production planner in the repair department. At the time of my study, she was the only female manager at the facility.

Suntech America had been a sales company in the U.S. since 1968 and the New Mexico facility was the first manufacturing facility located in the U.S. for the whole corporation. Headquartered in New York, and being a brand new facility, Suntech America's New Mexico plant (which I shall hereafter call Suntech America) had not yet been granted a large degree of autonomy by the New York corporate headquarters, nor by the parent company in Japan. This had caused much dissatisfaction, especially among American managers in the manufacturing department.

Suntech America manufactured medical instruments, and repaired (refurbished) the products. Like many other high-tech firms in the Sunbelt states, the facility was small in size. There was not a remarkable distinction between the office and the production areas. In contrast to those automotive plants in the Midwest, it was very quiet and clean inside the facility so that one got the impression of this facility being a small research laboratory. Although employees of the administration department and the upper-level managers tended to wear traditional business attire most of the times, employees (including managers) in the production and repair area wore blue jackets and tended to dress somewhat casually. In the manufacturing department the work processes were based on the auto conveyor which was called the round conveyor system. In the repair department, in contrast, work processes were based on piecework, an assembly (re-assembly) line consisting of seven module stages. For example, in the production (re-assembly) group, there were basically 23 different work processes for which 23 line workers were responsible. Those 23 workers were grouped into stages from "Module 1 Stage" through "Module 7 Stage." In addition, there were other work areas such as "training" and "inspection." In order to achieve a smooth work flow, the department utilized *"heijunka,"*[2] a method designed to ensure flexibility in work lines with quick set-up and short lead time. There was a large sign board in front of the whole work area which illustrated the daily target production number and the number that was currently being achieved.

The R & D department[3] was very small consisting of only seven (7) employees. Mr. Sakatani, a dispatched employee from Suntech in Japan, was a manager of the department. Mr. Sakatani was the only Japanese. The remaining employees in the department were all American, one (1) secretary and five (5) design engineers.

Finally, there was a warehouse area which was responsible for shipping and receiving of all materials. At Suntech, as in many other high-tech companies, the warehouse area was the only place which recalled the old stereotypical image of a factory. This area was the hottest in the whole facility during the summer time and the coldest during the winter. Shipping/Receiving and facility maintenance jobs seemed to be the only kind of work that entailed heavy physical labor in the company.

At Suntech the day started at 7:15 in the morning. Most of the employees started arriving to the company around seven o'clock and preparing for the day's work. The break-time varied depending on departments. For most employees, the lunch break was usually just thirty minutes, from twelve noon to twelve-thirty. Many employees, therefore, brought their own lunch instead of going out to restaurants. Those who lived near Suntech usually went home for the lunch break. The official work day for production workers ended at 3:15. Unless there was an overtime request (usually from Japanese managers) this was the time when most American line workers left the workplace. Among the American employees usually only supervisors and managers stayed after three-thirty, but most of them usually left the company by five o'clock. In contrast, the Japanese employees frequently remained in the workplace until six or seven o'clock everyday. In the next section, I will examine the significance of eight characteristics of Japanese organizational practices at Suntech America.

1. Lifetime Employment (or long tenure of employment)

To examine the significance of lifetime employment practices at Suntech America, I will look at Japanese managers' expectations regarding length of employment of American employees at Suntech. Though Suntech's New Mexico plant had only 118 employees at the time of this study, its parent company in Japan, Suntech Corporation, is a large organization with almost 7600 regular employees. As have many other large firms in Japan, Suntech Corporation had maintained the tradition of lifetime employment for its regular, male employees. On the other hand, the employment practice at Suntech America was different from these practices of large firms in Japan. Suntech America would, ideally, prefer that the American workers would consider lifetime employment. Japanese managers at Suntech America realized, however, that this practice of lifetime employment was unfamiliar to the contemporary American workforce. The management would have preferred to extend the lifetime work opportunity to employees, but were unable to do so because of the differences of the work environments between the U.S. and Japan. In Japan, employees in large firms usually stay with one company until they retire at the age of 60. Companies offer workers the security of lifetime employment and, at the same time, expect from workers a certain level of loyalty and commitment to the job at the company. In contrast, American workers at Suntech were used to changing jobs whenever they were offered improved work conditions, like higher pay and more benefits. Therefore, it was difficult for American workers to understand the Japanese expectations of loyalty and commitment to the job and to the company. As in transplants in the Midwest and in California, it was usually American white-collar middle managers and engineers who expressed their frustration with the Japanese managers' expectation of loyalty and commitment. Compared to the production workers at Suntech who did not have many job choices in New Mexico, American white-collar managers, and especially engineers, enjoyed more choices in their careers.

Like many other transplants in the U.S., the ideal of lifetime employment was expressed at Suntech in their commitment to prevent layoffs. Mr. Nogi, the repair department manager, referred to his ideal of a no-layoff policy. His idea of retaining employees as long as possible was generally a representative attitude of Japanese managers towards American employees.

> [A]bout layoff . . . instead of bosses laying off workers whenever they feel like it . . . If I were a president of the company, I would avoid layoffs as much as possible by planning the business cautiously. However, in reality I don't think it is true that there are no layoffs because this is a Japanese company. We will layoff workers when we need to.

Mr. Shibata related an idea similar to Nogi's regarding retention of American employees and reflected his expectation that American employees remain with the company for a significant duration (4-5 years), even if they were somewhat under qualified when hired.

> [I]t is better for us to have an employee who can work here with us for a long time even if the quality of the employee is a little one rank down, rather than an employee who is the best of all but who doesn't stay. No matter how good an employee is, you know, you can't accomplish anything within one or two years, and if an employee leaves in one or two years, this is a difficulty for us. So, we like 'A⁻' (A minus) kind of employees . . . those who keep working and staying here instead of getting bored soon and leaving here . . . that is the ideal.

The existence of this expectation toward employees clearly differentiated Suntech from other American counterparts, where the expectation for the employee was less personal. Rick Darnell, an American manufacturing manager, talked about his job responsibilities at Suntech being more personal than in his previous experiences in American companies.

> I feel like expectations on me personally are higher. In my last

company, there was an expectation in my position . . . and the company worked with an assumption that I would change jobs, quit and go somewhere else . . . but there was an expectation in that job. Whereas, it seems like here the expectations are on me personally. If I quit tomorrow my boss would be surprised. Okay . . . if this is American company and if I quit tomorrow, my boss would say, 'Oh, I'm sorry. Why did you do that?' And the next thought would be, 'How do I replace him?' Position versus person, I guess. I feel much more a sense of personal responsibility here.

For some lower level employees the more personal expectations from Japanese managers created a social context where employees saw themselves as an important part of the company and thus had become more self-motivated in their work. A sense of loyalty and commitment was thereby cultivated. There were, in addition, opportunities for promotion for production workers if they proved themselves. At the same time, jobs were certainly more demanding than in American companies. Libby Rodriguez, an assembly technician in the manufacturing department, expressed how she felt responding to this condition at Suntech compared to her previous experience in an American company.

[A]t Lukens you don't have a chance for promotion. At Lukens, you're just there to pull out their numbers, to get their parts out. It's an easy job, so they consider you an expense—you know, in today, gone tomorrow. They can replace you very fast. You don't need a brain to work at Lukens. You need a brain to work here. I want to use my brain. I just don't want to—I just don't want to sit and wind sutures all day, and abuse my arm, and take abuse, and not ever be anything. I want to be somebody. I know I'll never take [Mr. Shibata's] place in there. But I would like to move up, at least get [Terry's] (her supervisor) job.

Denise Staton, a personnel administrator, also referred to the Japanese managers' effort to retain American employees with problems instead of resorting to displacing them.

We have one case, where an employee had a lot of time off, a lot of time off. We were having problems, and a lot of unpaid time off. In an American company, he would have been fired. But it was Japanese managers that understood there is a problem in this person's life, and you know, worked with that problem and made sure enough that person straightened up because it was just an isolated incident. In an American company, the person would have been gone.

Mr. Shibata also related to the emphasis on loyalty through pay and benefits packages.

[I]f we expect loyalty from our employees, you know, it's a give-and-take. We have to do a lot of things for them in return, things like pay, and benefits and the like. Though I think we are doing this, it's not easy to do that perfectly.

In my study, "position versus person" characterized the general differences between American and Japanese organizations. The previous quotes from employees at Suntech show that Japanese managers at Suntech valued a sense of personal responsibility and commitment to the company and tried to retain American employees longer than American-owned companies. However, Suntech also differed from its home plant in Japan, where the management system relied even more on employees' personal attributes, and employees were more deeply inculcated into the company as a coherent social group. Japanese managers at Suntech realized that they could not isolate one element of all Japanese management practices or implement all aspects of lifetime employment practices in the U.S. The following statement by Mr. Nogi showed that Suntech tried to build a system that was prepared for the turnover of American employees:

Because this society is based on the individuality, not on the group, we think it is better to approach these problems in a systematic way. As a system, or as a method, or in some way, we try to deal with problems materialistically, not just moral advice or instruction such as 'Please be careful from now on,' or 'Let's concentrate more,' and things like that. Though this is in some way effective, we think it is more important to approach through tools, systems, and the concrete frameworks. And this lasts longer. Even if people change, the system is still alive. However, when we teach the person, and if the person leaves the company, there is nothing. So, it is important here to build a system in which we don't have to count on people.

Referring to the Japanese managers' tendency to take things personally when American employees leave, Mr.Shibata also mentioned the importance of preparing for the turnover of American employees.

In fact, I think it is good enough if 5 employees out of 10 employees stay in the long run. If we don't think this way, those Japanese staff who are relatively new here get so discouraged when Americans leave. They feel like, 'Oh well, we have been working together with Americans and making every possible efforts so far for two years only to see them leave,' feeling that Americans are cold and terrible. You know, this is wrong way to think. They should have included to their plans and calculations that this might happen to them.

Although Suntech's Japanese managers held to the company's ideal that American employees would stay for a longer period of time and had tried to motivate the American employees to do so, they had not attempted to institutionalize the practice of lifetime employment in the U.S.

2. Seniority-based wage and promotion systems

Although Suntech's New Mexico plant also utilized the combination of seniority and merit criteria in determining employees' wages and promotions, there was greater emphasis on seniority than on merit. In most of the interviews with Japanese managers, I was told that there was not a direct relationship between training and promotions. However, training provided an opportunity for increasing skills and thereby increasing the worth of the employee for the company. Although management was considering implementing a grading system (*"toukyu seido"*) in the near future, at the time of my study training only indirectly affected the promotional decisions in the sense that training improved the overall work performance.

Many Japanese managers thought that the company should be cautious of modifying this traditional pay and promotional structure unless the company could be sure that business would be steady, more predictable and profitable after the start-up period. Most Japanese managers perceived the start-up period as taking from five to ten years. In terms of the criteria for wage and promotions, Suntech America was inclined more toward the seniority systems, proceeding cautiously before implementing any major changes. This was a source of frustration to many American managers and workers who were accustomed to wage increases and promotions based upon specific guidelines and timetables. Americans perceived the caution of Japanese management to be ambiguous and indeterminate. Americans were accustomed to more immediate gratification for their efforts.

3. Elaborate welfare, bonus, and other benefits systems

The benefits package of Suntech America was different from both the traditional American and the traditional Japanese packages. As most of the transplants in the Midwest and in California, Suntech America did not provide such allowances for its employees that were typical among Japanese firms in Japan, except for the performance-based bonuses. Suntech's benefits package was also different from the typical American systems, which tended to favor the upper-level managers through exceptionally high bonuses. Except that Suntech's benefits structure showed more relative parity between managers and workers than those of American-owned firms, Suntech's benefits package consisted of several insurance plans, such as medical, dental, and retirement, which were typical of many organizations at the time. As shown in the following table (Table 3), the company's benefits package showed more resemblance to those of American firms, though there were minor variations in numbers of sick days, personal days, and vacation days.

Part-time workers in Japan usually do not receive any of the benefits described above. Except for the bonus structure that was clearly different from those of American-owned companies, the contents of Suntech's benefits package showed more similarity to those of American companies in general than to those of Japanese companies in Japan.

Table 3. Benefits and Vacation Days of Suntech America Corporation.

(1) comprehensive major medical
(2) dental plan
(3) life insurance plan
(4) long-term disability insurance plan
(5) retirement plan
(6) insurance plan for voluntary or involuntary termination
(7) sick leave
(a) non-exempt employees: 5 days per year, non-transferable from one year to the next.
(b) exempt employees: unlimited days
(8) $100 bonus for perfect attendance for non-exempt employees
(9) personal days
(a) non-exempt employees: 2 personal days per year, non-transferable from one year to the next
(b) exempt employees: no personal days
(10) vacation days
(a) full-time employees:

Hire Date	Year Hired	Next Year	Subsequent Years
Jan. 1–Feb. 28	5	10	11, 12, 15, 17, 20
Mar. 1–May 31	0	10	11,12, 15, 17, 20
Jun. 1–Dec. 31	0	5	10, 11,12,15,17,20

(b) part-time employees: employees who work less than 40 hours per week get 5 days of sick leave per year, 2 personal days per year.

Hire Date	Year Hired	Next Year	Subsequent Years
Jan. 1–Feb. 28	3	5	10
Mar. 1–May 31	0	5	10
Jun. 1–Dec. 31	0	0	5, 10

(Source: Suntech America's Corporate Guide, 1993)

4. Company-based labor unions

The parent company, Suntech Japan, had a company-based union. Suntech America, however, like many other Japanese transplants and American companies in the Sunbelt area, was a non-unionized company. Although there are some active unions, such as the plumbers and pipefitters, the electricians, and the machinists union in some American-owned firms, like other sunbelt states, unions' presence in high-tech industries is low in New Mexico. My interviews with both Japanese and American managers contained a great deal of antagonism toward American labor unions. One of the typical attitudes toward American labor unions that was shared among Japanese and American managers was reflected in the phrase, "If you get the union, you deserve the union." In addition to the managers at Suntech, many American production workers also held negative attitudes towards labor unions. As in high-tech transplants in California, Suntech's anti-union attitudes were more a reflection of the recent political economic environment of New Mexico rather than the fact that Suntech America was a Japanese-owned company.

5. Considerable inter-job mobility within a firm and emphasis on internal promotion

Interviews with some of key managers generally showed that Suntech America encouraged internal promotion. The emphasis on internal promotion was similar to the practice of the home plant in Japan in the sense that the company tried to cultivate employees and did not want to lose employees in whom the company had invested time and money for training. At Suntech America, however, the emphasis on internal promotion reflected Japanese managers' perceptions of themselves as being Japanese in America and their perceptions of Suntech as a Japanese-owned company. The repair department manager, Mr. Nogi, was concerned that certain Japanese practices at Suntech America, such as the emphasis on seniority in pay and promotions, did not attract "elite" Americans.

> [F]irst of all, we encourage internal promotion. This requires a tremendous amount of effort, like finding a diamond in sand. We try to develop employees from inside. We have this policy. Frankly

speaking, we are not a first rate company (*ichiryu kigyo*) in America. We are a second, or third-rated company. The 'first-rate' Americans don't come here. I mean, of course, this changes from time to time, but companies like IBM or Johnson and Johnson's, those excellent companies, those 'elite' companies. Also, we are not an American company, but a mixture of both Japanese and American. And, if anything, we are a more Japanese-influenced company. In addition, speaking of pay, we don't have an American system. In the American system, the 'elite' employees get enormous pay and the lower-level technicians are treated like a piece of shit. It's different here. We give mediocre pay more or less . . . and we are more or less mediocre, too. Your pay will increase as you stay here longer. So, to be honest with you, we can't say that this is a first-rate company. Our president may get angry if I say things like this. A 'super-star' employee in America will not come to our company. Those Americans will not come to Japanese company to be used by the Japanese. There aren't any 'elite' Americans who can put up with working for the Japanese. So, all we get here is second, and third-rate Americans. When we try to recruit from outside, these are the kind of Americans we get. In addition, we can't raise the pay that much higher, either. So, we get Americans of that level. Therefore, taking a lot of risk, we hire them, and train them patiently. It's like finding a piece of diamond out of the heap of sand. I don't really know what we do when hiring somebody for the big project, for example, at the headquarters in New York. This is another question. But here we try to promote them [mediocre Americans] from below, from within. This is my way of thinking.

As Mr. Nogi commented, Japanese-owned firms in the U.S. usually did not recruit a particular American employee with exceptionally high pay. This was true in the case of Suntech America. As I noted, one of the reasons why the company located the facility in New Mexico was relatively low living cost in the region. Companies in New Mexico, therefore, could still attract highly competent professionals (especially for managerial-level positions) with relatively low pay compared to other regions in the country, such as California.

The emphasis on internal promotions was particularly suitable when a company was located in a region where the local labor market was less mobile. In this sense, for Suntech, internal promotion was particularly emphasized for the locally hired shopfloor level American workers. Ideally speaking, the Japanese managers wanted to train the locally recruited production workers who would stay with the company, and promote them internally. The less mobile labor market of New Mexico served this purpose well because workers tended to stay with the company due to the relative lack of choices that were available to them.

On the other hand, the white-collar American professionals in managerial positions at Suntech tended to be frustrated and somewhat impatient with the slower promotion pace and the relatively slower increase in pay as compared to American-owned firms. Of course, the Japanese managers at Suntech generally wished that American managers would remain with the company. In Japanese companies, such patience was the norm and the expectation of higher wages was a matter of time. The issue of time (lifetime employment) and patience was a less common characteristic of American workers in general. It was not uncommon, therefore, that "headhunters" from other American-owned firms offering higher salaries were thus able to induce some managers and engineers to leave the company. As in other Japanese-owned firms in the U.S., therefore, the internal promotion policy was not particularly emphasized for American middle and/or high level managers. Instead, internal promotion was especially emphasized and much more successful among American assembly line workers and supervisors in the production area.

6. Small group activities on the shop floor level

Much research and many reports in the popular press have documented the widespread use of the team concept, quality control circles, and small group activities both in Japanese and in American companies. Suntech America also emphasized quality control circles and small groups in the production area. Interviews with American and Japanese managers, however, demonstrated many difficulties in implementing the team-based work processes in everyday worklife at Suntech. The interview data also illustrated significant differences of these QC's and small group activities between Suntech's New Mexico plant and its home plant in Japan. Rick, the manufacturing manager, talked about the difficulty in implementing teams in his department.

We don't have enough time to do that. One reason we don't have enough time is because we try to get consensus on too many things. We work too hard to make everybody feel good about too many things. You know, one of good things about American business is that there is a time when a manager asks to pick one or two people to do something and says, 'You do it, and tell everybody else how it's going to happen.' And everybody else has to say, 'Okay, that's what we are going to do.' But the guys I have here from Japan have real problems with that. And if we do that sometimes, then they start making phone calls to Japan, or [Mr. Shibata] will come over and talk to me, and it's like, 'Oh, everybody didn't talk about it enough.'

Though Japanese managers hoped that the team-based work processes be as similar as those in home facilities in Japan, they were very cautious not to impose this expectation or force American employees to practice QC circle activities. Mr. Shibata pointed out that workers in Japan did not get paid for their QC circle activities, whereas the company paid the American workers for such activities.

[F]or example, there are QC circle activities in Japan, the requirements for such activities are not written in job descriptions or anything. It's voluntary in Japan. But here in America, when implementing these activities, we have to do this during the work hours, otherwise we have to pay for overtime here, because they [Americans] are forced to do this. They will be taken out their private time, so, we have to pay for that.

Mr. Nogi, the repair department manager, also mentioned that the company was very careful about initiating these programs with American workers.

For instance, workers tend to break the IGs [4] very often. So, some workers on the level of the lead tech take the initiative and have a volunteer meeting with the line techs. So, looks like from October they have been doing this . . . [W]e do have now teams such as 'rescue group' and 'production group.' But we are not initiating those small group activities from the management side. It is good when workers are willing to do this. We encourage this if workers are ready for small group activities, and we pay for that.

Regarding the suggestion program of the home plant in Japan, Nogi also said that Japanese workers were more likely to make suggestions than were American workers. However, Nogi tried not to force workers to make more suggestions.

7. Intensive training and socialization of new employees by the management

Training at Suntech America was also very different from programs of the home plants in Japan. Generally, there was a tendency for training programs of a company to become more structured and systematic as the company grew. On the other hand, training programs in smaller scale companies were less structured and systematic both in Japan and in the U.S. Much of the literature on large Japanese companies in Japan has discussed the holistic and group-oriented training processes in which employees are socialized and form an identity with their company (e.g., Rohlen 1974; Cole 1976). Although the training programs of Japanese firms in Japan are a significant part of the traditional organizational practices, they are not as structured and systematic as the training programs of large American firms. Referring to the training programs of the home plants in Japan, Mr. Nogi said that the training programs at Suntech America were more commonly based in hands-on or on-the-job training. He explained the contrast between the traditional experience in Japan with operations in the U.S.

> There is a brother/sister program (mentor program), in which older employees are paired with new employees. An older brother pairs with a in-coming employee and trains him. In addition, besides company work, you know, they go to a mountain lodge and have a training workshops, like, 'All About Quality Assurance,' or something like that. So, training programs are quite established and we do it in big groups, group training. In contrast, we do it on the job here.

Suntech's New Mexico plant was only three years old when I conducted interviews. Managers and employees were both struggling to implement worker training programs in this new environment, often by trial and error. The training programs at Suntech America lacked any specific structure or organization. Although Mr. Nogi and other managers as well as employees recognized the need for such structures and systems, there were none yet in place. Like the transplants that I visited in the Midwest, a major difficulty had been the non-existence of senior veterans who had worked for decades in the company. In Japan, it was these veteran workers (*"sempai"*) with both knowledge and skill who trained new employees. In the U.S., however, the situation was such that new employees received training from people less familiar with the processes than their counter-parts in Japan. Additionally, if a manager or supervisor had to take a day or several days training each new employee, it impinged upon his own work and time. Furthermore, the sempai model of training implied a mutual responsibility from both the veteran and new employee. Here, again, a sense or bond of loyalty emerged as an intrinsic component of the Japanese work relationships.

Mr. Nogi realized that the Americans were unfamiliar with this type of training. The American workers needed an "A to Z" type of training, where every contingency and consequence was explained and systematized. He also certainly understood the difficulty this posed for the Japanese. The American workers at Suntech varied significantly in their education and skill levels, while Japanese workers at the home plant were far more uniform and standardized in their education and skill levels. Because of these social and cultural differences in the training environments in the U.S. and Japan, there were no established training policies at Suntech America. Mr. Nogi recognized these contrasts and appreciated the quality of those differences as he clearly explained in the following quote.

> We have a training session once a week, although this is only our department. There have been 32 or 33 training sessions so far at the staff level since we started. In Japan, employees take the initiative to learn new things with their 'sempai.' So, we don't really have to do much and things will go okay. In contrast, we can't expect this here. So, we have to instruct, advise them step by step. Employees here need systematic advice. In Japan, we don't have this kind of systematic training. So, here it is important to build this kind of system, where we can instruct employees systematically, rather than do some kind of spiritual training. Not that we train the importance

of loyalty. Not that we just tell them that they should work harder. Instead, we should instruct step by step, telling them that if you do this you will get there. So, in order to get there, you first should begin from here and then next go there. Things like this. In that sense, things like policy management [5] are more effective here.

On the other hand, American employees at Suntech thought that they had not received enough formal and specific training. In most cases the employees had to take the initiative and ask for guidance from their superiors. Don Grace, an assistant production manager of the repair department, was one of a few American employees hired by Suntech when the plant started production in 1989. He talked about his own experience of not receiving specific guidance or training before being promoted.

> I guess a good example of that is—I'm an assistant production manager, assistant manager level. And before, I was a supervisor. Before that I was a lead tech. There are no definite things that you have to learn to go from one stage to another. In other words, to be a manager, I don't have to understand how to forecast production. To be a supervisor, I did not have to take any training in how to handle personnel. There was nothing specific for me to learn to go from one level to the next level.

In contrast, he also mentioned the structured training program at the previous American company.

> [T]hey did have some structured training. For example, they had a couple of apprenticeship programs where, if you started as an employee, they would start you in the machinist apprenticeship program. And there you would work as a machinist apprentice for four years. And they would train you in all those job duties.

The repair department was the largest department at Suntech with more than seventy employees. This department was also the only department that had attempted to implement some structured training and offered certification for various levels of skills. However, most managers in my interview stated that there was no direct relationship between training and promotion. Don referred to a certification program in the repair department.

> We are giving people what we call a 'certification' in mechanical soldering or electrical soldering. And it consists of a written test and an actual skills test. And we do give the technicians a certificate. I was part of a small group of people that helped to implement that here at [Suntech].

Katie Springer, another manager in the same department, referred to the department's program as follows.

> We do have internal training within our department. It's for our management staff. And for management staff and for our lead technicians or floaters, the people that we want to develop into management staff within our Repair Center, it's official. We have a schedule, and we have training twice a month. Every month, what we do, though, as a management staff, is we share a presentation or training for the production staff. For instance, this month was mine. I gave one on the first of the month on policy management. And so, I present to the technicians what policy management is.

Katie also mentioned the on-the-job nature of the training program. According to her, the training was usually held within the business hours and lasted three to four months. She further described the training programs in the repair department.

> The training, I don't think, was really—it was more on-the-job training. Well, [for a] new hire—we have a system where the first day that they come in, they go through an orientation. And they learn about [Suntech] and about their benefits. And then, in the Repair Center, we also have an orientation that we put them through. They learn about a product, the endoscope, and they learn more about our business, and our business here, locally—what does it mean. And then, we have training within each group—Material Group, QA, and Production, and Engineering—'Tell me more about what Material Control means. What do you do? What does Production do? How does your system work?' We do that. And then, for the technicians,

they go through an additional training to learn their actual process.

Libby Rodriguez, a floater tech [6] in the manufacturing department, also mentioned that there was no specific program in which someone taught what she should learn step-by-step. Instead, she herself had to initiate learning the work processes.

> Nobody ever really took out a book and said 'Okay, [Libby], this is how you learn to do—,' because I learned to do everybody's stage. I know all ten stages on the conveyor system, and I can fill in for anybody. Nobody ever sat me down and said, 'Okay, this is how you do it.' I took the initiative and I learned it. I would get up and I would help other people, and I'd learn—I'd familiarize myself with all the parts of the unit. I would sneak a book home and read over the manual so I would know what parts were, and know how certain wiring went. And now I can put a unit together by myself if I had to.

Although there were no specific training programs in the manufacturing department, an employee like Libby who motivated herself and asked for a guidance received the appropriate training, but this was usually offered after work hours. Libby said as follows:

> When you first get started, they have a lot of training, like for your soldering. You're in a room, like, for a week, you know, just learning. But they do give you training after work. Like if you're having problems soldering, after work they'll give you more training. It's really up to you just to come up and say, 'Okay, I'm not—I don't have the soldering down. Can you help me after work?' And they'll put somebody to help you out after work.

Training for American managers was also neither structured nor systematic. Ron Peal, an operation manager in the manufacturing department, remarked as follows:

> I had no training. The only training they tried to give was policy management and 5S. [7] That's really the only real training I had precisely.

Denise, a personnel administrator, also made the same point and mentioned that she learned everything through informal on-the-job training.

> I don't really have any formal training, It was more of on the job. I guess Russ assuming, he told me something I would know exactly what to do, and something I did, something I had to. Just ask or learn, you know. I never went through any formal training. [It was] on the job, on the job training.

The training of manager level American employees usually involved a short (about a week) visit to the home plants in Japan. This was only offered to carefully selected American managers. Mr. Shibata stated that this was a risky investment for a company because there was no guarantee that these American managers would remain loyal to the company in the U.S.

> [A]bout managers, we send them individually to visit our factories and parent company in Japan. Now, [Bob Walker] happens to be in Tokyo. By taking turns, they, one after one, go to New York or to Japan, and in so doing, they can develop their knowledge and experience. But, you know, I am taking a risk when I do this because every effort turns into nothing if they leave.

The training programs at Suntech America differed from the holistic and group-oriented training programs in Japan. For Suntech's Japanese managers it was more than self evident that they could not expect the same training programs in the highly individualistic and mobile industrial environment of the U.S. In addition, they understood that there were not enough human resources, either on the part of the Japanese or the Americans, who were able to provide the kinds of training programs like those in Japan. As mentioned previously, there were no *sempai* on the shopfloor who could train American workers. Further, in the American social and cultural context, there was no model for such mentoring. The education systems that produced the uniform and standardized workforce in Japan differed greatly from the education systems in the U.S.

On the other hand, the training processes at Suntech America also differed from the training programs in large American firms in the U.S., in which programs were more systematic and structured. Although Suntech's Japanese managers tried to structure and systematize the training processes for American employees, there was a certain expectation of "apprenticeship duty" from Japanese managers toward American employees including both managers and workers. American employees were expected to take the initiative and learn what they needed to learn. This required that American employees would motivate themselves to learn new skills and would remain at the workplace even after normal work hours.[8] The training programs at Suntech thus resulted in unique processes that were different from either the programs of Japanese firms in Japan or from those of American firms in the U.S.

Finally, socialization of new employees to the work culture by the management was almost non existent at Suntech America, except for a short term orientation program for the newly hired Suntech employees. This orientation program at Suntech usually lasted only a few days, consisting of a brief introduction to each functional department and the managers, and an explanation of the company's benefits package by the personnel staff.. Unlike the home plants in Japan, there were no group-oriented sessions, including training, where new employees were introduced to the company's norms and values. Like many other Japanese transplants in the U.S., Suntech had not been able to form the established norms and values into which new employees were socialized. The company, however, sponsored opportunities for casual interaction, such as picnics, ski trips, soft ball games and tournaments, and an annual Christmas party. None of them was mandatory. In contrast to the socialization processes in Japan which was typically accompanied by significant peer pressure, socialization at Suntech was more characteristically recreational. In addition, there was little of the "familistic" atmosphere at Suntech America that has been discussed extensively in many previous studies on Japanese companies. Employees at Suntech frequently used the term "family" when they referred to the company in such a way as "we are a rainbow family." However, this rhetorical use of the term "family" should be clearly differentiated from companies in Japan, where the term "family" reflects the established norms and values of corporate culture of the company. In this sense, socialization at Suntech clearly differed from socialization processes of Japanese companies in Japan.

At the same time, socialization at Suntech also differed from socialization in American-owned firms. Katie, a manager in the repair department, referred to her previous American-owned company as having had a familistic environment.

> And they also had—it's just very family-oriented. They always had the parties for the families at Easter—bring the kids for Easter, and doing these things. And at Halloween they would do things. And you could get products. You could buy [MMS (pseudonym)] products at an employee discount. They have a big company picnic, and a lot of social gatherings at [MMS] for the company, too. You know, like maybe every two months we would get together and they would give us ice cream, or something like that, just so you would get time off with the people that you worked with—beer busts. You've probably heard of beer busts before. Ski trips, rafting trips, things like that.

On the other hand, Katie thought that opportunities for interactions among employees and their families at Suntech were more limited.

> If we have a meeting or we go out to dinner, it's never families. We have never done anything with the management staff, with each other's families or spouses. Never. Families are not allowed. Husbands and wives are not allowed.

As I have shown, socialization at Suntech America thus differed from socialization processes of both Japanese firms in Japan and American-owned firms. Finally, the issue of socialization is closely linked to the corporate culture of a company. Instead of emphasizing the socialization of employees to the company's work culture, managers at Suntech discussed the importance of social interaction between Japanese and American employees. I will examine the corporate culture of Suntech America in the next section.

8. Attention to developing a corporate culture and management philosophy

Among many large firms in Japan, management usually tries to create unique corporate culture. As I discussed in the previous section, the training of new employees is a significant part of the creation of a corporate culture. Some of the ethnography on Japanese companies, such as Rohlen's work on a Japanese bank (Rohlen 1974), shows how new employees are inculcated into the company's mold, and how each employee develops himself as a "company man" through the company's training processes in everyday worklife. The significance of a corporate culture and management philosophy of Japanese companies in Japan becomes meaningful only when we understand that since shortly after World War II until the present, the management of a Japanese company has exerted a hegemonic influence on employees' everyday worklife. Kenney and Florida acutely pointed out this dynamic of corporate culture that supported the team-based organization of work and production among Japanese manufacturing companies (Kenney and Florida 1993). Suntech Japan's manufacturing plants in Japan, as many manufacturing plants of other companies in Japan, also conforms to Kenney and Florida's characterization.

The ways employees at Suntech dealt with the concept of corporate culture may be similar to those of American non-traditional manufacturing companies in the U.S. in the sense that they talked about corporate culture and management philosophy without any significant influence or understanding of the corporate hegemony in their everyday worklife. Most production workers left the company at 3:15 p.m. unless they were requested to do overtime. Though most American middle level managers tended to stay after business hours and worked longer hours, we see a similar picture nowadays in many other American companies. At Suntech, American middle level managers tried to work longer hours because they desired to prove themselves to Japanese managers. Generally speaking, Japanese managers (and engineers) at Suntech wished that the production systems be as similar as possible to those of home plants in Japan. However, they were very careful about imposing their Japanese expectations on American employees. The nature of corporate control from Japanese managers was expressed when Mr. Shibata talked about his leadership.

> In fact, it is true of everything, not only in sales and production, that Japanese companies come from Japan to the U.S. and are allowed to do business here. I think we need these kinds of modest attitudes,

although this may sound too formal when I put in this way. So, when we work here, we will not be successful unless we make the best of Americans, I think . . . no matter how hard only our Japanese staff works here. I think it is important that Americans work with Americans for the U.S. That's one of my policies. The next is about my leadership. It is not good to have a strong leadership from top down, I think. Then you have an organization as a group that grows toward the future. So, for the leaders, it is okay if those front-line managers work together and lead the employees. A leader like me should remain behind the scene and make sure that work tasks are accomplished properly. What I am saying is very important here because we, Japanese, are here in America. We will never receive any attention no matter how hard we work if we only use Japanese employees. They [Americans] just look down on us even if we do this.

Mr. Shibata's remark clearly indicated that his management philosophy differed from the one of home plants in Japan because of the presence of American workers and because the company was located in the U.S. For him, the leadership that was implicit in his management ideals had to be changed in the U.S. when dealing with American workers. His ideal of management control in the U.S. also reflected his own perceptions of American society. Like Mr. Nogi, Mr. Shibata also related to similar perceptions of Japanese-owned company in America.

This is never publicly expressed. For example, in many publications, books and TV reports, there is something that is never told in public. For instance, these are never written, you know, about Americans in Japanese-owned firms in the U.S., which is also the same in Europe. It is that the 'first-rate' Americans absolutely never come to Japanese firms. For example, those Americans never want to work for us. That's because, suppose you are American, think about it, which is the same if you are Japanese. Think about working, for instance, for Korean or Philippine companies. Who will be very happy working for them? It is an another question if they treat you so well and pay you three or five times more. But, under the conditions of normal employment, think about it. If we Japanese force everything top down on Americans—when we say Americans, we generally refer to white people—they have a sense of superiority over people of color. They always say that they don't. But they absolutely do have this, I believe. They do, for sure. I can tell this from the over 20 years of my experience in this country. They do, for sure. If something happens, white people stay with white people.

Mr. Shibata's perception of the racial and ethnic relations in American society was generally rooted deeply in many other Japanese managers in the U.S. as well. In addition, understanding the cultural differences between the U.S. and Japan was crucial to modify Japanese management ideals to the American social and cultural conditions. Mr. Shibata further mentioned the cultural differences as follows:

That's more because of the cultural differences, the differences in the ways of thinking, the differences of the mode of imaginations and many others, rather than the language differences. In fact, Japan is basically like that. We are agricultural people. You know what agriculture is. [It is] that we build water canals together and share water-use on such a small land. So, we can't live unless we build teamwork. It's completely different from hunting and gathering society. In hunting and gathering societies, people don't have to do this. People don't have to cooperate. You can just do it in your way alone. So, there are these kinds of distinctive differences between us, the differences between agricultural and hunting and gathering people. So, we Japanese have to have this and that complex, intricate human relations, and determine the productivity of respective paddy, and form a group together in order to make our lives. We can't live otherwise.

He also thought that Japanese organizations were based on the prototype of agrarian community.

[T]he mass-repetitive production system, the system in which people manufacture the same products on a mass scale is adaptive for those people who are agricultural, people who have to cultivate the rice paddies. It's not that the Japanese are superior to Americans. I really don't think so. It just happened to be adaptive for the Japanese. And luckily, the Japanese are perfectly suited for this system of producing the same cars, TV's, and the same cameras, the same products with the same configuration through working together harmoniously. That's why we can do it. It's not because we are superior. There is this kind of innate (natural) tendency, or culture among the Japanese. Americans are not like that. If we don't understand this about Americans, we instantly start complaining that Americans are hard to deal with, and the like. It's not that Americans are not capable but that Americans are not suited for this. So, we have to change the way we approach Americans instead of forcing them to do our way no matter what.

The emphasis on corporate culture and management philosophy that existed at Suntech America, however, was handled very differently from either home plant in Japan or American firms in the U.S. At Suntech America there were no training programs that were aimed at educating employees to the company's mold. Instead, managers only emphasized the importance of social interaction between Japanese and American employees, though they had not been able to institutionalize the processes of interaction. In addition, management philosophy emphasized that Japanese managers needed to account for the perceived social and cultural differences between the two nations, and alter corporate control and management policies to enhance the relationships with American employees.

CONCLUSION

The existence of the eight elements of Japanese organizational practices at Suntech America differed from both traditional Japanese organizational practices in firms in Japan as well as American organizational practices. Lifetime employment was virtually non-existent in the U.S., although Japanese managers would have preferred that American employees remain with the company for at least five years, and if possible, even longer. American employees were accustomed to job mobility and company loyalty was, at best, a much lower priority among contemporary Americans. The pay and promotion structure and the emphasis on internal promotion were rather Japanese. At the same time, the slow promotion track and slow increases in pay tended to frustrate American employees, particularly

American managers and engineers. The benefits package showed a difference from both a typical American and a Japanese packages, though Suntech's package resembled many American firms. However, it was different from a typical American benefits package in the sense that the benefit structure did not particularly favor a few higher-level managers in salary and bonuses as in many American-owned firms. QC's, small group activities, and training programs have resulted in practices unique to Suntech America in an attempt to ameliorate the social and cultural differences between American and Japanese workers. The attention to corporate culture and management philosophy also existed, but was different in content compared to that of Japanese firms in Japan. Generally speaking, most Japanese firms in Japan have an already established corporate culture that was unique to each company. There is a unique corporate culture into which new employees are socialized through many intensive training programs and their everyday worklives. At Suntech, on the other hand, this kind of the established corporate culture was non-existent. Instead, the issue of corporate culture was mainly concerned with how the company could integrate American and Japanese managerial philosophies and the workforces. Japanese managers believed that the Japanese concepts of small group activities, the training, and socialization could not be implemented in the same manner because of the social and cultural differences and had, therefore, selectively adapted their organizational practices to the American industrial environment.

COMPARISONS BETWEEN THE CASE STUDY COMPANY AND FIRMS IN THE MIDWEST AND CALIFORNIA

Here I will incorporate the Suntech case study into the previous conclusions on the Midwest and California. As I have said in the last three chapters, the practice of lifetime employment was virtually non-existent, although Japanese managers preferred that American employees remain with the company for at least five years, and if possible, even longer. The pay and promotion structures and the emphasis on internal promotion exhibited some characteristics of Japanese plants. At the same time, slower rates of promotion and salary increases tended to frustrate American employees, particularly managers and engineers. All of the transplants were non-unionized; Japanese as well as American managers in these transplants displayed strong anti-union attitudes. The benefits packages at these transplant companies differed from both American and Japanese structures, though they resembled more closely those of American firms. A major characteristic of a typical American benefits package was the tendency to favor a few higher-level managers in salaries and bonuses.

QC's (Quality Control Circles), small group activities, and the training programs have resulted in practices unique to those transplants in an attempt to ameliorate the social and cultural differences between American and Japanese workers. On the shopfloor-level, the social and cultural differences between Japanese and American workers were reflected in the contrasting style of worklife: work hours, decision-making processes, the education and skill levels of workers, and attitudes toward the job.

American workers were accustomed to specific kinds of contractual relationships with the company, while, for Japanese workers, boundaries between company and private life were far less distinct. The frequent demand for overtime work and the expectation for perfect attendance were difficult for American production workers to cope with, particularly for single mothers. In addition, the slow and rigid process of decision making often frustrated American managers. For Japanese managers, it was difficult to deal with American workers whose skills and educational levels were not as uniform and standardized as workers in Japan. Compared to their American counterparts, most Japanese transplants were smaller in size and with a short-term history of U.S. operation, and had not accumulated a strong base of knowledge and experience for overcoming the social and cultural differences at the corporate level. Facing this reality, managers at transplants were continuously experiencing periods of trial and error in implementing team-based work processes with American workers. Most transplants did not have any established training policies, though managers recognized an urgent need to be more systematic in training American workers.

Both Japanese and American managers of transplants generally acknowledged the importance of social interactions between Japanese and American employees. Though management recognized the importance of such, there were few companies that paid attention to the process of such social interactions in any systematized, well-formulated policies. Like the processes of implementing teams and training, most transplants needed to gain wider experience in order to establish successful patterns of interaction. In most of the transplants, social and cultural issues at the workplace have been overshadowed by the companies' more immediate concerns with basic aspects of businesses. In this study, only one transplant had seemingly succeeded in improving relations between Japanese and American employees in their everyday worklives, and this was due to direct, intentional efforts on the management level.

Among most transplant companies, however, an emphasis on the socialization of new employees to the company's norms and values by the management was almost non-existent. Socialization, in the Japanese sense, inculcates new employees into the company's mold through intensive training programs and an everyday life course that is heavily influenced by the company. In transplant companies, this type of over-arching, systematized process is lacking. Although employees talked casually about the company's corporate culture in their everyday worklives, the majority of transplants, especially smaller and newer ones, were unable to formulate an established "corporate culture" into which new employees were socialized. On the other hand, the issue of corporate culture among transplants was directed toward integrating the Japanese and American workforce into a hybrid work culture, thus forming a "third culture plant" (Fuccini and Fuccini 1992).

The major issues in discussing corporate culture in transplants are the frustrations of both Japanese and American employees in everyday worklife, derived mainly from the differences in perceptions and expectations toward work. The issue of corporate culture in transplants, however, must also involve greater concern at the corporate structural level in the long run. As one American president of a transplant in California pointed out, creating a third culture plant eventually must involve changing the corporate culture of the parent company in Japan. The corporate level relationships between a parent company and its U.S. subsidiary becomes important here. In my study, some Japanese managers voiced their concern that they actually had a harder time in communicating with the parent company in Japan than with their American workers. There was also a case of a Japanese dispatched engineer who was unable to fit into the parent company in Japan after working for its U.S. subsidiary for five years.

Finally, the issue of corporate culture also necessitates localizing management of the transplants by hiring more Americans for significant positions. A general pattern among the transplants was that important positions, such as financial managers, production managers, and quality assurance managers were typically occupied by Japanese, while areas like administration and public relations were predominantly occupied by Americans. Japanese managers at transplants realized that such localization of these crucial positions for Americans in the future would be imperative. However, this may not happen as quickly as necessary, considering the struggles of both Japanese and American managers to overcome social and cultural differences, and corporate structural level differences between parent companies in Japan and transplants in the U.S.

At the present stage, it is difficult to determine whether they are succeeding or failing in creating this hybrid work culture. As previously identified above, there are some crucial social and cultural differences between Japanese and American workers that are difficult to overcome in a short span of time. In addition, many transplants have employed what Kenney and Florida referred to as the "unreconstructed American managers" (Kenney and Florida 1993), who were continuously frustrated with the company's slow promotion track, slower salary increases, and the glass ceilings. At the same time, some transplants, although not many, were succeeding in blending the Japanese and American workforces.

Finally, in order to further explore the issues of socialization and corporate culture, I need to examine the relations of power at the case study company, Suntech America in the following two chapters.

NOTES

1. I visited the company on an average of three times a week from July of 1992 through November of 1992. When I started the interviews there were about 120 employees, including temporary workers. During the course of the research at this facility the total number of employees fluctuated between 103 and 110 plus, mainly because of the change in the number of temporary workers. In addition, I deliberately concealed the name and kind of products as well as the name of the company for the purpose of maintaining confidentiality in this study.

2. "*Heijunka*" is a concept which loosely translates to "leveled production." This concept basically attempts to ensure that all work stages are

balanced so that the output of each work stage ("module") provides an even flow towards end-item production with no bottlenecks or slack time. Material and labor are balanced in each work stage depending on the potential output of each work stage. The purpose of the *"heijunka"* method is to achieve an even work flow and flexible work lines with quick set-up time and short lead-time.

3. During the fieldwork at Suntech I was strictly prohibited from entering the R & D lab. Although I interviewed with some of design engineers including a department manager, it is the only department which I was never able to get inside.

4. IG is a fiberglass element which constitutes an insertion part of an endoscope. The material is very fragile and expensive. Workers were instructed to pay extreme attention to IG's when assembling endoscopes so that they would not break the fiberglass material.

5. Policy management (*"Hosin Kanri"*) is a technique of translating the corporate vision into a series of management policies put in place through the joint efforts of everyone from the top down to direct employees. In policy management, the Suntech CEO sets goals every 6 months. Managers below him or her derive action plans to meet the goals, and managers below them do the same. Eventually this same procedure goes down to hourly employees. Everyone is involved in ensuring that company goals are met and maintained. There are usually visual aids posted everywhere so that all employees can see how others are doing. In many ways, policy management is similar to MBO (management by objectives), but more specific in terms of outlining basic activities that achieve management policies and goals.

6. A floater technician should be able to handle all different kinds of work processes on the line. When somebody is absent, it is usually floater techs who fill in and make up for the missing part of work. In the organizational chart, a position of floater tech is one step above assembly technician and below the position of a lead technician. A lead tech should be able to train other line workers. It usually takes a few years for an incoming employee to reach to this level. Both the manufacturing and repair departments had positions of floater and lead techs. In addition, floater techs in the manufacturing department performed tasks such as setting assemblies on the side of the line, or repairing units.

7. 5S refers to five Japanese words which start with the letter "S." *Seiri* (clearing up); *Seiton* (organizing and standardizing); *Seiketu* (hygiene); *Seiso* (cleaning); and *Shitsuke* (training and discipline). In a company document prepared by Suntech, it says, "These '5S' concepts facilitate the organizations

of the working environment to make workers more productive and comfortable in their daily duties." American managers in the manufacturing department did not like the concept at all.

8. Suntech usually paid overtime for this kind of work. In contrast, workers in Japan do not receive overtime for remaining at the workplace to learn new skills, or to participate in the team meetings, such as QC's.

CHAPTER 6

American and Japanese Interaction at the Workplace—Manufacturing Department, Suntech America

THE CASE STUDY—SUNTECH AMERICA CORPORATION

In the previous chapter I examined the existence of the eight crucial elements of Japanese organizational practices at Suntech America. At this point I can clearly state that the organizational practices at Suntech America did not significantly involve the common characteristics of organizational practices of Japanese firms in Japan. In addition, the issue of corporate culture, and the issue of social interaction between Japanese and American employees need further examination. As I mentioned in Chapter One, the power/control dimension in organizations becomes a crucial matter of concern. It is important to account for corporate structural level control (i.e., between parent companies and their local subsidiaries), on the one hand, and management level control (on factory floors, for example), on the other hand, that significantly influence employees' behavior at the workplace. In using fieldwork to explore corporate culture and social interaction processes, which imbue both corporate structure and management control, I will focus upon how management control is exerted over workers at Suntech, and, in particular, how American workers respond to the various forms of control by both American and Japanese managers.

TWO COMPANIES IN SUNTECH?: TWO FORMS OF MANAGEMENT CONTROL

Through my interviews with human resources managers, some high level managers like Mr. Shibata and Mr. Nogi, and my interviews with Rick Darnell, Ron Peal, and Terry Panko of the manufacturing department, I was able to understand the overall structure and organization, including management policies, of Suntech America. When I started shifting my focus from the office area to the production area ("*genba*"), I began to understand that there are two different "worlds" in the production area. At Suntech, the Japanese/American differences were manifested culturally in these two distinct areas - the manufacturing and repair departments. These two distinctively different work environments were the result of management antagonisms as well as cultural differences. Rick Darnell, the manager of manufacturing, felt much hostility and frustration towards the Japanese engineers. This had resulted in some confrontational episodes between Rick and the Japanese engineers.

Differences were also seen in the employees' responses to two different leadership styles which involved both positive and negative consequences in each department as characterized below. Libby, a floater tech in the manufacturing department, referred to the difference as follows:

> It's amazing. I'll sit with them. You know, sometimes I'll go out to happy hour, and I'll sit with a couple of them from repair. And it's like listening to a whole different—it's totally different. It's like two different worlds over there. You'll see now that you'll start interviewing them.

An operations manager of the department, Ron also characterized the difference between the two departments. He stated:

> [I]t's more of a wall [that] separates the repair from the manufacturing as I told you last night, that I believe that there is kind of experiment that hasn't been stated so. Okay, one side of the building we are going to be totally American in style. One side of the building we are going to be totally Aizu [Suntech] style. In two years, we are going to see who, we are going to look back to see who

did the best. Not official. But I believe that [Rick] and I have been resistant to change, to try to change us, stir us into Aizu or Shirakawa way.[1] We are going to say, 'No, No, No,' we learned the technical part of it and we leaned a lot of good points, but we want to be an American company. We want to push back on that. We want to. So, if you look at the manufacturing style, our style versus 5S and policy management indicators and stuff in repair, we are totally different. In manufacturing we are more American. In manufacturing—in the way we think, in the way we do business—we are more American. On the repair side of the fence, more Japanese.

In this chapter I will look at the hierarchical control in the manufacturing department by examining the relationships at the workplace between American managers and Japanese engineers, and the relationships between American managers and American workers. In the following chapter (Chapter Seven) I will analyze a form of management control in the repair department, which I have called poka-yoke (fail-proof) control, by examining the relationships at the workplace between Japanese managers and American workers.

Figure 1. Organization Chart of Suntech America.

Suntech America Corporation
Medical Research Group
Manufacturing and Product Research Division

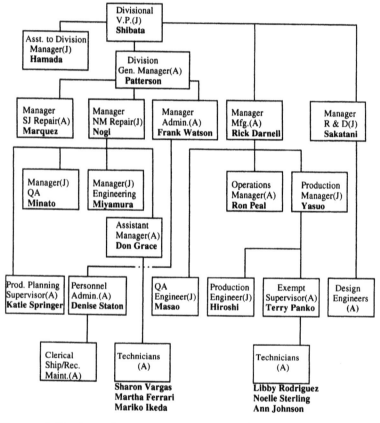

Note: * (J) refers to Japanese personnel.
          * (A) refers to American personnel.
          * Technicians are classified as non-exempt.
          * The chart was simplified by the author for the purpose of this chapter.
          *All names have been changed to protect informants' confidentiality.

Table 4. Characteristics of Hierarchical and Poka-Yoke Control at Suntech.

Hierarchical Control *Manufacturing Department*	**Poka-Yoke Control** *Repair Department*
Exerted by American managers over American workers	Exerted by Mr. Nogi over American middle managers and workers
A top down approach with militaristic attitudes	Heavily influenced by Japanese culture
Impersonal and bureaucratic	A top down approach with American middle managers who translate the Japanese expectations to American workers
Clear distinction between work and private lives	Less distinction between work and private lives
Workers are dispensable	Often involve elements of paternalism and apprenticeship
Loose attendance expectation	Strict attendance expectation
Loose dress code	Strict dress code
	Control of work attitudes
	Emphasis on punctuality, formality, loyalty, and dedication to the job
	Workers are indispensable
	Micromanagement on the job

MANUFACTURING DEPARTMENT

In the manufacturing department, there were two American managers, Rick, the manufacturing manager and Ron, an operations manager. There was one American supervisor, Terry. There were three Japanese engineers dispatched from Suntech in Japan. Yasuo served as production manager, and the other two, Masao and Hiroshi, were respectively, an industrial engineer (IE) and a quality assurance (QA) engineer. When I entered the production area, I often saw employees joking and laughing while they worked, and sometimes music was playing in the room. In contrast to the repair department, the atmosphere of the manufacturing department was somewhat more relaxed. As Ron said previously, the workplace was more "American" than in the repair department. As I mentioned in Chapter One, Richard Edwards has differentiated three types of management control—simple control, technical control, and bureaucratic control (Edwards 1974). Simple control involves the manager's personal exercise of power over workers. Technical control is where an assembly line or machines set the pace of work. Bureaucratic control involves institutionalization of hierarchical power through rules and procedures.

In the manufacturing department, management control involved all of the above three elements. Moreover, simple control was exerted in a militaristic manner which I refer to as "hierarchical/militaristic control." At Suntech this hierarchical/militaristic control was a significant element of the management control that was imposed by Rick and Terry. Both Rick and Terry were military retirees and boldly demonstrated hierarchical attitudes towards their subordinates. I should note, however, that this hierarchical control of Rick and Terry was not necessarily applicable to other American managers. For example, the top down nature of management control in the Suntech manufacturing department contrasted with the participative management practices that Lamphere observed in several non-traditional firms in Albuquerque (Lamphere et al. 1993). Thus, hierarchical control is not characteristic of all American managers. However, at Suntech, the hierarchical control exercised by two American managers conflicted not only with Japanese engineers but also with American line workers.

In addition, American middle managers, Rick, Ron and Terry, were quite frustrated about "remote control" or corporate control over their plant by the New York corporate headquarters and the parent company in Japan. One of the characteristics of this department was the power struggle between the New York office, the parent company in Japan, and this new facility, Suntech America in New Mexico. This struggle was obvious in the relationships among these American middle managers and three Japanese engineers.

MANAGERS

Rick was the department manager in the manufacturing department. Subordinate to Rick there was Ron, operations manager, and Yasuo, who had been recently appointed to production manager by the corporate management. Terry was a supervisor who was officially subordinate to Yasuo, and, at the same time, was supervising line workers like Libby (See the organization chart). In addition, two Japanese engineers, Masao and Hiroshi, were outside this chain of command in the organization chart, but reported directly to Rick and Yasuo, respectively.

In everyday worklife at Suntech, Yasuo, Masao, and Hiroshi, were strongly connected to the parent company in Japan. They were expected to report to Mr. Kitamura who had been a department manager at Suntech America but went back to the parent company in Japan two years ago. On the other hand, Rick, Ron, and Terry were strongly connected to one another, and tended to form an "alliance" against the three Japanese employees, Yasuo, Masao and Hiroshi.

Most of American line workers went home at 3:15 p.m. when the official business hours ended. They would remain after official work hours only when there was a formal overtime request. On the other hand, the three Japanese engineers, Yasuo, Masao, and Hiroshi, routinely stayed on the job after hours primarily because they had to communicate to the parent company, Suntech Japan. With the time difference between the two countries, the end of the business day in the U.S. coincides with the start of the business day in Japan. The Japanese engineers and managers, therefore, usually remained in the production area till seven or eight o'clock every night. When business required or when they were behind schedule, Japanese employees worked in the production area continuously until eleven or twelve midnight. These differences in the attitude regarding the company and work requirements were a source of frustration for both the American managers and the Japanese engineers.

This chapter focuses on the various power struggles at Suntech: (a) those between American middle managers and Japanese engineers, and (b) those between the New Mexico facility and the New York headquarters, and (c) those between the New Mexico facility and the parent company in Japan. Among managers at Suntech America's New Mexico plant difficulties arose because expectations differed widely between the Japanese and the Americans. As mentioned in previous sections, these expectations varied from different groups' perceptions of the duration of the workday and social interactions, to more mundane issues of rest room breaks. In addition, at least on the shopfloor level, there was an inherent sense of competition among managers that was heightened by the cultural differences. I will first describe the day-to-day, social and cultural issues that arose among the managers within the manufacturing department at Suntech America. Then I will describe some of the structural aspects of these power struggles that manifested in the relationship between the New Mexico plant and New York corporate headquarters, and between the New Mexico plant and the parent company in Japan.

Rick Darnell

Rick came to Suntech America in 1989 from another large American-owned semiconductor company in the Sunbelt area. He had a background in engineering and business finance, and was one of a few employees who had been working for Suntech since the facility opened in 1989. He came to Suntech both to enhance and further develop his career. He had felt some dissatisfaction with his former boss and with the management policies at the previous company. For him, having left the previous company had more to do with his professional development rather than, for instance, his pay or the possibility of being laid off. He was a manager who preferred clear boundaries between himself as a manager and his subordinates.

Like other American middle mangers in the department he also became frustrated about "remote control" from New York corporate headquarters and Suntech in Japan. In addition, he did not appreciate seeing the three Japanese engineers take enormous amounts of time in making decisions and working such long hours. He felt more comfortable with quick decision making and quick results. When his work was done, he was gone. Rick explained clearly how his work attitudes differed from those of his Japanese co-workers.

[W]hat I have seen in my trips to Japan, and what I have seen here is, I think people in Japan have an expectation that they are going to be working so many hours. So they have a certain number of jobs, and if they are going to stay till eight at night, they will stay until eight, but the same work gets done. But if you look at most Americans, if I know I have a lot of work, I will set my alarm clock a little earlier, and I will get here early and I skip break and I will take a short lunch, and then I work maybe an hour or an hour and a half over. When I am done, I am gone. Whereas people I saw in Japan, they come right on time in the morning, big rush in the morning, and then they take the full break, take the full lunch, and they take a break at the end of the day, and work for another two hours, maybe they will get together and take another break, and they stay a little longer, and about eight o'clock or nine o'clock, they start looking around, 'Is it okay to go now?'

Rick discussed at length a major difference in his attitudes towards social interaction among employees. Compared to the Japanese employees in Japan who tended to share many after-work-hours activities with their coworkers, Rick felt that his position required that he be more aloof, less socially available. He explained:

There is a cultural expectation of what I have to do in my job. And I think that most Americans expect me to be more impartial, more neutral, a little more removed. If I start being real friendly with six of the technicians this week, the other four start thinking, 'Oh, he likes them.' If I date a technician, the whole world falls apart I just—I can't do it. I had three different groups of technicians, when I was a supervisor [at the previous company]. I had three different groups, and I was a different kind of manager, or supervisor for each group, as I learned more and as I went along. You get a new group, you stop and think, 'O.k., I am going to do this differently next time.' With the first group I tried to be everybody's friend and went to parties at their house. I sit around, and you know, they come over and borrowed some stuff from me, and that worked for a little for a while. The first few months, it was okay, but then, somebody is not happy with your evaluation, like somebody else gets a fair raise, or somebody else gets some training that another person doesn't get. Maybe it's just American culture, but they start to take it wrong, get jealous and all because [Rick] went to the party at their house last week. I really think that Americans, at least, want their manager . . . they want to see me as someone who—it's like they want to believe that I am better than them. You know, I am cleaner, I dress better, better house, smarter, I know all the answers. I don't have to have friends, you know. I can go around. I can talk to everybody the same way, but I am not really too friendly with any one person, and I can never do those things that I saw [in Japan]. Like [Mr. Kitamura], I can never go play golf with the technicians. I can never date the technicians. That will destroy my credibility. You know, I have been to the dinners in Japan, where managers sit around and joke about the technicians or something. I would never talk about it. If I was stupid enough to do that. I would never talk about it.

Rick's experience in Japan was obviously enlightening, and illustrated clearly the social and cultural differences between Japan and the U.S. regarding social interaction among employees. It is not uncommon for a Japanese manager to invite co-workers, including subordinates to engage in social interaction after working hours. A boss, for instance, may invite his secretary to dinner. Rick perceived this as "dating," whereas Japanese would not necessarily perceive it as such.

Some other managers, administrators, and especially the three Japanese engineers, characterized Rick as a very difficult person to work with. Many employees perceived Rick, Ron, and Terry as being very close and protective of one another. They generally shared the same perspectives on discipline and employee behavior, and, in general, how management control should be exercised over workers in the department. They basically agreed that things should be done the "American" way, meaning hierarchical and immediate, always interested in short term results. They perceived Suntech America as an American company. The Japanese, in contrast, were more concerned with long range planning and goals. This elicited strong confrontational attitudes from Rick, as well as Ron and Terry, and eventually they clashed with the Japanese engineers. This had resulted in continuous power struggles between the Americans and the Japanese. Rick displayed a covert hostility in terms of work hours and the Japanese attitude toward such. In contrast to the three Japanese engineers in his department who worked longer hours, Rick deliberately worked shorter hours and stated as follows:

> I work about probably 9.5 hours a day. People who work for me, if you want to use that term, and, in the organizational chart, above me, work more. But, I work fewer hours for two reasons. One is to send a message that I want them to go home, and the other is that I try to force confrontations. I don't think—especially Japanese engineers who work so much—I don't think they work efficiently. So, I try to get them angry so that they will work more efficiently, so they will go home.

Although Rick had high regard for the company president, Mr. Shibata, he understood that Mr. Shibata did not have much experience in manufacturing, and thus gave Rick considerable autonomy on the job. Rick thought that his own manufacturing experience and skills were invaluable to the company and tried to take advantage of the autonomy in his everyday work in the department.

> He [Mr. Shibata] is—I think he is a very good manager for what we need to do here. He understands that he doesn't have manufacturing experience. He is really at my mercy. If I am totally incompetent, if I am incompetent, he looks very bad, because I work for him. So, he is responsible for me but he knows he doesn't understand enough [about manufacturing] to try to manage my department. I don't have problems with him.

Rick used his expertise, therefore, not only for the purpose of developing an efficient production environment, but also to secure and ensure his own power and status within the company. Certainly, all of the Japanese managers and even some of the American managers were aware of Rick's confrontational attitudes toward the Japanese managers and engineers. Rick exerted a hierarchical control over production workers which was impersonal and bureaucratic. This hierarchical attitude was common to Rick, Ron and Terry, and caused a considerable frustration, even some resistance, especially among American workers, which is described at length in the section entitled "Workers."

Yasuo

Yasuo was a production manager who had been sent to Suntech America by the parent company in Japan. His background was in mechanical engineering. He had never been a manager before, and therefore, being a production manager was a new and extremely challenging experience for him. In addition, he had never dealt with American employees before. He was expected to meet production goals set by the parent company in Japan. Before this New Mexico plant opened, all manufacturing operations had been handled by the home plants of Suntech Corporation in Japan, and the New Mexico plant was the first manufacturing facility in the U.S. for the entire corporation.

In a new company, it is rather common that things might not proceed as scheduled. The parent company in Japan, however, did not understand the reality Yasuo faced in the United States. Most of the managers of the parent company in Japan did not have any knowledge and experience of the American work environment, let alone the American workers. Yasuo found himself, even after a couple of years at Suntech America, being sandwiched between the parent company in Japan and the American managers. This had been extremely difficult for him. Initially, when Yasuo arrived at Suntech America, Mr. Kitamura was department manager, and therefore, it was less stressful for Yasuo. Rick took the position of department manager when Mr. Kitamura returned to Japan. Yasuo sometimes arrived at the workplace at five o'clock in the morning and sometimes remained in the production area until ten o'clock at night. Referring to his difficulties, Yasuo described his predicament as follows:

> Before [Rick] became a manufacturing manager, [Mr. Kitamura] was in his position. His policy for the production processes was to utilize Japanese know-how and practice the 'Japanese ways' of production as much as possible. When he [Mr. Kitamura] was going back to Japan, he made sure with us [three engineers from Japan] that we should never listen to [Rick]. Now [Rick] has taken the place of [Mr. Kitamura's] position, and tries to do things in his own way. In

addition, [Terry] is a manufacturing supervisor. In the organizational chart his position is below me. When I ask him to do something in a certain way, however, he has always done it in quite the opposite way. I don't know if this is intentional or not. But it looks like he is trying to fight against me. It is very hard to deal with this situation. In addition, all the production goals for the fiscal year are always set by Suntech in Japan. So, I as a production manager have a responsibility for meeting these goals, and when we cannot meet the expectations, I have to explain why to my bosses in Japan. They usually don't understand it.

Yasuo was promoted to a production manager over Terry a few months ago. Terry thought that Yasuo was promoted over him by the management merely because he was Japanese. Terry thought that he had considerably more experience on conveyor line production than Yasuo possessed. At the time of my study at Suntech, Terry had filed a complaint about Yasuo's promotion over him to EEOC (Equal Employment Opportunity Commission) for Suntech's discrimination against American employees in terms of promotion. This made Terry a "sensitive" employee. It was, therefore, impossible for me to interview him, since the company prohibited me from doing so.

Masao

Masao was sent to Suntech America by the parent company in Japan as an industrial engineer shortly after the facility opened in 1989. When Mr. Kitamura (Rick's predecessor) returned to the parent company in 1991, Masao became a QA engineer. After Masao became a QA engineer, he had mainly been responsible for the inspection of both incoming parts and outgoing products. He often worked closely with Yasuo, and Hiroshi, industrial engineers from the home plant in Japan. For the three engineers from Japan, Yasuo, Masao, and Hiroshi, it was much easier to work with American production workers than with American managers like Rick or Terry. After Terry filed a complaint to the E.E.O.C., Mr. Shibata strongly advised that they should avoid interactions with Terry as much as possible in their daily work. In addition, according to Masao, Rick, as an Airforce retiree and reservist, frequently used vacation time and personal days to participate in required Air Force activities. In contrast, Masao, Hiroshi, and Yasuo seldom used personal days or vacations, though they were, at least officially, entitled to take advantage of these benefits. Instead, they began the work day earlier and stayed after work longer than most of the American managers and workers in the department. Masao believed they, as Japanese, had a "mission" in their work at Suntech America until their return to Japan. First of all, he said they had to find and train responsible employees. Secondly, he thought that the Japanese must build a lasting system of organization that could be maintained even without Japanese presence at Suntech. Masao was extremely concerned that he would face continued challenges until these two goals could be realized in the manufacturing department.

Remote Control

As previously explained, within the company as a whole, Suntech's New Mexico plant was the newest manufacturing facility and the only such facility in the U.S. The New York office had been open for about twenty years and was well established as a sales office and headquarters for Suntech America. Suntech's facility in San Jose had been a repair site in California since 1976. Suntech Japan had been in existence since 1919 and was a large, well established, conservative enterprise. Prior to establishing the manufacturing plant in New Mexico, all manufacturing had been done at three different plants in Japan.

Management personnel at the New Mexico facility, particularly Americans, but even some of the Japanese managers and supervisors, were often frustrated and impatient with what they perceived as "remote control" from both Japan and New York. With obvious power/control issues escalating between Japanese and American managers, dissatisfaction and impatience increased overall. Additionally, the new plant was obviously "sandwiched" between New York headquarters and the parent company in Japan. American managers in New Mexico were continuously restrained by the lack of autonomy—remote control—from New York and Japan.

Ron Peal

Ron was the operations manager in the manufacturing department. He was responsible for purchasing functions, inventory control systems, and production planning and scheduling. Like Rick, Ron came to Suntech from an American-owned semiconductor company in southern California. Ron was one of a few American managers at Suntech who tried to work longer hours, usually sixty to seventy hours a week. Having been in a manufacturing environment in the U.S. for the past seventeen years, he was also accustomed to making immediate decisions with corresponding immediate results, often the standard procedure in American companies. He was, therefore, often agitated and frustrated about management practices at Suntech. He often referred to "remote control" from New York office and Japan.

> New Yorkers say, 'Why don't you do this?' to us. What is hard to the American fellows here at the same time is that Japanese come up to the people and say, 'Don't do that.' Yet New Yorkers don't understand that we have to get confirmation from Japan before we can do things. So, ask [Yasuo]. [Yasuo] is the worst. You can't pay me to have [Yasuo's] job. He is in tough position. I also feel sorry for him. Look at his face. You can't pay me for his job.

He expressed this frustration about the slow processes of globalization and localization of corporate management. The localization of corporate control was not being realized to his satisfaction.

> Talking about globalization. This company, really . . . I believe [Kuroki]'s [the president of Suntech Japan] corporate philosophy is local control. I don't believe he's just saying it to make Americans, you know, kind of okay. I believe that. I really believe that he wants that to happen, that he thinks that a German company should be a German company, an English company, or an American company. That was a one year plan. I don't care where we go. So, in the long run, we expect that. I want to break the ties. I don't want [Kitamura] running my business. I don't want New York to run my business. I would like to run it. Say, 'Here is a policy management. Here is your objective. As a corporation, we negotiated the budget. Improve it', you know? Poka [Poka-yoke system [2]] says, 'There are no light sources,' and stuff, and now, 'Go do this, go do that. Do whatever it takes. Meet your PNL [3] [profit and loss] bottom line.' I usually have

PNL responsibility. Give me self-objectives, send me off, and we will find our basic activities to get us there. I'd like to see this as a profit center. We are saying we are. Give us clear objectives, and give us a budget, which we negotiate, of course. You know, we may not get as much as we want, but once we agree with working on that, tell us what is the basic strategy, what the plan is—'We want you to build light sources. Do this.' And let us go. That's what I want to get. I am impatient to get there. I don't want to be listening to Japan for their opinions and New York for their opinions.

In fact, Suntech's management often talked about management's strategy of globalization and localization. As a multinational company, Suntech had its own corporate management in Germany and in the U.S. with local management staff. The subsidiaries were known in Germany as Suntech GmbH and in the U.S. as Suntech America. Since globalization of management was intrinsically linked to the process of localization of management, managers at Suntech (New Mexico facility) often used the term "glocalization," referring to the importance of the concept and the concurrent difficulty in implementing such practice. Mr. Shibata, when referring to the glocalization concept, often said that some managers in the manufacturing department are too impatient. He thought it was quite understandable that the New Mexico plant was still under remote control by both headquarters in New York, where he worked for 20 years, and Suntech in Japan.

For Mr. Shibata and for most of the other Japanese employees, three to five years of remote control was necessary until management felt certain that the new plant was able to succeed on its own. For a lot of American managers, this time framework was highly frustrating, simply because they were not accustomed to a perspective of as long as five years. Facing American managers' frustrations, Mr. Shibata often expressed his irritation and stated, "We made sure with them that the process would be very slow when started." Ron, of course, tried to understand this.

We get four-year manufacturing decisions. And they have to report to Japan and I understand that. They made that clear when we started that we work slow. It's going to take a while. Don't be impatient. They made that clear to us.

Regarding remote control, Ron thought it was a matter of corporate control coming from New York and Japan, where the New Mexico plant was perceived merely as a satellite work center, instead of a profit center. Though he understood the rationale on the part of Japanese employees, he became impatient.

> I am impatient. I like things to happen. And it's hard for me to understand long, long term planning. The strategy is to slowly bring Albuquerque up to local control, and I frankly think too slowly. I think we are ready to make our own decisions right now. I think we learned the system long enough where we can go on. [But] we are still getting, managed. I call it remote control. Mr. [Hamada] calls that remote control. We still have a lot of remote control from [Kitamura] and other people that I think unnecessary. It's not official, unofficial. Many, many dotted lines of this company. I have been with five companies that had divisions of parent companies. And at all five companies, we were profit centers. And if we met our profit and loss and our goals, we were basically alone. At this company, not only do we have the Japanese remote control, we had New York remote control. But control from Tokyo is not so clear. It's no experiment. We know it's there. Always there and you know you don't push for certain issues because you know it will be denied by Shirakawa, or Hachiouji [4] doesn't agree with it. So, you don't push it. New York is . . . you see it every day. It's clear.

Ron thought he was a strong negotiator but in actuality he was unable to easily come to terms with the issues. He described how he dealt with this situation.

> I want to apply what I have learned from my 17 years of experience to the situation where I am here, and override, 'Because that's not the way we do it in Japan.' Sure, call it, 'We do it this way.' I keep working on them. I don't give up. I don't get frustrated. I just keep working. I back off for a while, and I go back and tackle it again later. I am very persistent. If I am not, I back off for a while, and then I go back and get more information, and try it more, then I back off a little bit.

He recognized the underlying power struggle when he referred to his negotiation style with the Japanese.

> I know it's underlying. It's not a daily thing, but again, that long term strategy as I understand is, 'Do it our way for two or three years and then go off and do it your way if you want.' And people like [Masao] really believe in it. [Masao] is clear. He thinks that the sooner the better. I am not too sure that people like [Kitamura] and people over there [Japan] basically still have a lot of influence that way.

Ron continued to talk about remote control. He and other Americans often felt left out of opportunities to create plans, policies, and goals for Suntech America.

> There still are many meetings, Japanese-Japanese meetings, where they do not include Americans and which are not with a translation of what happened. [They are] not necessarily shared with American employees. I had to assume that if there is something for me to know, they would tell me, but I don't know that for sure. A lot of meetings and a lot of faxes are coming from Japan to [Yasuo], and other people that don't get translated. [Rick] and I don't know what's going on. That's the remote control. I believe that's because [Mr. Shibata] does not have 100 percent confidence in the American managers, even though he has been here 20 years. Plus his language is not 100 percent. He can't get clear answers for his Japanese staff, nor can he for the American staff. I don't know if he has as much confidence in his American staff as he does with Japanese staff. I think it's just our fault for not earning that confidence yet. I don't think [there is] some conspiracy to have secret table meetings to make all the decisions. As much as they can, they try to empower their American employees to make the decisions better. If the decisions are controversial at all—if it is a controversial decision—it would be balanced out. We [Suntech] are an American company. [However,] if questions come to the fore, they will always go back to Japan to get advice. I understand that when it comes to technical questions—'Can we substitute part A for part B? It looks completely different, doesn't work completely the same. It was designed in

Japan.' In most cases I was told that we don't have enough information to make those decisions yet. But operational decisions—how to do things operationally—I don't believe there should be any influence [from Japan] at all.

This remote control was certainly one of the main sources of dissatisfaction for a manager like Ron. Ron, however, also thought that the issue of remote control basically encroached upon most of the employees at Suntech, Americans as well as Japanese. Ron also observed that Mr. Shibata was sometimes frustrated by this situation as well.

He's got three problems. One of them is New York. Two, he's got Japan. Three, he wants it [New Mexico plant] to be a profit center. He wants to go out and make profits. [In reality, however,] he's got the same bureaucracy. But his disadvantage is that he is a market engineer type with no manufacturing background. He doesn't have the frame of reference and background to understand all the needs here to push hard enough for us. He needs a lot of detailed explanation to understand what our problems are. That's natural. He hasn't been in this background. So, that's probably frustrating for him also.

In addition, there were a lot of social and cultural differences between American and Japanese employees on a day-to-day basis. Speaking of staying late at the company, Ron said:

I stay. I don't leave before the Japanese leave because I don't want them do it all by themselves. So, you know, I work overtime. I shouldn't have to, and neither should Japanese employees. I don't think it's the American way. I am thinking it's not a good idea to have to work that many hours. A little bit, of course, a little bit if you are an exempt employee, or staff. Some extra hours. That's natural. I try to stay not because I am trying to match them necessarily, but I see them, blood pouring out of their hands, and I want them to see that American workers wouldn't put as much as blood into it as much as them.

In Ron's case, as with many other middle managers at Suntech, the frustration that was derived from power struggles was frequently obscured from the everyday work scene. As described above, there was not an overt "battle" going on between Japanese and American employees. It was, rather, that both American middle managers and Japanese engineers in the manufacturing department attempted to develop closer social bonds but the underlying competition, distrust, and power struggles still continued. Ron also explained his social relations with the Japanese.

> We try to go out to dinner together sometimes . . . having them over to our house. In Japan, one thing to notice is that getting invited to somebody's house, that's a big honor. They don't usually invite people over to their house. Here everybody is invited to go to barbecues together. So we had as many social things together as possible. We don't do it as much as we should do. But we enjoy each other's company.

As described in Ron's quotes, remote control from the parent company and the corporate headquarters in New York certainly influenced the daily work of Japanese and Americans at Suntech's New Mexico plant. It not only influenced everyday work, it also intensified aspects of power struggles between the three Japanese engineers and the American managers in the manufacturing department. Ron's case showed that corporate structure, such as the relationship of a subsidiary with its parent company and with headquarters, was a factor which influenced social and cultural factors at the workplace level—the differences in worklives between the Japanese and American employees.

Terry Panko

Terry was production supervisor for conveyor line workers. As I previously mentioned, when I started my study at Suntech in the summer of 1992, Terry had filed a complaint to EEOC about Suntech's allegedly discriminatory promotion practices. In my initial interview with Mr. Shibata, he told me that the company was waiting for case results from EEOC. Most managers whom I talked with, therefore, were particularly sensitive and nervous about me referring to the issue of Terry and EEOC. During my fieldwork at Suntech, Mr. Shibata strictly prohibited me from conducting an interview with him. Though I was not permitted to speak with him, I referred to his situation while interviewing other employees in the manufacturing department, such as Yasuo, Masao, and Ron. In addition, I was able to get some information on Terry from other American line workers such as Libby. Like Rick, Terry's management of line workers was quite militaristic and bureaucratic. Libby, one of his subordinates, recalled Terry's impersonal attitude when she first started working under him.

> You know, when I first started here, he told me,—I got into an argument with him, and I told him, 'You should try to become more our friend.' And he says, 'I'm not here to be your friend.' He told me straight out, 'I'm not here to be your friend. I'm your supervisor.'

Discipline imposed upon American line workers in the manufacturing department was usually enforced by the American managers, Rick and Ron, and Terry. Since Rick was a retired military man, his attitude and his subordinates' attitudes reflected a hierarchical and militaristic approach. The three Japanese engineers, Yasuo, Masao, and Hiroshi, on the other hand, acknowledged that they did not expect the same work attitudes among American workers as they would from Japanese workers at Suntech Japan. They were, therefore, more patient and displayed a "laissez faire" approach in allowing American managers to deal with their employees in their own way. Discipline was a crucial element of management control at the production area. An example could be drawn from Terry's use of discipline over the simple and yet necessary breaks employees took to use the restroom. Terry took measures to reduce time away from the line by attempting to impose a "no break" rule for female employees except during the scheduled break time or during the lunch hour. This became a point of frustration among female employees, in particular, and eventually could not be enforced.

In this section, I showed how three American managers in the manufacturing department, Rick, Ron, and Terry enforced their control over workers. The management control that was characteristic of those three American managers was hierarchical, militaristic, and bureaucratic. This strict and rigid control over American workers (especially on conveyor line workers) led to very high levels of dissatisfaction among line workers. On the other hand, the Japanese engineers, Yasuo, Masao, and Hiroshi attempted to allow greater autonomy for American workers and dealt with them more patiently in everyday interactions. Generally speaking, management control exerted over workers by American managers in the manufacturing department was more stringent and impersonal than the type of control used by Yasuo, Masao, and Hiroshi. This, of course, was not applicable to each and every situation. Attendance, for example is a crucial element of discipline that differs widely between Japanese and American managers. As I characterize in the next chapter about the repair department, the expectations of Japanese management were much stricter as compared to the more flexible and looser attitudes towards attendance among the Americans. In the manufacturing department, in spite of the hierarchical/militaristic approach to other aspects of discipline, attendance was regarded with less importance by the American managers than by the Japanese.

It is important, however, to note that the management control exercised by those American managers had formed as a response to Kitamura's—"This is the way we do it in Japan"—type of leadership. Both management control and corporate control in the manufacturing department reflected pervasive frustration and power/control issues. When I observed at social interactions at the workplace, the frustrations and power struggles were, to a large degree, due to the social and cultural differences between the Japanese and American employees and their differing perceptions of worklife. However, I should note that these social and cultural factors at the workplace were constantly influenced by over-arching structural elements, such as the relationships of the Suntech New Mexico plant to the New York headquarters and to the parent company in Japan. As I described, the nature of the relationship between the New Mexico facility and the New York office was often less shaped by social and cultural issues concerning the differences or similarities between Japan and the U.S. The corporate management of the New York headquarters mainly consisted of American managers who had known the company as a sales company and thus did not understand day-to-day processes of manufacturing. Corporate structural issues imposed by New York headquarters often impinged on manufacturing in New Mexico. In the next section, I will look at the workers' response to hierarchical/militaristic management control in the manufacturing department.

WORKERS

In the manufacturing department, the work day started at 7:15 a.m. Each day began with "warm-up" exercises which were instituted by Rick, an American manager and retired military man. This "warm-up" consisted of about five minutes of physical exercise - stretching and loosening up the body. At 10:30 a.m. all workers took a fifteen minute break in the cafeteria where they chatted informally and drank coffee or tea and perhaps ate a snack. Some of the workers who smoked would congregate outside and interact more freely with the Japanese workers, most of whom smoked cigarettes as well. The lunch break was from 12:00 noon until 12:30 p.m. when work once again resumed until 3:15 p.m. when the official work day ended for most employees.

Daily routine in the manufacturing department involved working on the conveyor system. As I mentioned before, the work processes in the manufacturing department were based on the "round conveyor" system. This conveyor had 10 stations with 18 palettes that went all the way around. There were five technicians on one side, and five technicians on the other side. The product was started at Stage 1 where the technician performed value-added work for one minute. The conveyor moved one stage and the next technician performed additional labor for 1 minute. This continued around through all 10 stations until the first "round" was completed. It took 20 rounds for one unit to be completed. The value-added processes continued so that each of the 10 stations could perform 20 or more different operations on each unit. This conveyor system enabled quick set-ups and flexibility in production, with multiple products being built simultaneously. For the conveyor line workers, on the other hand, this meant extra work pressure, because they had to deal with multiple work tasks at one time. Libby characterized the work on the conveyor as follows:

> Working on the conveyor is very fast. You have work allotted to you for one minute. But a lot of times, the work that's been given to you to do in that one minute is more than a minute's work. So you have to be thinking ahead all the time to get that done. At first, learning it

is stressful, because you think you're never going to be able to do this in a minute, you're never going to be able to keep up with everybody. But after two or three weeks that you've been there and you're familiar with everything, you start finding your own shortcuts.

Beneath each work station there were green and red buttons. When workers encountered problems they could stop the conveyor by pushing a red button. When this happened, a red light kept blinking until the green button was pushed. Libby described how this worked:

> You hit the light, but you try to get it solved as soon as you can. And I make the decision if it's on the line and it's going to take a long time to fix, then I'll just pull the unit off, and I'll work on it on the side and just catch up to every—body else's parts just to keep the other seventeen going, and so you don't have ten technicians sitting down doing nothing for X amount of time. You have to figure out your trouble rounds, try to find time to do a few things ahead to them so that when that round does get there, it can go a little smoother. Each technician has a light on top of their work stations. And then, once we get it fixed, we just hit the green button—because they have a red and a green switch by where they sit—and they'll just hit it, and the conveyor will go.

Daily routine was perceived differently among Japanese and American employees. For most American employees, as I mentioned earlier, the end of the business day was precisely at 3:15 p.m. when they left to go home. Japanese employees generally did not have the "time clock" mentality that American workers did. They would routinely stay on the job, whether or not it was required. Their expectations and sense of responsibility were quite different. Even among management level employees this difference was evident. Rick, the top manager in the manufacturing department might have remained for a maximum of thirty or forty minutes beyond the end of the shift, but then he, too, would leave for the day. On the other hand, Ron, the operations manager who worked under Rick, would remain at the company until 7:00 or 8:00 p.m. His motive for this behavior was to compete and prove himself to the Japanese.

In contrast to production workers, office personnel ended their work day at 4:30 p.m. Among the Americans on the administrative level, working hours, in general, tended to be less structured. Some of the Americans felt more responsible to stay beyond the designated work hours. Again the incidence of "time clock" mentality was less evident. Senior American staff routinely stayed an extra 30 to 60 minutes beyond the end of their designated work hours; among some Americans, in fact, work time was often until 6:00 or 7:00 p.m. To some degree this reflected not only a difference in routine, but also an adaptation to Japanese expectations, thereby eliciting both the respect and appreciation of Japanese staff in general. Referring to some of these differences between American and the Japanese workers, Denise, a Personnel Administrator stated:

> American managers have a harder time communicating on an everyday basis. I really do think the trouble is there on the senior manager level because decisions at that level, you know, Americans want to go this way, Japanese want to go that way. And, there are a lot of conflicts there. They don't want to adapt. American managers don't want to adapt—'It's our way, and I want you guys to do it my way,' you know? I think any American manager that comes to a Japanese company has to be flexible, and adapt. Then, they want to leave and go return to an American company. I just don't get it, they are not using it, they are fighting it. I am trying to use it to my advantage. And I don't understand why they want to fight it.

Denise perceived an opportunity to learn a new style or system of management and to use it to both her own and the company's advantage. She saw adaptation as imperative in a successful work relationship. In the following section, I will use Libby as an example of how workers responded to the militaristic/hierarchical control of Rick and Terry.

Libby Rodriguez

Libby, a floater tech, had been working for Suntech since the facility opened in 1989. She is an Hispanic American and a single mother. She used to work for an American-owned firm in Albuquerque that was located near Suntech. She came to Suntech because the previous company laid her off.

> And when they laid me off, they didn't even know that I was
> supposed to be an assistant supervisor for the night shift. And they
> laid me off. And then, afterwards they called me, you know, saying
> they were sorry, they didn't know that I was assistant supervisor, and
> asked if I would go back to work. And I said no, because if they
> don't know who their assistant supervisors are—that tells you what
> their management is like. And so, I just didn't go back with them.

She had been having problems with her American supervisor
(Terry) and managers since she started working at Suntech. Her
characterization of working for American managers made important
points about management control in the American manufacturing
environment, if not about the individual American managers. On the
other hand, she emphasized the positive aspects of working for the
Japanese. About American companies, she remarked:

> They don't realize or look at what you do. It's just if you're kissing
> their ass and doing things—their little projects. And then, if you
> don't agree with what they say and the way that they want things to
> go, then automatically you're pushed aside and you're not
> recognized, and you're not noticed. You're marked as a troublemaker
> for not doing things—or not agreeing to do it—their way. And that's
> very frustrating. And the Japanese, they won't always agree with me,
> but at least they'll take the time to sit and work it out, and say,
> 'Okay, what do you think?' Or they'll try to explain to me why it
> wouldn't work the way I want to do it. You know, they just don't
> throw it out the window. You know, they want to make sure that I
> understand. Before [Terry]—I think he just thought I was here
> making trouble. He's a military person. And when he told us to do
> something, he didn't want us to question him. He thought he was
> superior enough that we shouldn't question him, we should just do it.
> But he doesn't work the line everyday, everyday. And there was days
> that he would tell us to do something in a certain way. And I knew it
> wasn't going to work, because later on it was just going to make it
> harder to put in another part, or something. So, I would disagree with
> him, and we'd end up getting into it because I would disagree,

instead of just doing it his way. And that was one of our biggest problems, is that he didn't ever want anybody telling him— disagreeing with him. He's real military, real military. And he could never—our opinion doesn't matter. I think he thinks of us more like a machine, and you just turn us on and work, and we shouldn't complain, and we shouldn't do anything. We should just be here to work.

For Libby, dealing with Japanese engineers was much easier because she felt they gave her an opportunity to learn and grow, and demonstrated more respect for her, personally. She stated:

You know, I'm a single mother, so I don't have time to go to school. I work, and after work I got to go home and attend to my son. And I don't have time for school, and I sure as heck don't have the money for it. So, I appreciate them teaching me, because I'm only picking up on what I can't afford to learn somewhere else. I think it's great because they're not—they're not trying to close the book on me. They open the door and they teach me more. So, I appreciate that with them a lot.

On the other hand, referring to Terry's attempt to impose militaristic/hierarchical control on line workers, Libby explained as follows:

He would put it to where he told us that we had to control our bowel movement, and teach ourselves to go to the bathroom at break, which is at 9:45, or at lunch, which is at twelve to 12:30, because we couldn't be leaving the conveyor to go to the bathroom. But that one kind of threw all of us and we all complained about that. So that's been changed. Right now, basically, what we do is if we all have a round that we don't have to wait for the unit to be in front of you, so we work ahead. Or if I'm available, or even the person in front of you or behind you is, we'll cover for each other while we have to go, and then we come back. Honest, I confess, when he first said it, I was like, 'No way. I'm not doing this.'

These attempts to rigidly control employee behavior contributed to low morale in the department. Suntech management intervened by giving Terry a warning to allow women complete freedom in using rest rooms. In addition, they were no longer required to report directly to Terry. The morale of the manufacturing department improved somewhat after management warned Terry. Libby said that now they were being treated as adults and not children. Libby also thought that the militaristic/hierarchical management control characterized by Rick, Ron, and Terry generally held true among management and higher-ups in the corporate environment in the U.S.

In the following, I will explain how Noelle, who basically shared the same view about her previous American managers as Libby, addressed the power struggle between the Japanese and American managers at Suntech.

Noelle Sterling

Noelle used to work as a secretary in the manufacturing department. She changed her job two years ago and was, at the time of this study, an accountant in the administration department. Based on her own experiences with American middle managers in the department, Noelle described how the assembly technicians were being treated poorly by their American bosses. The majority of assembly technicians demonstrated a tendency to favor the Japanese over their American bosses. When I questioned Noelle about difficulties in the department, she felt that the American managers were responsible.

> [M]ostly [Terry Panko], who is their supervisor, and [Rick], because he did not have any control over [Terry] . . . He didn't stop what was going on. I think they are both false. You have a supervisor who is not in control, and a manager who is not managing a supervisor. The ones who are back there, assembly technicians, those are the people who deserve to be treated better than anyone in a whole company, I think. And the treatment that they are getting is just unbelievable. So many things are going on. It is really sad.

She was also aware of the conflict-ridden relations among the New York office, the parent company in Japan, and the Suntech New Mexico plant, as well as the power struggles between Japanese and American managers. In a very tactful manner, she referred to her previous workplace in the manufacturing department.

> There seems to be a real power struggle between the Japanese and Americans back there. Manufacturing is very, I found most of the managers back there to be, I don't want to say anti-Japanese, but there is definitely a power struggle. This is how it's done, and anything that is suggested by the Japanese, a lot of times, was totally ignored or done in the opposite way because things were suggested by Japanese. Yes, there is a lot more of a cultural battle back there. It is a totally different struggle, like I said. Back there it is more of Japanese versus American.

Suntech America was sourcing all the parts for production from vendors in Japan when the facility opened in 1989. Since then, the company had been sourcing in the United States, and later on approximately 75 percent of the parts were produced in the United States. According to Noelle, the struggle also involved quality issues.

> In the manufacturing department I think it has a lot to do with quality. I know a lot of other American managers. The way they do it is, 'Let's just cut this corner. We can do it faster this way. Fast, fast, fast, faster.' But not necessarily efficiently and that causes a lot of problems. It creates problems not only in quality but in inventory control, and the production line. And this attitude—that we can do it faster—is going to kill us. Japanese managers expect everything to be perfect. They want to be perfect. This is the way it should be put together, and it shouldn't be off 2 millimeters, or whatever. It should be perfect, you know. And an American manager is more like, well, if you juggle it this way and screw it in real fast, it will go together. Nobody can tell the difference. To me, that's what I thought. You know, you are too picky. They thought Japanese are too picky about quality issues. And, of course, I have been on both sides of the story, and the Japanese say in America, American vendors are not that great. You know, a lot of the products that we get are really bad. Quality is bad. But then I've also heard from Japanese that they have some of the same problems in Japan with their own vendors. But it's a pretty common claim.

When Noelle was hired, Mr. Kitamura was the manufacturing manager. Rick, who had hired Noelle, was in training with Mr. Kitamura. Noelle further discussed differences and the manner in which they manifested. Promotions, for example, were an area of concern and dissension as she described:

> When [Mr. Kitamura] was here I think there was a struggle between [Mr. Kitamura], [Rick], and [Ron]. [Rick] and [Ron] were very close. You know, [Ron] was like [Rick], and [Rick] was there for [Ron]. But I would have to say [Mr. Kitamura] was a Japanese person, because he came in here and said, 'This is the way we do it, and this is the way you need to learn it.' But I guess we as Americans, maybe even Japanese Americans, we always have that idea, or we can call this the only way. So, sometimes if you are taught something in one way, and you know that it will always be different. You'd better just be armed. They make light of American people. Japanese were promoted over Americans. Supervisors were not promoted.

Power struggles were underlying many of these issues, as was evident in the problems between American manufacturing managers, Mr. Kitamura, and Japanese engineers. Noelle discussed her view of the incident when Terry was not promoted to a production manager but Yasuo was.

> I think that number one, if you are not qualified for the job, you should not be put in that job. In America, you should know the qualifications for that position. I don't think that the American supervisor who is complaining is qualified for the job. And I think the way [Suntech] handled it was bad because they promoted [Yasuo]. They promoted a Japanese engineer without posting the job and giving people the opportunity to apply for the job, which even if you know that this is the person you are going to put in that position, you still have to post it for other people to have the opportunity to apply for the job. I think they [Suntech] made a very good selection. I think the selection was good but the process was wrong. And probably, knowing that there is already a struggle between Japanese and Americans back there, I think it just intensified the situation in manufacturing.

Noelle talked about how women were getting poor treatment by their American managers.

> Sexual discrimination against women. This is an American supervisor. They [assembly techs] were told, and I know this sounds stupid, but they were told when to go the bathroom and to go to the bathroom on the breaks so then they don't lose time in the morning. They told everybody try to go to the bathroom but on their time, not ours. Basically that's what it was. And the women, when it came time for evaluations of the staff, women were always picked on constantly. But the men, nothing. But yet some of the men I mean some of their behavior was not totally appropriate. But nothing was done. Yes, [Terry] and I had a run-in first. The first day that I came here. I was in [Rick's] office when [Terry] came and said, 'Oh, you are the new secretary. I like my coffee black.' And I had to step around and said, 'I like mine with sugar.' That's nice enough. So, by the way, it was like, 'Oh, you are a secretary, so you can serve me a coffee,' you know. This is a general attitude.

Like Libby, Noelle characterized American managers as imposing hierarchical control on lower level workers. In contrast, the three Japanese engineers tended to demonstrate a "laissez faire" approach and allowed American managers to deal with their workers in their own way. They tended to display more sensitivity to the needs of American workers and were inclined to be more patient with them, partially because they were always conscious of their status as "guests" in the United States. Because of this awareness among Japanese engineers, they tried to avoid direct confrontations with American workers, which they might not necessarily have done with Japanese workers. In the manufacturing department, American workers generally felt more comfortable working with the three Japanese engineers than with their American managers for these reasons.

In summary, management control in the manufacturing department was quite complex. As I have described, there were clear differences between the American managers and Japanese engineers in exerting management control. In everyday interactions with workers, Japanese engineers allowed more autonomy among American workers than did the American managers—Rick, Ron, and Terry. On the other hand, as illustrated by Ron's remarks, the remote control from Japan and the New York corporate headquarters did not allow American managers to have any significant decision making capability. This remote control had been a contributing factor in the power struggles that Noelle described. However, the power struggles were not exclusively between Japanese and Americans, though Yasuo's promotion over Terry certainly intensified the cultural aspect of Japanese/American power struggles. It must be duly noted that power struggles in the manufacturing department existed not only between Japanese and American managers but between American managers in the manufacturing department and the New York headquarters, which was also American managed.

The case of the manufacturing department at Suntech shows that what were seemingly cultural factors at the workplace level were strongly influenced by the over-arching corporate structures. In the next chapter, I will examine management control in the repair department, where Mr. Nogi's control differed significantly from that of the managers in the manufacturing department. The next chapter will further elucidate significant differences in the attitudes of the American workers and their reactions to Mr. Nogi's management control.

NOTES

1. "Aizu" and "Shirakawa" are the names of places in Japan, where Suntech Japan's home factories are located. At Suntech America, managers usually refer to those factories by simply saying "Shirakawa factory," "Aizu factory," or "Hachiouji factory."

2. "Poka-yoke" literally means "fail-proof." This refers to the systematic procedures of preventive maintenance, which enable employees to detect problems before they happen. This is a part of a pro-active approach to problems that is talked about among many other industries, including both Japanese and American companies.

3. PNL refers to "Profit and Loss" statement. At Suntech workers call this "Pop & Row" statement.

4. See Note 1.

CHAPTER 7

American and Japanese Interaction at the Workplace—Repair Department, Suntech America

REPAIR DEPARTMENT

The repair department of Suntech was a branch of the San José Repair Center. In contrast to the manufacturing department, where Rick, an American, was the department manager, Mr. Nogi, a Japanese, was the department manager in the repair department. Don Grace, an American, was the assistant manager. Beneath them there were two Japanese managers, Mr. Minato and Mr. Miyamura, and one American female manager, Katie Springer.

Inside the repair department the atmosphere was very different from the manufacturing department. Everything was very organized and clean. It was quiet. No one was talking while they worked. They wore uniforms. On the wall, there were diagrams and tables illustrating employees' skill levels, schedules for production, and the statistics of error levels in the past. Simply observing the general work attitudes among line employees brought to mind a picture of similar production areas in Japanese factories in Japan. Referring to the differences between the two departments within Suntech, Katie mentioned the following:

> [T]hat's hard, because even within the repair center and manufacturing, it's very different. For instance, the people that I manage work in the warehouse. The warehouse—it's one big room

in the back, and so it's shared by the manufacturing warehouse people and repair center warehouse people. There's no wall. They see everything that they do—each other. And yet we have different policies, different rules. For instance, my rule would be you have to wear your uniform. You have to wear your labcoat. You have to be back from break on time. You cannot make personal phone calls, whereas they can make personal phone calls. Sometimes they don't have to wear their uniforms. It's not so critical if they're late and they see that. So, it's—that's been very challenging for me to keep them focused and say, you know, 'That's okay. Please understand that I'm doing this for you, because I have expectations for you that you can grow and develop within the repair center. I make that commitment to you.' I don't know if they can do that, if their manager can do that for them. They don't have direction. Their manager doesn't go back there once a day. I have to go back in my warehouse probably every hour. So, it's totally different. They never see their supervisor, never. They see me constantly. So, there's pros and cons.

In addition to these rather obvious differences between the two departments, I should stress here that the repair and manufacturing departments differed significantly in importance because of their intrinsic relationship to corporate profits. As in the manufacturing department, structural factors, such as the relationships between Suntech America and its parent company, Suntech Japan, strongly influenced the internal dynamics of the repair department. Don Grace, assistant manager to Mr. Nogi in the repair department, described some of these differences between the manufacturing and repair processes as follows:

We are licensed by [Suntech Japan] to perform this repair service for the M[R]D Division—Medical [Research] Division (pseudonym), and they will not grant us permission to try and acquire parts here in the United States. The repair process is looked at, and always has been looked at, as a cost to the M[R]D Division. It has never been looked at as a profit center or as a money-making operation. The Medical [Research] Division, the sales group, they sell endoscopes, new endoscopes from Tokyo. They sell new endoscopes from Tokyo to doctors. When a doctor has that scope damaged, he sends it back to the service branch for M[R]D. There's about fifteen offices in the United States. If the branch can do a minor repair, they perform a minor repair on that unit and give it back to the doctor. If it requires major repairs, a major overhaul, it is sent to San José where it's disassembled, all the parts are inspected and put back into inventory. Everything usable is put back into inventory. I don't think it will be changed precisely because of the conservative attitude from the Japanese management, the head management from Tokyo. Because the system as it is has many built-in profits for [Suntech Japan] at the expense of [Suntech] Corporation of America, and at the expense of our customer service, it can always be—it can be used as a tool. A salesman can go into a doctor and say, 'Well, I can give you a major overhaul. It'll cost you 6,000 dollars. But I can also sell you a new endoscope—brand new from Tokyo—for 12,000 dollars.' Well, the doctor has a choice to make, then. If he buys a new one, those profits ultimately go back to Tokyo. If he has a repair, those profits will stay in [Suntech] Corporation of America. I think that, ultimately, manufacturing has the potential to be far and away much more important than repair, because they are actually manufacturing a new product. Those profits are going to go directly to the United States, to [Suntech] Corporation of America.

As Don explained, the repair department of the New Mexico plant had been regarded as less important than either the manufacturing department or the repair center in San Jose in California. The differences in importance of the two departments at Suntech that Don mentioned illustrates over-arching structural conditions at Suntech Corporation. The manufacturing operation functioned under stronger control from the parent company in Japan than did the repair operations, which had a more established base in the United States. Thus, in the repair department, management control differed significantly from that of the manufacturing department.

In the following section, I will describe management control in the repair department, which is characterized by elements of paternalism, apprenticeship, and micro-management. This form of management control is unique in that it differs from management control in either American organizations in the U.S. or in Japanese organizations in Japan. In addition, management control in the repair department differed greatly from the militaristic/hierarchical control so evident in the manufacturing department. This control also significantly differed from management control in the Suntech's home plants in Japan, where almost all workers are Japanese. In many ways management control exerted in the repair department was modified for the specific purpose of dealing with American workers. I have named this unique management control in the repair department "Poka-yoke" (fail-proof) control. I adopted this particular name from the title of a training session in the repair department, "Poka-yoke Process Improvement." I use it to describe the control exercised by Japanese managers when dealing with American workers at Suntech America.

MANAGERS

Mr. Nogi

Mr. Nogi had been working for Suntech Japan for more than thirty-five years. At the time of my case study, he had been an employee of Suntech America for at least fifteen years. He had been living and working in the U.S. since he started working for Suntech America. Almost everybody at Suntech would agree that he was very strict, both as a manager and as an individual. As the repair department manager, he preferred to maintain very tight management control from the top down. His top down management control, however, differed from Rick's hierarchical top down control over workers which is more commonly associated with American organizations. Mr.Nogi's rigid management control was tempered by his recognition of particular differences between American and Japanese workers. He attempted to express this understanding as follows:

> It is not good when we [Japanese] impose our ways on Americans. At the same time American ways of making things will not bring us anywhere either. So, the challenge is how we are going to bridge the gap and to find our own unique way.

On the other hand, Mr. Nogi was concerned that workers did not perceive him as imposing Japanese ways upon them. He strongly believed, however, that the Japanese way is better than the American way, and it was, therefore, difficult for him to make compromises. He felt that in educating American workers, they would come to recognize the greater efficiency and benefits of the Japanese way of production.

> I have to say wrong is wrong. I have to say good is good. And I have to say that I think I should. I can't compromise simply because I am in America. If I do we will keep going down . . . [B]asically, peoples' ways of growing up, or history, social environment, these are different, of course. However, the person as a human being is the same everywhere. So, educating people, changing people, and growing people should be basically the same to all human beings. Environment, culture, and personal history are secondary factors here. So, of course, I change my style a little on a case by case basis. But the basic approach to human beings will be the same. It has nothing to do with Americans or Japanese.

Mr. Nogi's perceptions of American society and culture are, in fact, similar to those shared among business people in Japan. In this view, the individualism of the West is always seen as a drawback for industrial activities which require a certain sense of collective effort. He stated as follows:

> The reason why the U.S. has gotten beaten by Japan in manufacturing, like automobiles and electronics, is largely due to the fact that this society is too individualistic. [American society] has disintegrated too much. On the other hand, Japanese society is based on groups. You can tell the process of group formation in Japan if you read Sakaiya Taichi's book. We have been like this for a long period of time. So, this kind of work is suited for the group oriented society. The individualistic society is much better for inventions and discoveries. But in this labor intensive work environment, like here, the power of the group is more than the sum of the power of individuals. In addition, individuals don't last long enough. This is not good. For example, almost 100 percent of the QC's and many other techniques that are in practice here were originally developed in the U.S. and have been imported to Japan. One of the reasons why they didn't take root in America was that this is a society based on individuals. The individual means that you are alone. It means that you don't have to teach to anybody even if I teach something to you.

So, although there are much more possibilities to make better things when two individuals cooperate with one another, everybody is separated here. Furthermore, individuals alone will not last. If there are three or four persons, when one or two are gone, the activity can last. So, the activities don't last long here. This is one of the reasons. Of course there are many other factors. Like the management's attitude, or not investing toward the future. There are many other problems. But, speaking of people, since this society is based on the individual, things don't last long. They end on the level of the individuals. There isn't anything like 'Sannin yoreba monju no chie.'[1] These are some of the big factors. It is that Japan happens to be excellent only in the area of industrial manufacturing.

Mr. Nogi's expectations, however, regarding training and work attitudes differed considerably from managers and supervisors in the manufacturing department. His attitude was almost like a high school teacher, quite patronizing in his approach to employees. His tolerance for absence and tardiness was much lower and his patience with such behaviors was minimal. His immediate subordinate, Don Grace, who was originally hired as a floater tech and worked his way up through the corporate hierarchy, was a highly loyal and even obedient employee. It was Don Grace who bridged the social and cultural gaps between Nogi and the American employees. He was also directly responsible for the hands-on training of all the technical staff in the repair department. The repair department was somewhat more collective, in the Japanese sense, because Mr. Nogi's management control was, strictly speaking, Japanese in style. Referring to the average workers' education level at Suntech, Mr. Nogi mentioned the differences in the ways Americans and Japanese have been educated on a general level. He especially pointed to the work attitudes of American workers.

They [workers at Suntech] are not educated, not at all. In Japan we used to get educated—though it may be different now—that the company is the place where you do your work. Here, in contrast, you don't get educated to understand that you have to work at the company, putting it in an extreme way. This is only a small example. In addition, the way you work, doing something cooperatively, analyzing the problems, what to do to improve the quality, these basics. In Japan, you are educated in these basics by the time you graduate college. Then, you will be educated 'naturally' after you enter the company about the group behavior, and the proper communication with your bosses. On the other hand, this society lacks education in this sense, or the level of this education is very low, or they don't know anything. In Japan people are just average. But this average is also high. The average Japanese is much better than the average Americans. However, the high level Americans are far more capable than the high level Japanese, which is no comparison. But this is also on the level of the individuals. This doesn't go to the grass roots or group level phenomena. That's why it doesn't last. High-tech [manufacturing] is the same here. It is also that a small group of people can go through college within a few years. But the majority of people are not able to do that. There are also some Americans who can't even write after graduating from high school. So, a few Americans are extremely good. But the rest aren't good at all. The level is extremely low. In this sense, those employees here are not educated very well at all. Some Americans here say that they have this and that experience at the workplace. But when I see them really working, they are not impressive. In Japan, people who say that they have this and that experience are somewhat better than those [American workers]. But here I don't see any who are that good.

One more thing. It is that they don't study at all, do they? Even when they are in a good position where they can learn more and get promoted, they relax and have fun at home. This also depends on individual preferences. Anyway, they don't study hard. In so doing they let a lot of good chances pass by. I think I am different. I don't know if it can't be helped. In Japan, there is much accumulation of knowledge through diligent work. In contrast, there isn't anything like this here. Some of them are really good, but the average people are not good.

Nogi tried to create the work environment based on a certain philosophy. The training programs in the repair department were basically for managers. Although the program was not as systematic and thorough as the one in Japan, there were sessions such as "Problem

Solving," "Basic Supervision," "Poka-yoke Process Improvement," "Quality Control," "Personnel Management," and "Improvement by Automation Device for RC (Repair Center)." They were initiated by American middle managers like Don. Nogi described the training programs in the repair department as follows:

> [I]f you attend ten sessions in a row, you get a small prize. I and [Don] deal with the lectures in the session. In so doing, we try to support the employees as much as possible. Usually they last 30 minutes to one hour, not so long. Also the material we deal with is not that difficult. It's more or less understanding a common sense. I am not going to boast, but I can say with confidence that these programs are based on a certain philosophy, not simply that we do this because they are doing that in Japan. There are certain consistent philosophies here. So, I try to approach problems in the light of these philosophies so that things go smoothly. Of course, here are tons of problems. On some nights I am too keyed up to sleep. But this program tends to go smoothly because these are consistent. They are based on a certain philosophy. In addition, I hate to see the gap between what you say and what you do. I don't give a good evaluation to Americans who don't act based on what they say. Though this is not perfect, these are consistent. Also I appreciate the person who can last.

He talked about the important factors which comprised the good worker at Suntech. The following comments capture the essence of the Japanese production system from a human capital perspective.

> This is an important factor [that] if the person can do the work as a matter of course . . . can deal with mundane everyday routines, and if the person can really understand what we say and mean. These are some of the factors to look at. There is at least some hope if the person comes to the company regularly. Then we can teach. As long as the person shows up at the company, then we can teach him and develop some kind of system that can support him. If you don't show up . . . no matter how super star a worker you are, there is nothing we can do if you don't come to the company. We can't do our business. I let many Americans go who can't maintain good attendance. It is

out of the question if you don't maintain good attendance. Because this is the place where you do work. No matter how brilliant, no matter how super star you are, you are meaningless if you don't show up. It is okay if your skill is mediocre, but it is crucial that you regularly come here to work. So, even if you don't reach to a certain level, although we can't give you a good grade then, you can be recognized as long as you keep coming here to work regularly and make certain effort to improve everyday.

The above statement by Nogi characterizes the human side of "the innovation-mediated" production system discussed by Kenney and Florida (Kenney and Florida 1993). Although the training system and implementation of the team concept in the repair department differed substantially from those of the Suntech factories in Japan, there were "Japanese" expectations, at least, on the level of management ideals at Suntech America. The management control implied in Nogi's above remark also stems from a different view of the capitalist system when compared to views found in the United States. Below, Nogi also showed his critical view of the Western capitalist system.[2]

To be frank, I think American system will only go down. There is no hope that this system will go up for the time being. America is now in the process in which many potential contradictions of the system are surfacing themselves. This country has been stimulating the industry-military complex under the name of capitalist world against communist world. But now those communist regimes aren't there any more. So, unless this country intervenes in other parts of the world, or intentionally creates wars somewhere, we can't hope that this capitalist world dramatically improves. Otherwise, the system will deteriorate itself. Not only the U.S. but now unfortunately, we don't see any alternative system, alternative economic arguments. The alternative system has been the one envisioned by Marx or Lenin, those so called socialist systems and communist economic systems. However, those countries followed the trajectories which they never envisioned. That is the question of people. Those systems could have worked out a little better if they went by the book. I'm not a communist, or anything, you know. I am sure that this world [capitalist world] will end sooner or later if we go the trajectory which we have been following. This system is not a forever kind of thing. History has proved this, you know. The slavery system started, then feudal system, then we entered a modern period through capitalism. Then, what's coming next? There must be the next, of course, you know. It was Marx and Lenin who came up with the alternative. I know because I graduated from Economics department. This was a highly possible alternative economic argument. They reached to a certain point. However, it was unfortunate that there was the problem of the individual person. When humans get power, you use the power in the way that favors you, instead of using the power for the sake of the society. That's why the system degenerated. That system could have developed much more if they separated private desire and interests from the economic structure. However, unfortunately, since we humans have a limited time to live, we all die. So, when you get power, you try to prosper using the power you have while you are alive. When that happens, the socialist system turns out to be much worse than the capitalist system. But, if the systems they envisioned should work out at all, that would have lead to the true utopia. But this could only be realized when we get rid of human desires. Unfortunately they only proved this. We have to have something intermediate between that utopia and this capitalism, I think. But we have not had this argument yet. So, there is a question of 'Where are we going?' I don't think I can see the new system while I am alive. Maybe your time or in your children's generation. What kind of economic system can make people feel happier? The only thing that is clear now is that the capitalism isn't the one. This is for sure.

In the political context of North America, Nogi is not, by any means, a politically active person who would be perceived as "socialist," or "communist." Nor was he ever a radical student activist in his college days who had made a political turn around and become an integral part of the Japanese company. In fact, it is not uncommon to come across Japanese middle managers, like Nogi, who consider western individualism a drawback in the industrial production which require a collective effort and standardization. Nogi's view of the "conforming," and "standardized" individual in relation to industrial group work was deeply woven in his perceptions of the performance and evaluation of employees. When discussing this, Nogi emphasized that the following factors were important:

> Quality. In my department, it's quality. And dependability, attendance, and attitudes for cooperation. There is an evaluation chart for this. So, we do it according to the chart. We do this 2-3 times in a fiscal year.

In addition, inspection was an important part of everyday work.

> [W]e do inspect every stage of the line work. Like QA [Quality Assurance], all of sudden [a QA supervisor] goes to a certain part of the line and observes the job. Just like you saw before. We do this all the time. So, we do correct the work process all the time. But we don't retrain the whole of the work process.

Strict attendance and promptness were, as previously mentioned, crucial to Mr. Nogi's management control. Although no formal sanctions were imposed upon employees for infractions, they were met with a certain amount of aloofness and some degree of humiliation as a result of tardiness and absenteeism. Workers' appearance and style of dress were also important to Mr. Nogi. Any deviation from the company's norms, (e.g., exaggerated hairstyles, tattoos, torn jeans, and so on) were met with tacit disapproval by Mr. Nogi. He expected all employees to be well-groomed and neatly dressed. Lab coats were worn by all workers and provided a sense of uniformity and cohesion in the repair department.

As described above Nogi tried to implement tight management control from the top down. How was this accepted by American employees? At the most superficial level, their response was mirrored by the company's high employee turnover rates and low attendance figures. The turnover rate at the repair department was 15-30 percent at the time of study.

> [W]e hired some bad ones at the beginning because we didn't know very much. We just hired workers at random. We didn't know what to do. Also I was in Miami at that time. I asked somebody else to hire workers here. I did not know the conditions of this facility. Those

employees have already left here. In addition, we hired younger person at that time. So, the hiring process was not really down to earth. Now we changed the standard of hiring. We try to hire middle aged people as well as young people. We also try to hire people who have almost done with child rearing. Since we changed, it's been more stable.

Nogi also explained the attendance rate in terms of the race and ethnicity of employees.

There are differences, of course. For example, Asian workers here, or Thai, or Singapore. They have a better attendance, putting vacations aside in this case. The data taken there [San Jose] has included vacations. But if we exclude vacations, they usually have 99.9% of attendance on average. In contrast, here, we have about 90%. So, it's totally different. So-called white and Hispanics, they are totally different from them [Asians at San Jose plant]. That's because they have a different way of thinking. That is, they [Asians] think a company is the place to work, instead of thinking that a company is the place where you work as little as possible and try to get paid as much as possible, putting everything in a simpler way. Of course, it's more complex in reality. If I make a sweeping characterization in this way, there are these kinds of cultural differences. And if we go in this way, since they [Anglos and Hispanics] are laid back, Asians will go up very much, I think. They are easier to deal with. I don't have to worry about them being absent. One very serious problem in places like here is when workers don't come. Things will go on anyhow if workers come here. I am trying to be very strict on this [attendance]. There is no excuse when you come late because you had a flat tire. You will be on time if you leave home 15 minutes earlier even if you get a flat tire. What I have been instructing is that everybody should be here at least 15 minutes before starting time.

As shown here Mr. Nogi's management control was very strict and had even an element of paternalism. When he talked about "educating" American workers at Suntech, Mr. Nogi implied that managers had to patiently teach employees how to work at Suntech. His teaching involved instructions on attitudes toward work, how to dress at work, and how to "think" about work. This necessarily involved the process of apprenticeship for workers. In the following, I will illustrate the cases of American managers, namely, Don Grace and Katie Springer, and their responses to Mr. Nogi's management control.

Don Grace

Don was the assistant production manager to Mr. Nogi in the repair department. He was a typical example of an employee at Suntech who had developed his career through internal promotion. When he came to Suntech he was a line worker. He was promoted to a QA lead tech, and then to a supervisor, and had just recently been promoted to assistant production manager. As an American, he was expected to basically supervise most of the production workers. At the same time Don was expected to represent Mr.Nogi to all the American workers at the repair department. He demonstrated much frustration at being "sandwiched" in between his Japanese boss and his American subordinates. He was in a position of having to support Mr.Nogi's tight, very strict, and even somewhat paternalistic management control, which most American line workers did not understand well.

> I like him a lot, but there are times when I just hate him. And for me, and a lot of the people that I work with, when he is gone on a business trip, a lot of the comments are, 'Things are running so smooth.' 'There's no problems today.' 'Everything's operating very, very smoothly.' He has a tendency to over-manage, to micro-manage. Well, he expects me to stand up in front of everyone and tell them to be quiet. And that has a very—many times, the things, the actions that he asks me to take are very demoralizing on the people that I have to manage. I have, right now—right now I have thirty-three people that work for me.

Don further explained his frustration.

> [H]e can be tremendously difficult. He sees things either in black or white—'do it this way or that way.' And he really doesn't—he always puts the company first. Well, almost all the Japanese managers have worked for the same company since they were eighteen. Mr. [Nogi's] worked for this company thirty-five years.

And he's still what I consider a young man. He's, I think, fifty-two years old. And there are just some things that I just—I just cannot agree with him—I can't agree with him on. And it's okay if I don't agree, but I'm going to do it his way, anyway.

In the repair department Mr. Nogi basically decided matters concerning promotion of employees. For Don, promotion also depended on Mr. Nogi's judgment. Don did not really understand the way Mr. Nogi was promoting him, because it did not fit well into the American system of promotion. Although Don was frustrated about the way Mr. Nogi promoted employees, he was fearful about confronting Mr. Nogi.

And I've—that's one of the hardest things for me to deal with at work, because I—if I don't do what he wants me to do, what he asks or tells me to do, I fear for my own growth in the company, for my evaluation, you know. I was promoted to assistant production manager last January. I expect to be promoted to a production manager this January. A lot of that is going to depend on him. It's his judgment. And what I have been told, what he has told me, is what he told me last year, is that, 'You'll be working as a production manager.' He means just that—that I will have all the responsibilities to work as a production manager. But he will not pay me that because in the Japanese philosophy, you cannot go from being a supervisor to a production manager. First you have to be an assistant, and then you can be a manager. And even as a supervisor I was doing many of the things that a production manager would be expected to do. And I've worked all this year, basically, as a production manager. And hopefully, at the end of this year I'll be promoted to that. But that doesn't—you know, that's—that's secondary to what I'm actually paid. In America, if you're doing the job description of a higher level than what you're at, you should—you should get paid for that.

Mr. Nogi was increasing Don's job responsibilities but not his salary. Both in the repair and in the manufacturing departments, according to Don, American workers perceived that Americans at Suntech were very poorly paid for the jobs that they were expected to do. Don talked about how his pay at Suntech was below standard for the manufacturing environment in the United States.

> Okay, well, when I was a technician I was making about—with overtime—with the overtime that I was expected to work—I was making about twenty-one, 22 thousand dollars a year. When I was promoted to a supervisor, I made 22 thousand 500 dollars a year, which for me was no raise at all, but my expectations were greatly increased. When I was promoted to assistant production manager, now I'm making 30,000 dollars a year. And it seems to me that, when I have looked at statistics from the Department of Labor, that those salaries are very low for those job positions.

Speaking of salary, Don thought that he would be making significantly more money than he was earning at Suntech if he performed the same job at American-owned firms.

> I know the people in San José, some of the people—exempt people in San José feel the same way—that I could go to another American company and make 25 or 30 percent more than what I'm making now with the same job description. And it's uncomfortable because I think that in many ways, I'm trying to be developed as a good employee, but the compensation at this point is very poor—not very poor, just maybe not as adequate as it should be. I have to ask myself a question. If an American company called me—I'm sure you're familiar with business head-hunters—if a head-hunter called me up and said, '[Don], you know, you've got three years of management experience in a Japanese company and we'd like you to come over and be our production manager. We're going to pay you 40 thousand dollars a year.' Sure it's tempting. Well, what does a production manager make at a large corporation?—maybe 50 thousand dollars a year. How about in California, where this other facility is? Supervisors make 40 thousand dollars a year. Supervisors for [Suntech] make twenty-four, 25 thousand dollars a year. That's something that's real hard to—it's hard to deal with mentally.

Don said that salaries were a serious matter of concern for many American workers at Suntech. Many American workers felt that they should be paid more for the amount and the intensity of the jobs that they were expected to do at Suntech. However, he was still interested in staying with Suntech because of the job security that the company offered. Don thought that Suntech demonstrated a certain commitment to job security as compared to many American-owned companies. He talked about the job security at Suntech as highly appealing when he compared the situation to the previous American-owned company that he worked for.

> 30 thousand dollars that I know is coming this year is better than 40 thousand dollars for half a year next year. And I felt very strongly about that when I left [General Machine] (pseudonym). I was making a lot of money, but the job ended. And I want to work and be confident of making a paycheck, a good paycheck, every week. That job stability is number one. And I don't have confidence in other companies—in other American companies—that they have the same attitude towards job stability.

DO YOU REALLY THINK THAT WAY?—CULTURAL DIFFERENCES

In the repair department, most frustration among American workers was directed toward both Mr. Nogi's and other Japanese managers' management control which the Americans found difficult to understand. For Don, Mr. Nogi was very aloof and impersonal, yet he felt like Nogi was constantly monitoring what he did.

> His command of the English language is fine. But his ability to say things that make people feel good about what they're doing, or make people feel bad about what they're doing—his control of that ability is poor. In general, I always feel like he's looking over my shoulder, and I don't know when he's going to decide that what I'm doing is no good. I might be doing something the same two days in a row. One day it's okay, the next day he comes up to me and says, 'This is terrible, unacceptable. You cannot do it this way. Is this the way you really think?' And he's—again, getting back to him—he's not personable at all. He—most people have some kind of personality. You know a little bit about their likes, their dislikes. You just don't

know anything about him, you know. He plays golf, but I don't know if he likes it. You know, I don't know if he just does it because it's business.

Nogi expected Don to tell American workers that they were not meeting his expectations. Don often had to focus on how poorly they were doing. He thought that Nogi's control was demoralizing for many American workers.

[F]ollowing Mr. [Nogi's] instructions, we were being stricter and stricter and stricter with employees. And they were—you could see they were just feeling pressured. Our production numbers were not high. But following his directions, everyday we would come out and tell them how bad things were, 'You made ten errors yesterday— totally unacceptable. We must find a way to overcome this.' And then they'd make fifteen errors. And the next thing, we'd come out, 'Oh, fifteen errors. We just can't live with this. What happens when our production doubles?' And then they'd make eighteen errors. And—we had very poor quality. People started feeling like they didn't want to come to work. So, 'Ohhh, I don't want to go to work today. I'll call in sick.'

For Japanese managers, always the job comes first. Nogi and other Japanese managers in the repair department were explicit enough to tell American workers that they were expected to sacrifice family matters for work at Suntech. This was, of course, a significant source of frustration for American workers, including Don.

I've had many people tell me that the Japanese are cold fish. You know, when they say that they mean that there's no emotion. They feel that people like Mr. [Nogi] or Mr. [Miyamura], that you just cannot communicate with them, that whatever you say, they are always right, you know, they will not recognize your viewpoint. I'll look at them and I'll say, 'Sure. Please take care of your family.' The Japanese would never grant that. Never. They would say, 'Please do it after 3:30.' 'Please find another way.' There's just no recognition that sometimes you have to sacrifice work for family. It's always sacrifice family for work. I think fundamentally it's because Japanese society and culture always focuses on sacrificing the individual for society. And in America, America is just—it's as far opposite as you can get. America and the Constitution have always said 'Sacrifice the society for the individual.' And it's caused our own unique set of problems.

As Don described above, the differences in management control between American and Japanese managers, in general, reflected some basic differences between the two societies, and how the Japanese and the Americans perceived the individual in relation to their own society. What was implied in the management control exerted by Nogi and other Japanese managers was that company life should have a priority over the individual's life. Yet the domination of company life over individual life was and remains very rare in the United States. Don talked about his observations of the ways Japanese worked at Suntech.

[T]he Japanese management really expects a lot of sacrifice, individual sacrifice for the good of the company. I feel that they would want me, or that they want me to give up all of my time, and—I have—I have a lot of respect for my family. And they're fundamentally why I work, to try and make life better for them—and myself. And I always make a point to take my wife's birthday off— small thing. It's important to acknowledge the work that she does when I'm here. And by taking her—I don't take my own birthday off, I take her birthday off. And I was asked not to do that this year. My manager, Mr. [Nogi], he came to me and asked me—he said, 'You have to be here that day.' I said, 'I'm sorry, but I've already made plans and I cannot come in.' And he was—he was very disturbed by that. He did not like it at all.

Mr. Nogi's attitude, as Don described above, is a reflection of how Nogi's management control involved Japanese social and cultural elements. One of the most characteristic Japanese elements was the demand for overtime work. Don referred to overtime work in the repair department, which was usually requested by the Japanese managers.

I had over 500 hours of overtime [within the department] in August. And I had over 300 in September. We estimated it would take each employee one hour of overtime everyday for those two months. So, they have a lot of overtime—not just everyday, but many times Saturdays, and sometimes Saturday and Sunday.[3]

In addition, management control in the repair department involved a certain amount of exclusion of Americans from the main decision making processes. Don talked about the sense of exclusion he felt from Japanese managers who seldom included Don in their meetings.

> You know, I guess there are times when I have seen—I've seen the other managers back in the Repair Center going to Mr. [Nogi]'s office, the Engineering manager and the Quality manager. And they go and they have a meeting. But I don't go in, even though I'm working as production manager. I'm not included in that meeting. And then, after that meeting I'll be told, 'Well, we're going to do this in the Repair Center.' Well, why am I left out in that—in that meeting? It doesn't happen as often as it used to. But I have never gone into a meeting with the other managers and Mr. [Nogi]. Their meetings have reduced. But I have never been called into a meeting with the other managers and Mr. [Nogi] in an effort or an attempt to discuss some issue.

I mentioned before that what I characterize as poka-yoke control involves micro-management. Don referred to Nogi's micro-management which also related to how the Americans and the Japanese in the repair department perceived problems in different ways.

> He [Miyamura] had—he has never had any training in how to deal with American personnel problems or American—American employees. And I think that is—that one point is one of the most critical factors in getting Japanese and Americans to work together. Because most Japanese, they have no idea how American workers are going to act as a group or as individuals. And, again, we don't—you know, it's a problem on the American side because we're not prepared at all for the expectations of the Japanese management. And there are many times when a Japanese manager will point to some really small, almost insignificant item and say, 'This is a problem that needs to be fixed.' And a typical reaction by the Americans is,

'We have so many big problems to focus our attention on, and here you are looking at that. That's a waste of time right now because there are more important things that require our attention.' And I guess the term we use is 'micro-managing.' And it's a difficult transition because it really—I think it's where the weaknesses of both cultures clash.

Don cited examples of how American workers and Japanese managers in the repair department identified problems differently.

Well, for example, Mr. [Nogi], my boss, he will—he will say that, uh, pick on one thing, something that seems not very important. And he will say that the technician is not cleaning their desk properly. He will say that, 'That's a problem and I want you to take some kind of action on it and report back to me.' Well, first, I have to go and watch and see why he thinks the technician is doing it wrong. And then I have to make some kind of judgment as to what his expectations are as to the right way. And usually that's not complicated. Usually to me it's a very simple problem. But the same day, maybe we have lost—the same day, we lost 5,000 dollars worth of product—that's two endoscopes. And that's a very big expense for us, and it's something that really does require immediate, concentrated attention. We need to find out what is wrong so we don't lose another NS unit [4] for another 2500 dollars.

Sometimes the way that Nogi identified problems was almost unbearable to Don. Don thought that Nogi's tendency to identify problems in the workplace was more or less consistent with all the Japanese with whom he had worked. Japanese managers perceived as immediate problems what seemed to the Americans minor or trivial.

Mr. [Nogi] comes up to me and tells me that he thinks that employees are not cleaning their bench correctly. Well, I think that's a stupid problem. Why does he think it's so important? I don't understand that—he says something like, 'If you don't take care of—if you can't take care of these small problems, why should I trust you on taking care of the large ones?' So, I feel like I have to address this bench cleaning problem when I have these other big problems to deal with. And it's—and it's something that has been consistent with all the Japanese. You know, they'll come up and tell me that this technician is wearing pants with a hole in them.

Employee's appearance on the job was also a significant matter of concern for many Japanese managers. Don could not understand why management control would concern itself with personal matters like hair styles and tattoos on workers' arms.

You know. I have another technician. And local hairstyles—she wears her hair up like this, okay? And I had a technician—we actually had the president of [Suntech] Corporation worldwide, Mr. [Kuroki] (pseudonym)—he came and visited this facility. And he sent a letter to Mr. [Nogi] about the girl with her hair up, wondering if she is an acceptable employee. Just because of her hair! To me it's stupid. But that's—that's typical of something that happens almost daily. And it's something that's real frustrating. And, again, that's the culture in Japan. And at the same time, it's the culture in America. You know, I really can't go over to an employee and say, 'I think you should comb your hair differently,' or, to a man, 'I don't think you should wear long hair.' And they [employees with tattoos] are two of the best employees that we have. When I was interviewing them [for the job], all of the Japanese managers were concerned because they had tattoos. And I asked them why—it's just a tattoo. To me, you know, it's a tattoo. So what? Well, you know, people don't wear tattoos in Japan. But they're wearing them here.

Many American workers were concerned about how they were being treated by the Japanese managers. They perceived that they were being treated poorly, micro-managed, and over-controlled by Japanese managers. In addition, Don felt that he was getting lost because he did not clearly understand what Japanese managers expected of him. He pointed out that communication was a problem. He felt pressured by the need to communicate expectations of both American workers and Japanese managers.

I think a lot of the frustration that there is now is because of the way we are being treated, the way we perceive that we are being treated.

We have met our production goal 100 percent every six months over the last three years. We have had incredible challenges to overcome. We've had lots of part shortages. We've had personnel problems, absenteeism, expansion, quality problems. But we've always met everything a hundred percent. And there really doesn't seem to be much recognition of that. I still get told that I'm not managing people closely enough because I'm not watching them clean their bench or how they clean their bench. You know, I—everytime I talk to Mr. [Nogi], I don't know—when he calls me into his office, I don't know if he's going to tell me something good or tell me something bad. I just don't know. I don't know what to expect. I don't know what he expects. You know, I don't. That's—I have tried to interpret those things. And he surprises me both ways. Tuesday I was not feeling well, and I had made a couple of bad decisions for production that day. And I was sick yesterday. And I just had not been feeling good, and I was having trouble concentrating on my work. And I was trying to do those things that I thought he wanted me to accomplish, or the way he wanted me to accomplish them. And he called me into his office to talk about something. And we ended up discussing production that day. And he just totally surprised me by telling me something that I didn't think I would hear. He told me not to worry about the production numbers that day, that he knew that we were having a difficult day as far as personnel, and that we should focus on trying to make production as smooth as possible for the next day, and not worry about output for Tuesday. And that really surprised me. And it made a lot of sense, it made me feel good. I never feel like I'm really up to his expectations, doing what he thinks I'm capable of doing. I just—I never know. I never know.

Expectations as articulated by Nogi and other Japanese managers in the repair department certainly involved very "cultural" elements. As Don described in the preceding quote, communication problems did not simply refer to the language barrier in an instrumental sense. By communications, Don referred to pinpointing the cultural differences between the Japanese and the Americans. Recognizing cultural differences entailed understanding why the Japanese and the Americans were the way they were. On the level of day-to-day interaction at the workplace, these cultural differences often manifested as the differences in perceptions of worklife and the company. Nogi's comments on American workers at Suntech, on the one hand, and Don's response to Nogi's management control, on the other hand, strongly reflected the differences between the individualism in American society and the collectivism in Japanese society. Don mentioned the importance of educating both the Americans and Japanese about cultural differences.

> [I]t's—it's something that—for the Japanese and Americans to really work well together there has to be some understanding of those cultural differences. And I know that most of the Americans—it's difficult for them to understand the culture that the Japanese managers come from, or any of the Japanese employees. And they really need some education. They need to understand—why the Japanese are the way they are.

Don attempted to bridge the gap. However, the reaction that Don received from the Japanese managers was not tangible.

> I have tried to make them understand how Americans are as a group, or how they think and feel as people. And I don't know if I've been successful. But I always feel like I am—like I'm describing something that's not realistic to them. And usually what I get is a big smile from them and, 'We'll see. We'll see.' So, I don't feel that it's accepted very well.

There were occasions when the cultural differences between Americans and Japanese managers manifested in power struggles as in the manufacturing department. However, these differences were often subtle, underlying everyday interactions at the workplace and, therefore, obscured from direct observations of interactions among workers. The following comment by Don captured the reality of how cultural differences were experienced by American workers at the workplace, where the differences in perception were a source of frustration for both American workers and the Japanese managers.

> I think there are some times when I have told them that I thought that what they were doing or what they were proposing was—was silly,

or not—didn't make any sense to me. And they've looked at me like 'Do you really think that way?' And that's a common phrase for them to use—'Do you really think that way?' And no, I don't really think that way. I just don't understand what they really want to accomplish.

As the assistant production manager, Don understood his position and the necessity of supporting Mr. Nogi's poka-yoke control over Americans. He understood the difficult position he was in—supportive to the unpredictable Mr. Nogi and responsible for American line workers whose responses to ambiguous directives varied from incredulous to acquiescent. At the same time, as an American, he was very frustrated about Nogi's management control because he himself did not really understand its orientation. In the following section, I will show a case of an American female manager and her response to Mr. Nogi's poka-yoke control.

Katie Springer

Katie came from a large American-owned computer company where she had been responsible for material planning and material scheduling. She was the only female manager at Suntech and was responsible for scheduling and daily production in the repair department, and would decide, for example, how many products they should build for the day. She reported directly to Mr. Nogi. When comparing Suntech with the previous American-owned company for which she worked, she recognized major differences. She found that working for Mr. Nogi demanded strict discipline and a strong work ethic. She also realized that managers were constantly monitoring employees' work at Suntech. Comparing Suntech's work environment to the American company, she explained as follows:

[A]t first, it was very hard for me, because I worked for a very large corporation that—American companies, I guess, that I've dealt with before tend to be a little bit more lax. And the work ethic is just not quite the same. I always thought that I had a good work ethic. But when I came here, I realized that I really didn't. At [MMS] (pseudonym) a lot of people goofed around. A lot took long breaks, long lunches, all this stuff. And that was just the normal. No one really monitored you and told you, 'Not right.'

Like many other workers at Suntech, Katie thought that Mr. Nogi exerted extremely strict and tight management control, and lacked the flexibility that is more common in American-owned companies. When she described the work environment of the repair department at Suntech, she acknowledged that she missed the flexibility of the previous American company that she worked for.

> I miss the flexibility—at [MMS], flexibility of, I guess, working hours, or being at a professional level or an exempt level and being able to not be watched all the time, 'Oh, you're five minutes late. Oh, no, you can't take a long lunch.' You know, and I can do that here, but somehow it just—I really have to be an example here. Everything I do, I have to set an example, for everybody.

For Katie working for Suntech, especially working for Mr. Nogi, was tougher and more demanding than working for American companies. She believed that there was a more dependent relationship between company and employees. At Suntech she was always thinking about what she could do for the company.

> I didn't learn as much there [the previous American company]. I learned a lot there, but I'm sure it took me a long time to learn it, whereas here, in a shorter amount of time I'm learning much, much more. And also, here, it's more team-oriented. I am dependent on you. You are dependent—we're all dependent on each other. And at [MMS], it's—it was pretty much everybody out for themselves. Everybody wants to—they're looking out for themselves. [There, it's,] 'How can I make myself look better? Where can I be?' And here, it's, 'How can I make my department look better? How can I make [Suntech] better? How can I save money here?'

Katie acknowledged that because of the strict environment, many American workers left Suntech.

> It [Suntech] wasn't what they expected it to be. Some of them weren't used to working—first of all, they weren't used to working

in a manufacturing environment. And then, to come into [Suntech] is a very strict—especially in the Repair Center—I really believe it's very strict. You must be on time—not only on time, early. You must wear a uniform. You must not sit on the table or a desk—I mean, just everything. No yelling across the room—quiet, be professional at all times. It's very strict.

Among American employees Katie was one of very few who had adapted well to this strict work environment. As a manager she believed it was a good for the company that those workers left Suntech.

I would also comment that the people that have left are—it's good that they left. So, I would say that we have not lost anybody that we wouldn't have wanted to lose. But we've all agreed that these are people that we've had problems with, and it's been difficult people, and not very good employees—poor attendance or very negative influence on other employees, very poor quality, unreliable—I mean, just everything. The majority of them have just not been very good—not model employees

When she came to Suntech, Katie experienced culture shock for several months. In contrast to the American company that dealt with Katie as an adult and gave her a certain autonomy, Katie felt that Japanese managers at Suntech, especially Mr. Nogi, treated her like a child and constantly watched over her shoulder. The following comment by her captures what was it like to work under the poka-yoke corporate control.

At first, it was hard for me. I was—I was not real happy when I first came, because, to me, it seemed too strict. And it was offensive to me, because I worked for [MMS] who I felt treated me as an adult, and nobody baby-sat me—and watched me all the time, and did this. I could come and go as I pleased. And now, all of a sudden, I had to be here early. I had to be here late. I felt like I couldn't laugh.

Like Don Grace, Katie also mentioned that she had a difficult time in understanding Nogi in terms of his everyday interactions. Mr. Nogi's management control was, for Katie, very different from the management control that she was familiar with in American companies.

> Well, first of all, communication was hard, and understanding the work ethic was very hard for me, you know, because my manager was—I didn't really understand what he wanted—where he was coming from. I couldn't really understand his philosophy. It was different than what I was used to.

Though she went through a difficult time learning how to sense the Japanese managers' expectations at Suntech, Katie felt that she had gained in her ability to comprehend their expectations. For many other American workers, meeting these strict expectations was problematic. However, like Don Grace, Katie responded favorably to the reciprocal nature of the management/worker relationship. Katie was motivated to dedicate herself to Suntech because the company offered her the job security and possibilities for career advancement.

> I understand where they're coming from. We're being paid to do something here. Of course, we're expected to be here on time. We have responsibilities. And the things that [Suntech] can offer us, if we have potential and if we work hard and strive to do our best— [Suntech] can offer us lifetime employment and advancement, and things like that. And I don't think that there's a lot of American companies that can do that right now.

Katie realized that Suntech was a company that would provide ample opportunity for advancement if she worked patiently and diligently.

> I really see that this is a company that hires people with the intention of their future advancement, instead of hiring people and saying, 'Okay, this person can do this job for twenty years and that's all they're going to do,' . . . I don't see that. I see that there are a lot of opportunities here—if you work hard enough for them.

In addition, Katie came to realize that tight management control is necessary for the sake of productivity. Referring to the "loose" management control in her previous American company, Katie thought that the tight management control by Japanese managers had led to greater efficiency and improved productivity because workers were forced to work harder.

> The workers here are great. They're great. They have efficiency and productivity. And now, I understand why [MMS] is not doing so well. I understand. It's obvious. Well, people wasting time. Too many people. Not enough tight control. No improvement. No continuous training in their employees and development where there should be. Too lax, too much letting the employees do—and including the managers—everybody do what they want to do. Too much laughing, and—too much. I know that we can do a lot more with a lot less people here, because it forces you—because you don't have people to do it—it forces you to gain the skills yourself. You are forced to learn these things. You're forced to do them.

Like Don, Katie sometimes felt great annoyance with the Japanese managers' tendency to regard even small matters as highly important, things which to most Americans would be of little or no importance.

> I mean, let's worry about the big problems. As an example, today— actually, for a week—we have some carts where we keep parts on them. And there's a little like a foot that goes over the caster. It's a little rubber piece over the caster. And Mr. [Minato] is obsessed with insisting that we dust those things. It's like—and I feel like, 'Don't you have anything to do, [Minato]-san? Take the time and dust them.' And I keep thinking—I'm worrying about our production rate, and making sure we have enough parts, and we're having a short week next week, and I've got to make sure all these things are happening, and training goes on, and all this stuff. I'm not—I can't focus on dusting these things. And it's just driving me crazy.

In the context of management control on the shop floor, Katie referred to the Japanese managers' attitudes towards new employees. She explained how Japanese managers in the repair department discounted workers until they had proven themselves to managers, especially to Mr. Nogi. Katie was one of the few American employees who had proven herself to the Japanese managers at Suntech.

[T]he thing I noticed here, it seems like you really have to prove yourself. Prove yourself. Prove that you're going to be stable, that you're not going to give up, that you're not going to break. Because it can be very hard on you, and sometimes you want to go home and—I've gone home many times and cried. I've been so frustrated because I don't understand why—And I'm sure a lot of people have. I know a lot of people have. Because something that to us might seem so minor, not a big deal, has been—you have been made to feel this is such a big deal, you made such a mistake.

In addition, the Japanese managers were not accustomed to giving positive feedback that American workers expected regarding their performance on the job. This lack of everyday feedback with workers reflected the traditional *"sempai"* (senior workers)–*"kouhai"* (junior workers) relationship [5] in Japan, where the sempai do not usually praise the kouhai's performance on the job until their skills reach a certain level. This sempai - kouhai relationship is one of the significant elements in the process of apprenticeship in Japan. For American workers, the withholding of positive feedback by Japanese managers was perceived as disapproval. They needed positive "strokes" regarding their work from bosses. The R&D department's secretary, Susan (pseudonym), also pointed to her Japanese boss's tendency of not giving enough feedback.

[A]nother difference is working for an American manager, you get lots and lots of feedback on how you're doing your work. Working for a Japanese manager, I don't get much feedback . . . There's no criticism, but there's also no praise . . . You do your work and turn it in, and you don't hear later on, 'This was wrong, that was wrong. Next time, why don't you do it this way?' Or you never hear, 'That was really a good job.' You just don't hear any of that. I mean, once you turn in the work, you never hear about it again.

Katie commented about her own experience of receiving very little positive feedback from the Japanese managers in the repair department.

When I first started working here, I was real frustrated because I didn't know how I was doing. I had no idea. 'Are you satisfied with

me? What's wrong?' You don't tell me. 'How am I?' And the
comment I got was, 'Don't worry. When you're not doing good,
you'll know.' That was the response I got from Mr. [Nogi]. 'You're
doing okay. You'll know when you're not doing okay.' And I was
like, 'What about when I am doing okay?' No. No. One of his
favorite sayings, too, is—he has a hard time telling you, 'Hey, you
did really good.' He'll say, 'That's not so bad.' And so, we joke, you
know. That—to him—but we interpret that when he says, 'That's not
so bad,' that means it's okay. So, we're learning. We're learning.
'Good. I got a *not-so-bad*. That's good.'

According to Katie, most American workers were not used to Mr.
Nogi's strict management control and micro-management.

It's tough. It's tough. [Americans are] Not used to working that hard,
and not used to having—we call it 'micro-management.'

Compared to working for American companies, Katie thought that
working for Suntech, especially in the repair department, was
extremely tough.

I think that we do a really good job. I think the Repair Center does—
And a lot of that's because you're expected to give a hundred and
fifty percent, or a hundred percent, okay? And in American
companies—if you give a hundred percent, then you are exceptional.
And here, [if] you give a hundred percent, you're average.

Like Don, Katie also mentioned her frustration over the intangible
cultural gaps that she noticed in everyday communication with the
Japanese. She talked about the ways that she responded to the Japanese
managers at Suntech when she faced some cultural gaps.

Don't just accept—yeah. And that—and we used to get so frustrated
over that. How can they just accept this? But then, we also learned,
don't argue. Don't argue. Don't argue with the Japanese. That's an
important thing—Don't argue. It's not worth it. Because then, they
don't hear you anymore. All they hear is you're arguing, you're
closed-minded. So, instead, you should say—okay?—and try and

take it in and interpret it, and use it, and say, okay. What are they really saying? It is important to me? Naw. Throw it away. Or, you know, if it's not important, throw it away. If it is important, what they're saying, okay. Use it and improve. If it's not important, they just want to blow off steam, throw it away.

During my interviews with Mr. Nogi and Mr. Shibata, they sometimes referred to Katie as an American employee whom they could trust with responsibilities. They had quite a high opinion of her. At the same time, some American line workers, like Sharon, perceived her as a strict manager who was "trying to be like the Japanese." Both Don and Katie were successful in gaining recognition from the Japanese managers at Suntech, especially from Mr. Nogi. Mr. Nogi's attitude and behavior towards American workers in his department were more like a strict high school teacher who patiently tried to educate his students. In his interview, Mr. Nogi stated that the Japanese should not impose their ways on American workers. Most American workers at Suntech, however, saw Mr. Nogi as doing precisely that— trying to impose upon them Japanese standards typical of the home plants in Japan. Nogi strongly maintained that the Japanese work ethic and attitude were necessary for the sake of the company's efficiency and productivity.

Mr. Nogi's management control, or poka-yoke control, demanded that Americans be punctual, dedicated, loyal, and diligent workers. Under this system, workers were expected to put a greater priority on their job than on their private lives. Workers were controlled and monitored to a great extent by their managers. Such control was exercised to the extent that even the worker's everyday appearance, attire, grooming, and mannerisms at the workplace were under close scrutiny. Mr. Nogi believed that consistent and punctual attendance of workers on the line was a prerequisite for this type of management control to properly function. Managers did not require superstar workers but workers who were steady, patient, and loyal to the company even if the worker's ability was mediocre.

The characteristics of poka-yoke control that I described here resemble management control in Japanese factories in Japan. Poka-yoke control at Suntech America, however, also differed in significant ways from the management control that is exercised in Japanese factories in Japan. First, poka-yoke control was exercised over American workers by the Japanese managers. Since poka-yoke control was exercised specifically to deal with Americans in the North American industrial environment, there existed a potential for social and cultural differences to arise.

Second, poka-yoke control exerted over workers in America was top down. This differs from the type of control utilized in Japanese factories in Japan, where day-to-day control originates from senior veteran workers, or "sempai," instead of the top-level department managers. In Japan, it is usually these "sempai" workers who make decisions about everyday work. In the case of the repair department, Mr. Nogi exerted poka-yoke control in a top down fashion over American workers and American middle-level managers such as Don Grace and Katie Springer. In addition, in the context of poka-yoke control, American middle managers tended to be "sandwiched" between the Japanese managers and subordinate American production workers. Third, with poka-yoke control, the Japanese managers usually remained in the background, while they allowed American middle managers to assume the front and center role in everyday worklife. At a glance, it might have appeared that the American middle managers (Don and Katie) were in charge of workers on the shop floor. However, in actuality Mr. Nogi typically directed, advised, and monitored every action of these American middle managers. In this situation, the rationale of the Japanese was "Americans are best to deal with Americans."

Finally, and most importantly, the way that poka-yoke control was exerted often involved culturally conditioned dualistic dimensions. These dualistic dimensions can be characterized by the Japanese distinction between "*omote*" (front) and "*ura*"(back). [6] In Japanese factories in Japan, management control over workers usually lacks this distinction because both managers and workers are Japanese. At Suntech America, in contrast, Mr. Nogi's excessive micro-management clearly illustrated this distinction.

For example, he talked about Americans at Suntech as second-rate or mediocre in comparison to some first-rate professionals in this country who would probably be less interested in working for a Japanese-owned company. Nogi could only refer to Americans in this way in his private conversations in Japanese with me, because I, too, was Japanese. This conversation between Nogi and me clearly illustrates the situation of "ura." Only within the context of "ura," could he speak with me so openly. He would not have made such a statement in the area of "omote" partially because as a manager it would have been improper to refer Americans at Suntech as mediocre, and partially because if he stated such feelings publicly, it might have jeopardized his position as a department manager. At the same time, his perception of Americans at Suntech helped to shape the manner in which he exerted the poka-yoke control on American workers. When he stated that educating American workers was like "finding a piece of diamond out of the heap of sand," he implied the importance of carefully selecting American workers and then educating (training) them patiently. This process was seldom necessary in Japan because newly hired workers are very standardized in terms of their education, skill levels, and potentials.

Mr. Nogi expressed at length his perception of the probable future decline of the "American system." He would not have discussed such ideas with American workers. Instead, he could only share these perspective with Japanese workers/managers or with a Japanese student like myself and, indeed, perhaps because I was an outsider at the workplace. Again, Mr. Nogi's perception of the American system with its lack of standardization influenced the way he exerted poka-yoke control over American workers in everyday worklife on the shopfloor. His real feelings remained unspoken. Mr. Nogi expected American workers to be punctual, dedicated, and loyal workers on the job; in addition, he expected Americans to place a priority on the organization's (the company's) interests over their individual interests. This attitude toward company life was based on Nogi's critique of the American (or the Western) system, in which the pursuit of individual freedom has been extended to the point that it counteracts the good of the group, company, or society. The prototype of what Kenney and Florida termed the "innovation-mediated" production system (Kenney and Florida 1993) was indeed Mr. Nogi's poka-yoke control at Suntech. As Don Grace commented, the Japanese production system is based upon sacrificing individual needs for the good of the company, whereas American society is based fundamentally upon the notion of individual liberty. It is the preeminence of individualism in the U.S. which contrasts so vividly with the collectivism inherent in Japanese culture. Nowhere do these ideas clash more noticeably than in the areas of labor and production processes. Poka-yoke control as exerted by Mr. Nogi at Suntech was, at best, an experimental attempt to create cohesive elements that would enable American workers to adapt to the Japanese industrial production systems. In the following section, I will elaborate the responses of American workers to Mr. Nogi's experiment in exerting poka-yoke control.

WORKERS

The work day in the repair department began at 7:10 a.m. Typically, a short managers' meeting was held for about five minutes. At 7:15, all forty nine employees gathered in the workplace for a group meeting. Don would usually stand up in front and assess the production of the previous day and new production goals for the day. The purpose of such meetings was to motivate employees and offer a quick pat on the back for previous work accomplishments. The meeting usually concluded with Don's statement, "Okay, let's do 5S (Five S)." Everyone then cleaned the work area in preparation for the day. Again, there was no talking, no joking, no smiling. 5S refers to five Japanese terms which start with the letter "S"; *Seiri* (clearing up), *Seiton* (organizing and standardizing), *Seiketu* (hygiene), *Seiso* (cleaning), and *Shitsuke* (training and discipline). These "5S" concepts are commonly utilized among many firms in Japan. The Japanese managers of the repair department had adopted these concepts in an attempt to raise morale at the workplace.

In the repair department there were fewer power/control problems between managers than those which existed in the manufacturing department. Power/control issues were apparent, however, in workers' attitudes toward Mr. Nogi. He was perceived to be overly strict, regarding more highly the employee who was obedient to him and was dedicated to the job. Many workers perceived that Mr. Nogi favored some particular Japanese workers and promoted them faster than others. This was a point of dissatisfaction and anger among American workers. Work stress was much higher in this department since the work load was much greater. Workers felt that they should have received better pay, and should have been able to expect more promotions within the department.

Sharon Vargas

Sharon had been working as an assembly technician in the repair department since the company started in 1989. When the company began its operation, there were thirteen workers. At the time of this study, there were only six workers because many had left the company. Her job was to solder wires together on various products. She was irritated by Mr. Nogi's strict scrutiny of her work, and felt that she should have been paid more because of the extreme demands of the job. She felt highly stressed because of the constant monitoring by Mr. Nogi. In addition, as a single mother, she often felt the need to leave the company and attend to her child. This created frequent conflict especially regarding overtime requests from the managers. She sensed the subtle pressure to accept overtime requests because Japanese managers in the department tended to hold it against her if she did not work overtime.

Sharon had previously worked in the manufacturing department of an American company nearby with Libby. The repair department at Suntech was far more strict and demanding than the American company where she had worked previously. She felt that Mr. Nogi expected her to stay with the company and to be a perfect worker. She related an opinion similar to Libby's about working for the previous company. Her comment below illustrates the general differences in management control on workers between American-owned companies and Mr. Nogi's repair department.

> I used to work at [LabTech] (pseudonym) across the street, and they weren't paying too good. And it was like I couldn't handle that kind of job because sometimes we'd work and then there were times when they didn't know if we were going to work that next day. Or we'd work nights and—they switched it around too much. So, I just— there was no—couldn't tell when you were going to work or when you weren't. And then, they were laying off a lot. [I]t's—at least you're always guaranteed a job here—[Suntech's management] is not always laying off. At [LabTech], all we did was make sutures. And that was—all we did was package them and that was it. It wasn't— you never had to think about it, whereas over here, you know, you have to always concentrate and make sure you do it right. And over there it was more like, you know, it didn't matter. If you messed up,

they kind of, well, you know, 'Just send another one.' Plus, in American companies, I noticed they tend to just leave you alone, you know. They're—you know, you come to your job and you leave. And over here it's like, you know, 'Don't just come and do your job,' you know. You kind of have to enjoy your work, I guess, whereas in American companies they don't really care, you know, 'Just come and do your job and we'll pay you.'

Sharon referred to Suntech, especially the repair department, and told how workers have to be motivated for the job.

They want you to be perfect. But in a way it's kind of—it gives you more motivation, because then you think, well, you know, I've got to do the job right. And the American companies, it's like, well, if you mess up, they don't really—it's like they don't care. So, they just let you go about your business.

What Sharon notices everyday was the constant monitoring by Mr. Nogi and his expectations that work tasks be conducted quietly and properly. Mr. Nogi monitored Sharon more than some other workers whom he favored. This was a source of irritation for Sharon.

Mr. [Nogi] and—mostly the Japanese don't like for the employees to talk. And there's times where even though the Japanese are talking, he don't say anything, but he'll tell [Don], you know, well, 'These people were talking.' But it's mostly—he won't mention like the ones that he gets along with, or something. He mostly mentions everyone else, you know, that doesn't really get along with him. And he's always watching you to make sure that, you know, that you're not doing it. But yet, if it's someone else or someone that's real good friends, he kind of—he passes you by, whereas with us he's like, you know—he'll stand there and he's always watching, you know. So, you can't really be talking. And that's kind of hard, because there's times where you have to ask somebody something, or something's wrong, you know, and you kind of try to tell them, you know.

Other Japanese managers in the repair department, not only Mr. Nogi, generally demonstrated a clear tendency to observe and monitor

American workers. For American workers, this was a very uncomfortable experience; they felt that somebody was looking over their shoulders at all times on the job.

> I feel a little better than when I first started working here, because I guess now there's not as many Japanese in our department as there used to be. So, it's a little bit easier. You don't feel as much that they're really just watching over you. because before, it used to be that that's all they would do, is made you kind of feel like . . . well, don't they have something to do other than just come over here and watch you working, you know? Because they'd do that sometimes. They'd come all day and watch you and just—you know, it was like—and it's hard for you to even try to do your work because you don't want to mess up, because they're standing there watching.

What was hard for Sharon to reconcile was Mr. Nogi's expectation of perfection all the time on the job. This expectation from Mr. Nogi gave Sharon so much pressure that she felt like she could not make any mistakes on the job. In contrast, Sharon saw Don as more flexible in his treatment and attitude toward line workers.

> And [Don], he's not so hard on you as the Japanese are. Even though he expects a lot from you, he's not as—it's like it's okay for you to kind of mess up, you know. He doesn't hold it against you as much as they do. So, he—and then, he kind of—he can make it, you know, to where you don't feel too bad about what you did, even though it wasn't—you know, it depends on what it was. And Mr. [Nogi], it's like if something happens or goes wrong, he's like really mean about it. And he tells [Miyamura] or somebody, 'Well, you know, you've got to keep an eye on this person now.' And [Don] kind of—he'll come and talk to you and he'll ask you, well, you know, 'What happened?' And he doesn't tell you, 'Well, you did this wrong and now we're going to . . . ,' whereas Mr. [Nogi] kind of, you know— he just, 'You did that wrong' and that's it. He doesn't like that. So, whereas [Don], he kind of—he knows. He says, you know, 'It happens.' And Mr. [Nogi] kind of—like I say, he wants you to be perfect. And it's like he expects you to be per-fect.

Mr. Nogi constantly monitored American workers. He especially observed some workers whose behavior he perceived as problematic. What was unique about his poka-yoke control here was that he let American middle-managers like Don directly confront these workers. Mr. Nogi remained in the "ura" (back) thus forcing Don into the "omote" (front). Using Don to exert management control over workers put him into a difficult position. Sharon further explained as follows:

> Especially, like I said, if there's—somebody's talking or something, he's like—he'll stand up there and see who does it the most. And he'll tell [Don], you know, 'Well, this person, every time I looked over there, is always talking,' or something. And then, you know, I mean, [Don] won't really say anything. And then, if Mr. [Nogi] tells him something, then he goes and tells somebody, you know, 'Well, Mr. [Nogi]'s over there. You'd better . . .'

The implication was clear. Don was forced to confront issues with employees at Nogi's request. Don, however, tried to ease the situation as much as he was able. The following comments by Sharon show that Mr. Nogi was trying to enforce the Japanese standards of work attitudes on American workers at Suntech.

> Well, Mr. [Nogi] and [Don] are kind of like that, but Mr. [Nogi] mostly. [Don], he's kind of—he'll be kind of open about it. He won't be so obvious about it, you know. He kind of gives you a chance, whereas Mr. [Nogi], I guess if it was up to him, maybe he would just want Japanese workers, because they wanted all of us to work standing up and we're not supposed to sit down. And then, they kind of use that, too—'Well, in Japan, you know, at [Suntech Japan], the employees there don't get to sit down,' and, 'You guys expect too much.' So, Mr. [Nogi] kind of had them, 'Okay, everybody needs to stand up.' But there's a lot—there are some stages there that you need to sit down to do the job, you know, and they're kind of trying to get rid of that.

Although Nogi repeatedly stated that the Japanese should not impose their standards on Americans, American workers like Sharon perceived that Nogi was attempting to run the repair department the same way as in Japan. Sharon further described the situation as follows.

[L]ike I said, they want you to be perfect. I guess they feel that their company over in Japan—their workers are—they've already— they—he tells us, 'Well, over here in Japan, you know, the workers this or the workers do that,' you know. And they kind of—they want our company to kind of be run the way the Japanese have theirs over there, in Japan, you know. We—we're not used to that kind of conditioning. He kind of—especially, like I said, he'll kind of tell you, 'When I went to Japan,' you know, 'the employees over there are doing this and you guys over here aren't even there yet.' A lot of times they'll just tell us, 'Well, our Japanese employees can build this many scopes, and you guys haven't even reached that capacity yet.' They kind of make us feel like maybe they're faster than us or something, you know? So, it kind of makes you feel that they don't think we're capable of working as fast as their Japanese employees.

Sharon felt that she had to work as fast as Japanese workers in the home plants in Japan, and do the job without making any mistakes. If she made any mistake on the job, the Japanese managers never let her forget about her mistake and tended to hold this against her for a long time.

The IG is the light source, where you plug it in. There's times where—the IG is the most important thing on the scope. If you break it it's like they can't use it. You kind of destroy the scope. And there's times where they really, really get on you for that. You know, if you break it it's like they don't let you forget. They're always looking over your shoulder and stuff. It's just—they put a lot of responsibility on us and they expect us to be perfect, you know. And it's kind of—if you make a mistake, they kind of hold it against you for a long time. And they're [Nogi and Miyamura] always watching you to make sure that it doesn't happen again. And you kind of feel real stressed out about it, because you're worried, 'I don't want to do this again.'

For Sharon, this attitude of Japanese managers toward perfection put her under so much pressure that it became counterproductive to her job performance.

> Because they do tend to treat you a little bit better if you show that
> you're not making as many errors, you know? It's like—like I said,
> they kind of—they don't want you to do anything wrong. So, they
> kind of—that's the worst thing, is like you know you're just—you
> don't even want to make any mistakes. And that's the thing you
> worry about, like, all day long at work.

Under the constant scrutiny and pressure to work hard, Sharon was
forced constantly to think not how to do the job right but to just keep
up the pace. Ironically, this conditioning further contributed to creating
a greater possibility for work error.

> [W]ell, like I said, you know, you're trying to make yourself work
> more, which makes more—it makes—gives you more room to make
> more errors. Because you're trying to keep up, and at the same time,
> you're so worried about keeping up that you just totally forget about
> what you're doing, and you just want to keep up.

Mr. Nogi's poka-yoke control required perfect attendance of
employees. For workers, therefore, it was extremely difficult to be
absent from the workplace. The expectation of Mr. Nogi was that
workers should prioritize their jobs at Suntech over other personal
matters, even family issues, which especially for the single working
mother is the main priority. Sharon described how difficult it was to
miss a day of work.

> Like I said, it's hard for you to miss work. But you do have sick
> days. But it's like you've got to be really, really sick. because there's
> times where if you call in, they'll ask, you know, well, 'Can you
> come in for half a day,' or something. You know, they kind of—they
> want you to show up.

Sharon also related to the circumstance of Suntech in comparison with
the previous American company that she worked for.

> In—well, my other job, it was like they didn't really care if you went

to work or not. And here, you know, it's like you're an important
part of it. If you missed work, it's like, God, they don't know what to
do when you're gone.

For example, managers of the repair department were unwilling to let
workers leave the workplace even when they needed to attend to their
children who were sick in bed.

[M]y daughter's sick or something, and I still come to work, you
know, and I'm at work thinking, you know, I wonder if she needs to
go to the doctor or something, you know, and I'm over here. And it's
hard to even miss work, because you miss work and it's like
someone tries to take your place and do your job, but they can't keep
up. And so, the next day you come to it again and there's like—
you're so behind. So, it's hard to miss any days . . . [T]here was one
girl worked here, and she had a lot of problems. Her children were
always getting hurt, or something. And they kind of—if she could,
you know, they'd make her stay. You know, they didn't want her
leaving. But there's times where—well, like, I've gotten called—you
know, my daughter's sick or something—'Can you come and get
her?' And they're kind of, 'Well, can't you send somebody to go get
her?' You know, they really don't want to let you have off to go tend
to your child.

In addition to the strict expectation of perfect attendance, workers
were often requested to work overtime. At the end of each fiscal year
much overtime work was requested frequently by the managers to
make up for the delay of the production schedule.

So, that puts a lot of stress on us, because we're trying to meet the
schedule before 3:30. And there's times where the line is just—
there's a lot of problems in the line, and it holds everyone else up,
and we can't catch up, you know. So, that's when we usually have to
work overtime, or then they usually send us home and then they tell
us, 'Well, tomorrow expect overtime.' And it's like we're always
trying to make sure—we know we have to do so many before break,
so many before lunch, just so you'll know you'll finish at 3:30. And
that's kind of like if you know you're waiting, you can't wait too

long, because that really sets you back, and then you can't catch up.
It's harder to catch up. So, they usually try to have somebody help
you catch up, or they'll make it up in overtime.

Officially, business hours for the production area at Suntech ended
at 3:30 p.m. Nonetheless there was no way of meeting the production
goal of the day by 3:30 because workers in the repair department
sometimes had to repair (refurbish) 80 scopes a day. Doing a few hours
of overtime was thus not uncommon.

> We've barely started now that we get off at 3:30. But it was—we
> were so behind because we had a lot of part shortages and stuff. So,
> that really put us behind. And then, we were doing like eighty scopes
> a day, so there was no way we could do them before 3:30. You had
> to do overtime, no matter what. Some people do 'til six.

An additional difficulty for Sharon was that managers created a
social context in which Sharon was unable to refuse overtime requests
by the managers. If Sharon refused the overtime, she believed they
would hold it against her. Sharon actually had never refused such
requests because of this atmosphere of subtle coercion at the
workplace.

> There's this one girl, and it was—see, she did the stage before me.
> And a lot of times she's—she wasn't too fast, so there was times
> when we couldn't even do sixty-four scopes before 3:30. We were
> lucky if we maybe did thirty scopes by 3:30. And she was just so
> slow. And then, every time they asked her if she could stay overtime,
> she always said no. But yet, she didn't realize it was her fault that the
> rest of the line couldn't leave, you know. And they kind of—and
> then, I asked [Don] about that. I told him, 'Well, she always goes
> home, you know. What happens if one of us says no? What's going
> to happen?' And he said, 'Well, you know, that they kind of frown
> upon that and they're watching her, and they know that she always
> says no and she leaves, and they always know who stays and who
> doesn't,' you know. And he said, 'We're always—we watch that,' he
> says, 'and we might have to do something about it.' So, it's like they
> kind of force you—if you say no, it's like they hold it against you. It

was kind of—that's why I really never said no.

Mr. Nogi's poka-yoke control created a social context in which both workers and managers were unable to leave the workplace because of private matters. This condition at the workplace was extremely difficult for a single mother like Sharon.

[I]t's like sometimes it makes me feel like they don't understand, you know, because I have my daughter. I have to go for her. And I can't expect her to wait for me 'til six o'clock. Or, you know, it was like maybe—because I guess—I don't know. Mr. [Nogi]—his kids are all grown, or something. It's like—it seems like most of us don't really have young children. So, maybe he just didn't care whether we had a family or not, because some had to go home and they had to take care of their families. And it's like—it made me feel like he didn't care, because he could stay, you know, we should be able to stay. But there's times where, we had to say no and we couldn't, you know. And I've always had to—there's times where I couldn't stay but I had to make arrangements just to have my daughter picked up, you know, and that was kind of putting a burden on whoever I had to call. And it was like, I couldn't say no, because I knew he would kind of get upset.

Many American workers, including Sharon, perceived that the Japanese managers felt more comfortable when workers were obedient and even submissive to the managers' control.

And they—there's a lot of people that've complained about it. But we really couldn't say anything to Mr. [Nogi] or any of the Japanese staff because they kind of—they don't like for you to really complain, you know. You just kind of—you work for them and that's what you're supposed to do, and not say anything.

Though management in the repair department included Americans like Don and Katie, Sharon clearly blamed the Japanese managers for creating the intense pressures. Don basically understood American workers, particularly single mothers like Sharon, would sometimes need to leave the job because of family situations. Don, however, chose to comply with Mr. Nogi's control. Don tried, however, to avoid the responsibility of allowing workers to decline overtime request. The situation characterized by Sharon illustrated that Mr. Nogi assumed authoritarian control over the matters of absenteeism and overtime work.

> Well, sometimes we had to kind of—if we really, really that we couldn't stay, we could tell them. But they were like, 'You'd better talk to Mr. [Nogi] about it.' So, it was—no matter if you tried, they would say, 'Well, we can't really do anything about it and you have to talk to Mr. [Nogi],' you know. So there was—either way, if we tried to talk to our supervisor, we had to go to Mr. [Nogi], no matter—even if we told him. So, it was up to him, you know. And it was kind of hard trying to explain to him, 'Well, we can't stay because, you know, we've got this, or something.' It seems like sometimes he didn't understand, or he kind of—he didn't really care. You know, he said, 'Well, you didn't finish, and now you want to leave?' He's kind of—it's hard to talk to him. He's real set on his ways, you know. He already knows—Nogi will not help you anyway.

In this setting many American workers believed that the Japanese managers looked down on them because they were not as precise, as fast, and as dedicated as the Japanese workers in Japan. Under poka-yoke control from Mr. Nogi, therefore, Sharon felt that she had a problem committing herself to her job at Suntech. At the same time, she was fearful if Mr. Nogi perceived that she had too little commitment to the job, he would be tough on her.

> I don't think I have commitment. I just—I don't want them to look down on me, so I try to make sure that I don't make any errors, because I don't want them holding it against me, kind of. And I don't want them—I think maybe if they knew that I didn't have no commitment, they'd kind of, like, always watch you and see, you know, well—because they do that a lot. They—the ones that—they can tell, I guess, you know, if you [have no commitment].

Like Don, Sharon was also one of many American workers who

were considering other job opportunities elsewhere. She thought that she should have been paid more because of the high intensity and pressure of the work. Sharon spoke about her pay at Suntech.

> Pay is a little better at Suntech, but sometimes I don't think we get paid enough for what we do, because they expect a lot out of us sometimes. And it's like, you know, they're expecting too much for what they pay us.

As Mr. Nogi commented previously about the Japanese-owned companies, the Japanese-owned firms generally offered slower promotion tracks and more mediocre salaries for employees. This is one of the reasons why Nogi thought the Japanese firms usually did not attract first-rate professionals in the United States. In addition to the low pay at Suntech, Sharon also referred to the low and infrequent raises that workers receive compared to typical American-owned companies.

> A lot of people aren't happy with what they pay. And then, we're lucky if we get thirty cents raise, and that's only once a year, which isn't much. They think that it's a lot, I guess. You know? And it's like, well, they start you off now at $5.50 [per hour]. And I've been here already—let's see—three years, and I barely make $6.25 now. And it took me about three years just to even make that much. And I started out at $5.25, and that's with the once-a-year raise that, you know—that's the only reason I even make that much. But they usually—the first year that I started working here, they only gave us like ten cents, a raise, or something, you know?

In relation to the low rate of pay and slower raise schedule, Sharon perceived that promotions made a big difference in whether or not Mr. Nogi favored a worker. Generally, Sharon also noticed that the Japanese managers tended to prefer workers from Japan. There were two locally hired Japanese women who worked as floater techs. Although Sharon had been working for Suntech as long as these two Japanese women, she noticed a certain difference in the way Mr. Nogi treated American workers and the two Japanese workers.

Sometimes it seems like they kind of favor you more if you're from Japan like they are, because a lot of times they'll have—like Mr. [Nogi] will have—a party or something and he usually only invites only the Japanese employees. There's times where he just kind of— even for lunch or something—he kind of takes them out to lunch and stuff.

Speaking of Mariko, one of the two Japanese line workers, Sharon thought that she was promoted to a floater because she was a Japanese and because she got along well with Mr. Nogi.

Maybe, too, a lot of it has to do because I don't really get along with Mr. [Nogi]. But, you know, there's like [Mariko] got to be floater, but she's Japanese. So, it's always . . . She wasn't as fast as some of the other ones. They're always looking at something. There's a lot of us in there that probably will never get promoted. We're always going to stay there, you know.

Sharon believed that Mr. Nogi's favoritism was the major determinant in promotion and hiring processes. There were, of course, American workers who got promoted. Sharon thought those Americans were promoted primarily because they made obvious efforts to please Mr. Nogi.

I think more of the people that kind of kiss up to Mr. [Nogi] . . . because there's a lot of people get promoted. It's—you can tell, you know, who's trying to get promoted because they start being nicer to him or doing things for him or just trying to please him. There's one lady that works here, and he spends a lot of time at her house and she makes him dinner and everything, and they go together like to games and things. And from what the employees talking and stuff, it kind of—she's trying to get her friends in to work here, you know. And that's the way it is. Mr. [Nogi] makes like the final decision on who gets hired and who doesn't. And she—you know—she's always telling him, well, 'My friend this,' or 'My friend that,' you know. And he kind of, well, 'Tell her to come in and talk to [Don] and interview and then I'll . . . ,' you know.

Mr. Nogi's poka-yoke control certainly reflected his strong personal characteristics. It is also important to note that workers were not just passively accepting his control over them. Sharon mentioned a certain resistance among American workers against his control. Workers sometimes tried to cover their mistakes so that the managers would not find out.

> [I]f I want to improve it, people are going to say, 'Well, she just wants to get her way,' or, you know, get a promotion, I guess. And a lot of people around here, it's like they don't really like that, you know. You try to be their friends—with Mr. [Nogi] or somebody, you know—they kind of hold . . . they're like, well, then you probably—if, we try to fix it, you know, so they don't find out. So, we try to make—fix our own. Something happens, you'll probably go tell them, you know. Because there's times where if something happens—errors—and then, they feel that if you're friends with Mr. [Nogi], you're going to tell him. Well, you know, 'This person's been doing this and we've been letting him get away with it.'

Sharon's description of the way American workers were treated by the Japanese at Suntech brought to mind stereotypical images of the maquiladora industries.

> Maybe they don't want to pay us much. Maybe we're kind of like the ones that are from Mexico, you know, like Americans. If they hire someone from there, they kind of—they know they work for cheap. So, kind of—maybe that's what they're doing to us.

As Don mentioned, the problem for most American workers in the repair department was low morale; they perceived themselves as being poorly treated by the Japanese managers. Sharon's case was also no exception. She knew that she would eventually perhaps go to another company that would pay her more than Suntech. As I mentioned in the beginning of Chapter Five, workers in manufacturing companies in New Mexico generally have a very hard time finding another job if they quit a job. They usually do not have many options other than to remain with the company that they work for. Sharon perceived herself as being trapped in this situation.

[T]here are not too many of the people that are happy there—mainly the ones that like it there, like the ones that get paid more—you know. A lot of us are just—we're just working here because we can't just up and quit, you know, because I can't do that. And if I—I would have already did it a long time ago, I think.

Ideally, under poka-yoke control, workers were expected to be loyal and to stay with the company for a longer period of time. For the company, this stemmed from training costs and the training time that the company had invested in each worker. In the repair department, however, Mr. Nogi's expectation had been modified to cope with the reality of the workplace in the United States, where workers more frequently change jobs than their counterparts in Japan. As Katie mentioned, the rationale here was that it is good for a company to lose workers who were not motivated. Sharon explained what one of her supervisors told her.

There's a lot of people that quit, and they don't stop them. They just tell you, 'Well, we'll hire somebody else to take your place.' You know, they just—that's how they feel, you know. They say—or, Dan's [Repair department's supervisor] told me, 'Well, you people want to go out and look for other jobs. You think it's so easy,' you know. And he says, 'It's not,' he says. And, 'You think you have it hard here,' he says. 'Wait until you try to get another job,' he says. 'But that's up to you,' he says. 'If you want to try to get another job,' he says, 'we're not going to stop you. We'll just replace you.'

As this comment illustrated, the expectations of managers toward retaining workers under poka-yoke control had been adapted to the reality of the work environment in the U.S. For a worker like Sharon, the situation posed a serious dilemma. She did not see any possibility of getting promoted in the near future. The work environment was too rigid, too intense, and too stressful for her. The salary was not enough to balance the stress and the pressure of the job. On the other hand, in American-owned companies, managers usually did not even care whether she came to work or not, so there would be even less job security. At the same time, Sharon perceived that Suntech offered some sort of job security providing she was able to get along with Mr. Nogi and subject herself to his poka-yoke control. For a single mother like Sharon, salary was a key issue in making choices. In New Mexico's labor market, however, there were few jobs available to her. She felt as though she was trapped at Suntech due to the lack of choices.

In the following, I will discuss Martha, who shared with Sharon many similar reactions to Mr. Nogi's poka-yoke control, but perceived more cultural differences in the way this control was exerted over workers.

Martha Ferrari

Martha had been working for Suntech as a department secretary in the repair department since the facility opened in 1989. As the department secretary, she was responsible for processing all the paper work for the department, not only for Mr. Nogi. Her responses to Mr. Nogi's rigidity and strict poka-yoke control were very similar to those of Don and Sharon. From Martha's point of view, the difficulties many American workers had in dealing with Nogi's control arose from his high expectations for job performance, which differed greatly from the expectations of Americans. She explained her perceptions of Nogi's strict attitudes toward perfect attendance and punctuality.

> But sometimes, you know, I feel like, well, you have to take into consideration that people are human and they make mistakes. But occasionally, you know, people, I feel, are allowed to make a mistake every now and then. And I don't think he really sees it that way, you know. I mean, little mistakes, of course, is not a big deal. But if, for instance, I was to have a car accident coming to work one day, I'd probably get in trouble because I was late. And I—and he would feel that I should have accounted for the possibility that I might have a car accident, so I should leave my house a half-an-hour earlier.

Martha also referred to Mariko, the Japanese floater tech, and described how Mariko's work attitudes differed from those of many other American workers. Mariko had a perfect attendance record.

> [W]hen she was a technician, she would come in early—I don't know what time, because I usually get in about ten after seven. But she would be here—I think she used to get in about 6:45 in the

morning, and she would go to work. And maybe her and one or two other people would do that. Everybody else pretty much waits, you know, until it's time to start, and then they start work. And I don't know if that's because she's Japanese and that's the philosophy, or . . . .

Martha pointed out what she perceived of as cultural differences. In her everyday worklife, Martha often felt that she could not agree with Mr. Nogi. Nonetheless she usually avoided confronting him because she assumed that it would be disrespectful to him if she confronted him on these issues. On the other hand, Martha felt that American managers would not be offended if she disagreed with them.

I wouldn't want to say anything that might offend somebody, like, with Mr. [Nogi], let's say, because he's my boss, also. But I don't agree with him. I have to most of the time just keep quiet about it. I would be more apt to argue, let's say—I don't want to say 'argue,' really—but to speak my mind with an American manager than I would with a Japanese manager, because I think they might think it's disrespectful. Like, if I said to Mr. [Nogi], 'Well, I don't agree with that,' I mean, he would probably think that was disrespectful. If I said that to one of the American managers, I don't think—maybe they would see it that way, but I don't—I don't think so. They would just take it as a difference of opinion.

The Japanese managers' attitudes toward the difference in social position had also upset Martha in the past. At Suntech America, when new employees were hired, Martha had been introduced to them because she would be working with them, keeping track of work schedules, time cards. On the other hand, the Japanese managers at Suntech would not even bother introducing her to the Japanese visitors from Japan. Martha felt that it was because of the cultural difference that she was not introduced to those Japanese visitors. The Japanese management Suntech, she felt, did not consider her important enough to require such introductions.

The way you were brought up, you know, the cultural differences are so great sometimes that you don't—at least, I don't want to—. Like, for instance, this has nothing to do with it, but—when I first started working here, you know, we have visitors a lot. A lot of the times, they're Japanese from either [Suntech Japan], or just from wherever. And I was never introduced. You know, they'd come around, and they'd be introduced to the management staff. And they'd just walk by me. And at first, I thought, 'Well, gosh. What am I—nothing?' I mean, they can't, you know. And [Ann] went up to—and this was the president of [Suntech Japan]—she went up to him. And I guess, you know, they had brought him around, and there was a couple of other guys, also—brought them around. And she got up and walked over to him, and shook his hand and said, you know, 'I'm [Ann Johnson].' And she was told later on that she was way out of line for doing that. Now, I knew that that would be way out of line for me to do that, so I didn't do it. But I still thought it was—and they still do that. I mean, they still don't introduce anybody to me. But I think that's the cultural difference.

An interesting contrast between Martha and Ann, the secretary in the manufacturing department, demonstrated a different approach to a similar situation. When Ann, behaving in a very American way, introduced herself to Japanese visitors, the Japanese managers perceived her behavior as "improper" in that situation. Martha used to get upset with these cultural differences. By the time of my interview with her, however, such attitudes no longer offended her as deeply. She understood that it was just the difference in culture, although she was not particularly comfortable with it. What still bothered Martha in everyday worklife was what she perceived as "unfair" treatment by the Japanese employees at Suntech. She talked about the sense of exclusion that she felt when the Japanese managers and Japanese workers like Mariko shared among themselves, without offering Americans an opportunity to join them.

[O]ne who's a floater now and the other one's still on the assembly line—sometimes, you know, they have—they'll buy stuff like fish and other products that they get from some company—I don't even know—and they'll only ask the Japanese people if they want it. Well, what if somebody wanted it, you know, who's American? Like, they wouldn't have the opportunity. Do you know what I mean? Like the newspapers that they circulate are the Japanese newspapers. And these people are not in a high position, but they get these because they're Japanese. Like the other Americans who are at the same level don't have that opportunity. See, in that sense, I think maybe that's not—that's not fair. You know, I mean just because you're not Japanese doesn't mean you don't like Japanese food. You know what I mean? And maybe the other manager staff who isn't Japanese, you know—maybe it would be nice if they asked, 'Would you be interested?,' and give them the opportunity to say yes or no.

The Japanese managers (Mr. Nogi and Mr. Miyamura), and workers such as Mariko, did not mean to deliberately exclude Americans' participation. They assumed that Americans would not be interested in fish or the Japanese newspapers. Whereas Americans such as Martha perceived these distinctions as exclusion from the Japanese circle. The way poka-yoke control was exerted, of course, involved dimensions that were intrinsically influenced by Japanese culture. In everyday worklife one of the dimensions most obvious to both Japanese managers and American workers was the communication barrier. For example, Martha talked about how Mr. Nogi's evaluations could be construed as cultural.

He evaluates my performance, or he'll ask the management staff also, you know, 'How do you think she's doing?,' or this and that. And see, now, there was one item that really bugged me one time in one of the evaluations. They have the different categories, you know, that I was explaining to you. And—not the attendance issue, because I know the attendance hasn't been that great. But there's one item, 'cooperation'—you know, how you get along with others. Now, I think I get along great with everybody. I mean, I'm never rude or nasty, or anything like that, okay? And this was not last year, but the year before. He said—he made some comments to me about cooperation. And I was, like, 'What are you talking about?' And—. Not to him personally, but he had interviewed some of the Japa—not the Japanese staff, some of the management staff. And somebody claimed that I either refused to do certain things or . . . And I was like, 'That's insane.' And to be honest with you, I thought that it may have been the Japanese staff only because maybe they misinterpreted what I was saying. I told him what I said to them is, 'I cannot do it right now, but I'll do it, you know, either now or . . .' as being uncooperative. And I was like, 'But that's not fair, because that's not how it's meant to be.' I have ten people that I do work for. So, I'm not always going to be able to stop what I'm doing and drop everything just for one person. I have to tell them, you know, 'This is when I'll be able to do your work. Is that acceptable?' And that's what I've always done. And somebody, somewhere interpreted that as being uncooperative. And that's not fair to me, you know. And it's the communication difference. Now, I'm not absolutely sure that it was one of the Japanese staff. But I have to assume that it was because I know the American staff would understand what I was saying if I said, 'No, I can't do that right now, but I'll do it, you know, tomorrow or whatever.' They wouldn't view that as being uncooperative, because it's not. [Katie], or [Ed], or [Brian], or any of the other guys. I mean, there's so many of them that—you know, I have never, ever said to anybody, 'No, I won't do that.' To me, that's being uncooperative. But I have never—and I would never even think about saying that to anybody.

Martha also suggested that a common vernacular or idiomatic expression can be problematic. For example, a commonly used phrase in the United States, "No problem" could be understood differently by the Japanese managers than by American workers.

'No problem, no problem.' And that just means, like, 'Yes, I'm agreeable with what you're saying,' or—and it's sort of like a . . . Well, anyway, we used to say that all of the time. Like, if Mr. [Nogi] or somebody else asked if we—if there was a problem, you know, we'd, 'Oh, no problem, no problem.' And he viewed it as we were trying to cover up a problem. But that's not what it is at all! You're just saying 'no problem,' like 'everything is okay.' But Mr. [Nogi] used to think—and I don't know if he still thinks that—but this is maybe in the beginning—he used to think that it meant that we were trying to cover up a problem. So, in that sense sometimes you have to be very careful about this common terminology that you use. And a lot of times, you don't even think about it. I still say 'no problem,' you know, just because it's something that you're used to saying. It's just an expression that you're used to saying.

Simple use of everyday language, therefore, caused unpredictable results.

The ways management control was exerted over workers involved a certain cultural element, either in poka-yoke control or the militaristic/hierarchical control in the manufacturing department. At least on the shopfloor level, the differences in the ways management control was exerted over workers partially stemmed from the differences in the significance of the company in each individual's life. Like Don, Martha pointed out the general differences in the attitudes towards the company's work among the Japanese and the Americans.

> Well, also the way—the way things are viewed, you know, interpretation of your outlook on life. I think [with] the Japanese, it's like work is number one. And a lot of American people—not that their work isn't as important—it's not their whole life, you know. It's like as I was explaining, my family, you know, is just as important to me. I work because I need money. I like what I do, but I'm working because I need to live, because I have a house and I have a family, you know. If I had a lot of money, I would still do something productive. I wouldn't sit at home and be a bum. But I wouldn't be working for somebody else. I'd have either my own thing—you know, I'd be doing—I would be doing something productive. But I wouldn't be working for somebody else if I had, you know, as much money as I wanted. So, of course, you work to support yourself, you know. And that's, I think, how most Americans probably view things.

For the Japanese managers, and for most workers in Japan, once they begin working, the company becomes the first priority in their life. Most of the other aspects of everyday life will be geared around the company. Poka-yoke control essentially demands that workers conform to this expectation. For the majority of Americans, this has been one of the toughest aspects of working for Japanese-owned companies. Martha recalled her previous job in an American company where the managers were far more flexible in their work attitudes, allowing workers to leave the workplace when they needed to.

I'm sure that at my last job I probably made plenty of mistakes. But I never got yelled at. I never had an argument. And I got along very good with my boss. If I ever needed anything, you know, he understood. If I had to—my son was sick, and I had to take him to the doctor, or whatever, you know, it was like it was no big deal. And I feel like if I had to do that—I've only done that once since I've been here, when I thought my son had strep throat. And—no, no—I'm sorry—I thought he had an ear infection—and so, I wanted to take him to the doctor. And I couldn't expect a baby-sitter to take him to the doctor. I mean, he's my child, he's my responsibility. And I just don't think that that was looked upon in a very favorable way. Now, I'm not saying that it's okay to always take off because your kid's sick. I never take off when my kid is sick. You know what I mean. And in that sense, I have to put my family first. And I don't think that the Japanese staff understand that. They feel the work comes first. And my work is important to me. My job is important to me. But my family has to sometimes take priority. And—you know, in the case of an emergency or sickness, or whatever—[it] has to sometimes take priority.

At Suntech, most of the manager-level employees, including the supervisors, frequently stayed until five o'clock everyday. Some of them stayed even longer. Since production at Suntech started at 7:15 a.m., almost all of the line workers immediately left the company when the official business hours were over at 3:15 p.m. unless they had an overtime request. Observing how they were expected to work, Martha was uncertain about her desire for advancement in her career. She described the situation as she perceived it.

See, now, that's another thing that I think might hold me back a little bit. You know, some of the lead techs or people like management that are in a higher position, you know, they're expected to stay until five o'clock or 4:30, whatever. And I just can't do that because I have a family to take care of. And if they want to eat at ten o'clock at night because she's got to work late, they can do it. I can't do that because my child needs to eat, and I have to feed him, and make sure that he does his homework, and put him to bed. And, you know, I don't have that flexibility. And that shouldn't mean that I shouldn't be able to advance, if that's what I want. But I think that's what holds me back, you know. I mean, I can work late, you know, from time to time, but not—like, I'm here tonight, you know, late—but not every single day because on Wednesdays I have certain things. I have to be out of here by four o'clock at the very latest, you know.

In this section all American employees whom I have described were subjected to Mr. Nogi's poka-yoke control. Both Don and Katie expressed their difficulties as managers. Sharon and Martha expressed their frustrations as workers. However, each employee faced different realities at the workplace. Don, as the assistant production manager, believed that he had to support Mr. Nogi's poka-yoke control even though he did not understand it well. Though he was able to understand the frustrations of American line workers like Sharon, he tried to support Mr. Nogi's control over them. In contrast, Katie was more ingrained into poka-yoke control in that she was gaining a good grasp of its rationale and advantages. Katie was less sympathetic with workers than was Don. Except for Katie, who did not have children and had a supportive and understanding husband who respected her ambition, everybody had a family to support. Sharon felt very uncomfortable with Mr. Nogi and was resistant to his poka-yoke control. In addition, Sharon was always considering other job opportunities because of the high stress at Suntech and salary considerations. In contrast, Martha was a highly committed worker although, as a secretary, she was unable to see any possibility for further advancement at Suntech. Though Martha was often upset about the ways that the Japanese managers treated Americans, she tried to understand these differences as cultural and still tried to prove herself to the Japanese in her everyday worklife.

Though each individual's situation was different, it is important to note one significant and shared characteristic in their responses to the poka-yoke control from Mr. Nogi. The lack of flexibility poka-yoke control featured in dealing with various needs and wants of American workers significantly conflicted with the concept of the worklife that was shared by American workers. In poka-yoke control, like it or not, workers were expected to be inculcated into the "corporate hegemony." Workers (even managers) were, and had to be, very controlled in this production system. There were Americans like Katie who were adapting well to the conditioning of poka-yoke control. However, it is fair to say that Katie's case was rather unique. Katie did not have children to care for. Katie also perceived ample opportunities to advance herself. On the other hand, most American workers, especially those Americans with family responsibilities, struggled with the rigid expectations of poka-yoke control for perfect attendance records and frequent overtime work.

CONCLUSION

Discussing American and Japanese experiences at the workplace, and worker's opinions about cultural differences and similarities, has always been very frustrating for both researchers and informants. Social science has become increasingly aware of the importance of accounting for intra-cultural variability when discussing cultural differences and similarities. In some manufacturing environments, such as the various workplaces of Japanese transplants, most workers have focused on intercultural differences.

Most of my informants at Suntech America responded in terms of the framework: "Americans are . . ." and "The Japanese are . . . ." The degree of difference between the two cultures in this environment was generally perceived as much greater than the degree of difference among individuals within each culture. This perception existed primarily because there were both specific and implied cultural categories for things Japanese and things American, and there was little overlap between the two. When discussing the interactions between Japanese and Americans, all of the Japanese managers I interviewed dealt with the topic in terms of an "American versus Japanese" cultural frame of reference. This was the major reason why I also used the perceived distinctions, such as "Japanese" and "American" when I discussed militaristic/hierarchical control in Chapter Six and poka-yoke control in Chapter Seven.

Hierarchical/militaristic control in the manufacturing department was exerted over American workers mainly by American managers like Rick and Terry. In this form of control, the manager enforced control in a top down fashion with militaristic attitudes. Manager's attitudes toward workers were impersonal and bureaucratic. In the manufacturing department, because of this militaristic attitude toward workers, workers' frustration and hostility were directed at the

American managers. The three Japanese engineers were not directly involved in the dynamics of management control. American managers like Rick, Terry and Ron expressed their dissatisfaction and hostility more toward the structural level of corporate control (remote control) by both the New York headquarters and by the parent company in Japan. American line workers like Libby and the department secretary, Noelle, demonstrated more understanding and affinity with the three Japanese engineers. Moreover, the structural conditioning of corporate control, i.e., remote control, further stimulated and intensified the American managers' hierarchical/militaristic control.

In contrast, poka-yoke control in the repair department was exerted by a Japanese manager, Mr. Nogi, not only over American workers, like Sharon and the department secretary, Martha, but also the American middle managers, Don and Katie. Though poka-yoke control was exerted in a top down fashion by the Japanese managers, there were American middle managers, like Don, who tried to translate the expectations of Mr. Nogi to the American workers in the department. As its essential characteristic, poka-yoke control demanded workers to be molded into the corporate hegemony. Since this control was exerted by Japanese managers over American workers, it often involved elements of paternalism and apprenticeship. The manner in which poka-yoke control was exerted over American workers by Mr. Nogi, as I described, often involved cultural dimensions that Americans did not well understand. The frustration among American workers like Sharon, even managers like Don, therefore, was directed at the Japanese managers and especially at Mr. Nogi.

Even within the one company, Suntech America, there were two contrasting departments in which the forms of management control were significantly different. Workers in the manufacturing and the repair departments also responded differently to these two different forms of management control. However, I should note one significant characteristic that held true in the different conditions of these two departments. In the manufacturing department, it was American middle managers who resisted the hegemonic influence of Japanese corporate worklife. In the repair department, it was both the American line workers and the middle managers who resisted the hegemonic conditioning of Japanese corporate worklife.

Although workers and managers in the manufacturing and repair departments at Suntech responded differently to the different forms of management control, both cases illustrated that cultural differences were significant factors in the workplace and greatly challenged the creation of a unique corporate culture of Suntech. At the time of my study, Suntech New Mexico's facility had only three years of history since its opening in 1989. Like many other transplants in the Midwest and in California, issues of corporate culture at Suntech were mainly concerned with the question of how the company might possibly integrate the Japanese and American workforce, and create a unique corporate culture at Suntech.

The case of the manufacturing department strongly demonstrated that corporate level, structural conditioning (remote control) contributed negatively to the integration of the Japanese and American work cultures. In addition, cultural differences regarding worklife styles, e.g., length of time and personal involvement with the company, hindered the integration of the Japanese and American employees. In the repair department, the relative significance of dedication and loyalty to the company by the Japanese managers and the priority Americans place on their private lives also created a vast cultural gap, making such integration extremely challenging. While these cultural differences were a daily and on-going problem in both departments, so was the issue of remote control upon managers, both Japanese and American. It was, I believe, problematic and unduly stressful and the cause of a yet greater breach in understanding between the Japanese and the Americans.

EPILOGUE

I conducted my fieldwork for this study from the summer of 1992 through October of 1993, and therefore, some of the data that I collected might well be updated. I stayed in touch with some of the employees at Suntech after I moved on to visit other Japanese transplants in the Midwest and in California. When I was preparing for the second phase of my fieldwork in the Midwest, I heard from Tomoko, one of the Japanese employees at Suntech, that Rick Darnell had left Suntech and went back to the American-owned company for which he had previously worked. Shortly after, I learned that Terry Panko had also left Suntech. As I mentioned, Terry had filed a complaint to EEOC about Suntech for a discriminatory practice in the promotion process. Although the Japanese managers and American human resources staff were concerned that the case might be brought into the court, the case was settled favorably for the company.

At the end of the summer of 1993, after I came back from my research trips in the Midwest and California, I heard that Suntech had hired a new manufacturing manager. Suntech headhunted this new manager with the lure of an exceptionally high salary from an American company. Tomoko was somewhat excited about this new manufacturing manager because he was from a company in the same field and was very experienced. From some of other employees at Suntech, I heard that the company, especially the Japanese managers and engineers, had very high expectations for him.

During the spring of 1995 I was working as a technical translator for another Japanese-owned high-tech transplant in the same region, which had just started its manufacturing operations. During this time, I heard a rumor from some American managers at this new company that Suntech was not doing very well. I contacted Tomoko and found out that the manufacturing department at Suntech might be closed, but that the repair department would probably continue functioning as before. Tomoko also told me that she was thinking about leaving Suntech for another Japanese-owned company in California. During the conversation with Tomoko, she often told me that it was quite hard to be sandwiched between the Japanese managers and American workers. She was afraid that she would never be able to make any friends at the company as long as her work situation remained the same at the company. Shortly afterwards, all three Japanese engineers, Yasuo, Masao, and Hiroshi, returned to the home factory in Japan, and Tomoko also left the company.

During the summer of 1995, I heard that the operation manager, Ron Peal, left Suntech for another American-owned company. It was at almost the same time that Tomoko told me that Frank Watson, the administration manager, left Suntech. When I ran into Mr. Shibata once in a Japanese restaurant during that summer, he told me that only the repair department was functioning. He did not tell me much about what was going on at the company at that time.

Partly because of the intensity of dissertation writing process, I lost touch with my informants at Suntech after the summer of 1995. It was in January of 1997 when I finally discovered that Suntech's New

Mexico plant had actually closed down in October of 1996. I located an article on Suntech's plant closing in a local newspaper. The article stated as follows:

> [Suntech America, Inc.] will close its 7-year-old [New Mexico] plant and dismiss all 46 remaining workers at the end of September. The closure follows the layoffs last year of 45 to 50 employees at the plant, which repairs and helps assemble [endoscopes] and other medical products. [Suntech] plans to shift the repair and assembly duties to a plant in San Jose, California . . . [Suntech] searched the nation in the late 1980's for a manufacturing site The company said in 1989 that it selected New Mexico because of the availability of qualified labor and a perceived work ethic that surpassed those of other potential U.S. locations . . . The company will provide out-placement services to the laid-off workers
>   (Albuquerque Journal, 4 star, 2C, August 1, 1996).

I contacted Tomoko who confirmed that Suntech had officially closed its plant in October of 1996, and that Mr. Shibata had gone back to headquarters in New York. He actually had been demoted from a senior vice-president to a vice-president. Mr. Nogi had been sent back to the repair facility in San Jose, California. He also had been demoted from the repair department manager to a position reporting to Freddy Marquez who is currently the repair center manager at the facility. According to Tomoko, Suntech's business declined quickly mainly because the company could not keep other Japanese competitors from entering the same field. Secondly, she mentioned, the plant lost many strong American managers, especially in the manufacturing area, because of the tight and rigid corporate level control by the New York corporate headquarters. I asked her about the role social and cultural factors had played in the closing of the plant. These factors were of little significance in her opinion. I believe that Tomoko's position as a go-between and the accompanying stress and isolation speaks more than any further observations or opinions she might have offered. Like both Shibata and Nogi, she was caught in the tangled web of power relations which eventually led to the unfortunate demise of Suntech America in New Mexico.

The preceding epilogue originally concluded my dissertation

which was submitted to the University of New Mexico in May 1997. My relationship with some of key informants from Suntech including Tomoko, however, continued even after the plant closing. In the spring of 1998, when I was in the midst of revising my dissertation for this publication, I had an another opportunity to share information with an American ex-employee of Suntech about the plant closing.

According to Daniel (pseudonym) , who used to work in the R&D department, one of the most significant reasons for the plant closing was the failure of the R&D operation at the New Mexico facility. During the years of 1992 through 1994, the R&D department was designing a new product that turned out to be incompetent in the market. After this failure of the R&D operation at the New Mexico plant, the New York headquarters started losing confidence in the manufacturing operation in the New Mexico plant, and started shifting its corporate focus back to the repair center in San Jose, California. As I mentioned in Chapter Two, when I was conducting fieldwork at the plant in the summer of 1992, I was strictly prohibited by Mr. Shibata from obtaining any information about the R&D activities. I could conduct interviews with some employees from this department, but could hardly obtain any significant information at that time.

Daniel also pointed out the nature of the manufacturing process at the plant. As I described in Chapter Six, the manufacturing department was utilizing a conveyor belt system. According to Daniel, this system was totally outdated, by any standard, even at the time of 1992.

Finally, he also pointed out the New Mexico plant's relationship with the parent company in Japan. In 1996 the recession started seriously affecting Japanese economy; most firms in Japan were forced to reduce the scale of their operations. Suntech Corporation in Tokyo was no exception. In order to retain employees and prevent layoffs at their home plants in Japan, Daniel said, they wanted to return manufacturing operations back to Japan. Daniel's information reinforced something which had been related to me in 1992 by Don Grace, an assistant manager in the repair department at Suntech America. Don felt that Suntech America would always be less important than its counterparts in Japan and, in fact, would be sacrificed if necessary, in order to maintain stability and profits of the parent company in Japan. Don affirmed clearly this idea, ". . . the system as it is has many built-in profits for [Suntech Japan] at the expense of [Suntech] Corporation of America . . . ."

NOTES

1. "*Sannin yoreba monju no chie*," literally translates to "When three persons get together, we have great ideas." The proverb signifies that the power of the whole group is much greater than the sum of its individuals. Although this is a Japanese proverb, this is also a familiar idea in the U.S. The idea is emphasized quite frequently in the non-traditional manufacturing environment in the U.S. where people try to utilize the team concept.

2. Nogi is not the only manager who is critical of the Western capitalist system. In fact many high-level managers in corporations in Japan share similar views, if not necessarily in terms of Marx or Lenin. This comparative difference between capitalism in Japan and in the West are discussed by Johnson (1993). Turner (1991) also refers to the comparative differences in the ways in which capitalism and technology are realized in Japanese companies in Japan.

3. At Suntech, overtime work hours per month are calculated as a total sum of the number of overtime hours that each non-exempt workers has to work. For example, there were 49 workers in the repair department at the time of my study. When Don said he had 500 hours of overtime in August, each worker in the repair department did overtime on the average of 10 hours per week.

4. The NS unit is the insertion part of the endoscope.

5. As I noted in Chapter Two, "*sempai*" literally means a predecessor or an experienced senior. "*Kouhai*" also means a follower, or an inexperienced junior. The sempai–kouhai relationship in Japan is typically seen in the process of apprenticeship or in the process of learning in general. The relationship usually accompanies the traditional paternalistic relationship, in which a sempai takes a good care of a kouhai, who humbly asks help and guidance from him.

6. "*Omote*" in Japanese literally means a surface or the front as opposed to "*ura*," which means the back. This relates to Ervin Goffman's distinction of "front" and "back." Although this duality in everyday interaction exists in any human society, the distinction between omote and ura is often influenced by another set of distinctions between "*ko*" (public) and "*shi*" (private) in Japan. The relationships between "*ko*" and "*shi*" are based upon the tradition of Confucian ethics. See "The Japanese Business Value System" by Motofusa Murayama in *Japanese Management* (Lee and Schwendiman, ed. 1982: 108).

CHAPTER 8

Conclusion

In this book I examined the transferability of Japanese organizational practices to Japanese-owned transplants in the U.S. in terms of the eight salient characteristics of Japanese practices outlined by Murakami and Rohlen (1992). Although there are some exceptions, my findings on transferability generally do not conform to previous studies that have argued that some Japanese organizational forms and practices, such as the team-based work processes and extensive benefits systems, have been successfully transferred to transplants in the U.S. (Hatvany and Pucik 1980; Ito 1987; Johnson and Ouchi 1974; Starr and Bloom 1985; Starr and Hall 1987; Wakabayashi and Graen 1991; Womack, et al. 1990; Kenney and Florida 1993). Instead, my findings agree with Abo's study (1994) that organizational practices of the Japanese transplants have resulted in practices that significantly differ from those of both home plants in Japan and their American counterparts. For example, I showed that the transplants in my study utilized various forms of work teams, but that they were not precisely the same as those in home plants in Japan.

I frequently referred to Kenney and Florida's work (1993) in my study mainly because I agreed with their insightful point of view concerning the organization of work and production of Japanese factories in Japan. However, my emphasis on power relations, particularly on corporate control by parent companies in Japan over their U.S. subsidiaries, led me to a somewhat different conclusion from that of Kenney and Florida. Kenney and Florida (1993) argued that the successful transfer of innovation-mediated production systems from home plants in Japan to U.S. subsidiaries would eventually enable Japanese transplants to instill their work ideologies among American workers and, thus, bring stronger corporate hegemonic influence to American communities. However, I found little evidence for the successful transfer of Japanese organizational practices to the industrial environment in the U.S. There was little evidence for the all-encompassing worklife that Rohlen described in his study on a bank in Japan (Rohlen 1974). Among the transplants in my study, there were no holistic training processes for workers, nor an everyday lifecourse by which newly hired workers were shaped into the company's mold. These practices were not transferred to the transplants mainly because of the ideological differences of the worklife between Japanese and American workers. In addition, I emphasized the significance of corporate structural level influence on everyday interactions among employees at the workplace. As the case of Suntech America exemplified, remote control by the New York headquarters and the parent company in Japan intensified power struggles between Japanese and American managers, and thus hindered the process of integration of Japanese ad American workforces.

In this book, I argued that the successful transfer of organizational practices from Japan to the U.S. would be difficult, not only because of the social and cultural differences in work ideologies between the Japanese and American workers, but also because of the pre-existing relations of corporate control between parent companies in Japan and their transplants in the U.S. These relations of control on the corporate structural level often prohibited the successful integration of Japanese and American employees at the workplace.

While the transplants exhibit elements of both Japanese and American organizational practices, the creation of a truly viable hybrid corporate culture was not evidenced by any company in my study. One transplant, Yamadadenso, was successful in integrating many Japanese and American organizational practices and had made great efforts on the corporate management level to accomplish a more integrated workforce. At Suntech America, in contrast, the process of creating a hybrid-mix of Japanese and American organizational practices was incomplete since American and Japanese elements co-existed side by side rather than becoming integrated.

1. REASONS WHY BASIC PRACTICES WERE NOT TRANSFERRED

The findings from the automotive related transplants in the Midwest, the high-tech related transplants in California, and the case study company in New Mexico exhibited many similar tendencies. As examined in chapters three through five, my findings generally showed the existence of the elements of both Japanese and American organizational practices at the transplants in the U.S. Many elements of the practices that are common to firms in Japan, such as the practice of lifetime employment, seniority-based wage and promotion systems, extensive benefits packages, company-based labor unions, intensive, holistic training and socialization programs were not transferable to the U.S. transplants. These practices were not institutionalized in transplants because of the differences between the industrial environments of the U.S. and Japan, and because of the social and cultural differences between American and Japanese workers.

An organizational practice is not an isolated entity, separate from the influences of the larger social and economic environment. Both seniority systems and internal promotion are based on the assumption that employees will remain with a company for a long period of time. Intensive training and socialization of new employees by management becomes meaningful only when employees work with a company for many years. The lifetime employment practice, therefore, implies an expectation of loyalty to the company. American workers are not accustomed to this expectation, and tend to change jobs far more frequently than their counterparts in Japan. In providing intensive, holistic training programs, management in Japan also assumes a readily available workforce adequately prepared by the educational structure, where skills and educational levels are far more standardized than those in the U.S. In addition, social and cultural differences between Japanese and American workers are reflected in the worklife, work hours, decision-making processes, and attitudes toward the job.

The interactions among employees at the workplace also reflect significant social and cultural differences between the two countries. For example, a Japanese boss tends to work more closely with and takes personal responsibility for the work processes and progress of his subordinates. In addition, the Japanese boss cultivates a more personal relationship with his subordinates. In contrast, American employees are accustomed to a contractual relationship between themselves, the company and its management. Further, the contractual nature of the relationship between American employees, management and the company is also evident in the way work tasks are accomplished among American and Japanese employees. American employees tend to draw stricter boundaries regarding their own work responsibilities than Japanese employees do. In general, American employees are unaccustomed to sharing their responsibilities with other employees. American employees are used to specific job descriptions and delineation of tasks and responsibilities. In the context of the American workplace, therefore, sharing job responsibilities is often perceived as a threat to one's own area of specialization.

For their part, Japanese managers maintained a set of "Japanese" expectations toward American employees, at least on the level of management ideals. Loyalty to the company, diligence, and dedication to work were greatly valued, reflecting a collectivism inherent in the Japanese culture. The slow rates of promotion and salary increases also reflected the Japanese attitude toward the development of employees' skills. All these tendencies have resulted in the juxtaposition of Japanese and American elements in which many American elements are derived from the wider pre-existing industrial environment, and co-exist alongside, but are not integrated with a set of Japanese expectations shared among Japanese managers.

2. CONSIDERATION OF CORPORATE STRUCTURAL LEVEL INFLUENCE ON THE WORKPLACE

The existence of rather traditional Japanese expectations in transplant companies whose corporate structures more closely resemble those of American-owned firms, creates a unique social context at the workplace, in which American and Japanese employees interact, contradict, and negotiate their power relations in their attempt to create a hybrid corporate culture.

In chapters six and seven, I further explored the issue of a corporate culture in my case study company, Suntech America, by examining the processes by which Japanese managers and engineers tried to translate their expectations into the American context. I examined forms of management control and illustrated the ways in which management control was exerted at the workplace. As I described in Chapter Seven, Japanese managers, such as Mr. Nogi, hoped that American workers would become as similar as possible to their Japanese counterparts in Japan in terms of their attitudes towards the company. He attempted to exert poka-yoke management control and to translate his expectations to American workers through American middle managers, like Don and Katie.

The case of Suntech America illustrated the difficulties of forming a hybrid corporate culture; American and Japanese elements are still not successfully integrated in everyday worklife within one company. The hierarchical/militaristic management control exerted by Rick, Ron, and Terry of the manufacturing department was clearly American in style, and took an extreme militaristic form. It contrasted with the more open, participative management practices in non-traditional American plants that Lamphere described in her study (Lamphere et al. 1993). Compared to participative management practices, the hierarchical/militaristic control at Suntech involved a top down decision making process which discounted the process of consensus decision making. The managers' attitudes were impersonal and bureaucratic, which resulted in lowering employees' morale at the workplace. In the repair department, on the other hand, the management control exerted by Nogi, i.e., poka-yoke control, was heavily influenced by Japanese culture. Given these two forms of control, American workers responded to each, negotiating how willing they were to meet the demands of their American or Japanese managers. Most importantly, these workplace level phenomena were constantly influenced by the corporate structural level factors, such as remote control from the parent company in Japan and the headquarters in New York.

In all the data chapters (chapters three through seven), I carefully presented the means by which transplants were constantly influenced by structural level corporate control from the headquarters and the parent company in Japan. At the workplaces of transplants, most obstacles arose from the social and cultural differences between Japanese and American employees. At the same time, it is important to note that the corporate level structures indeed heavily influenced these workplace level interactions. The case of the manufacturing department at Suntech clearly illustrated that remote control from the parent company in Japan and the headquarters in New York further intensified the power struggles between the three Japanese engineers and American managers at the workplace.

In Chapter Three, I discussed the case of Dan Dooley at Yamadadenso who believed that the social and cultural differences between the Japanese and American employees at the workplace could be overcome if the company paid significant attention at the management level to the issue of social interaction between Japanese and American employees. It is important to note here that Dooley was one of few American managers who was able to earn the trust of the Japanese management at the parent company in Japan. In Chapter Four, I presented the case of Bob Mosser, who strongly opposed Japanese influence at the workplace. Like Dooley, Mosser was able to achieve a high level of autonomy because he had earned the trust of the Japanese management at the parent company in Japan. His case also showed the significance of corporate structural level influence on the workplace. Carolyn Monroe of Nippon North America also believed that the social and cultural differences between the Japanese and American employees at the workplace could be overcome only with strong efforts at the management level. Freddy Marquez at Suntech's repair facility in California also realized the importance of a continuous exchange of personnel between the parent company in Japan and its U.S. transplant in order to successfully integrate work practices and expectations of both Japanese and Americans at the transplant.

All of these cases pointed to the significance of influences and pressures from both the corporate structural level and the management level on the relationships among employees at the workplace within one company. As I illustrated in Chapter Three, Yamadadenso was successful in integrating the Japanese and American workforces, mainly because of management level efforts from the beginning of the start-up phase of the plant. In contrast, as I mentioned in the Epilogue, Suntech's New Mexico plant closed down, at least in part, because of remote control from the headquarters in New York and the parent company in Japan. Although the end results were opposite, the cases of Yamadadenso and Suntech clearly demonstrated the importance of accounting for both the corporate and management level influences on the day-to-day relationships among employees at the workplace.

In this web of power relations some American managers become immobilized in the Japanese transplants. In Chapter Three George

Donald of Oyama America clearly illustrated the "unreconstructed American manager" (Kenney and Florida 1993) in the transplants. Unreconstructed managers are powerless to influence conditions at the workplace in any significant way. They are literally "stuck between a rock and a hard place," the "rock" on one hand being the corporate structures that determine policies, processes and production modes, and the "hard place" being the job of go-between for Japanese management and the American workers. The American managers in the manufacturing department at Suntech, Rick Darnell, Ron Peal, and Terry Panko clearly represent those managers at transplants who "got stuck" in the corporate structures. They held on to the ideals of American management practices which value immediate results, such as quick decision making, faster promotion and pay increase. These ideals were not easily accomplished at Suntech, not only because the Japanese managers and engineers retained Japanese work attitudes and expectations, but because of the power of the parent company in Japan. Most importantly, they did not possess any substantial power to transform these conditions. In addition, they were frustrated with the work attitudes of Japanese managers and engineers, but they were not able to change these Japanese employees.

The three American managers at Suntech left the company before it closed, returning to work for American-owned companies. They indeed fell between the cracks of American management ideals in which they believed, and Japanese management ideals that were shared among Japanese employees. Facing social and cultural differences with Japanese employees in their everyday worklife, as well as corporate structures that they were not familiar with, they became dissatisfied with their work conditions, and yet, they realized that they did not possess any substantial power to change these structures.

Japanese workers, likewise, bear a similar burden and face a similar, perhaps greater risk, in terms of their career development than the unreconstructed American managers who can return to the more familiar setting of American companies. What I call the "altered" Japanese employees are those who are unable to fit back into the corporate structure of the parent company after working for years at the U.S. subsidiary.

Along with the proliferation of Japanese industries in the U.S. came large numbers of Japanese engineers, managers, and technical workers and their families. Their perspectives of themselves as members of the team—company men—has not been diminished by the distance from the home company. Whatever new experiences, new understandings and perspectives working in the U.S. has brought to them, it has not reduced the necessity of strictly adhering to the internalized work attitudes and ethic they brought with them from Japan. In addition, they are not expected to remain in the U.S. for more than a few years. Their underlying assumption is that they will go home when the job at the transplant is done. Thus, these Japanese employees are confronted with the choice of allowing themselves to become somewhat "Americanized," or retaining their identities as company men. "Americanized" Japanese employees, for example, tend to assert their individual opinions far more strongly than is expected within a social group setting. They also tend to separate their private time and space clearly from the public time and space that is required of them by the company. In the context of workplaces in Japanese organizations in Japan, these employees tend to breach the sense of solidarity that is strongly shared among the members of the traditional organization. Therefore, if they should in the least be perceived by the homeplant as having become Americanized when they return, they may well be ostracized from work groups, and eventually excluded from the promotion track at the parent company in Japan. Bob Mosser, in fact, referred specifically to a Japanese engineer who was unable to fit back into the corporate culture of the parent company after staying in the U.S. for five years. His case might well represent the existence of such altered Japanese employees at parent companies in Japan. Unreconstructed American managers at transplants in the U.S. and altered Japanese employees at the parent company in Japan are indeed the embodiment of the social and cultural differences in the organizational practices of Japan and the U.S.

Basic differences in attitudes towards an individual's responsibility to the company reflect differences in ideology of worklife between Japanese and American employees. To the Japanese, loyalty means dedication, cooperation, and diligence, while for the American such characteristics are not inherent. To be sure, the Japanese manager may at times envy his American counterpart leaving the company at 5:30 or 6 p.m. after a 9-10 hour work day. He realizes, however, that such latitude of individual choice is not available to him because he will eventually return to Japan. This was clearly elucidated by Sakamoto of Y.K. Manufacturing in Kentucky. He stated:

> Cultural differences—[To Americans] work is not their whole life. They can think of work as fun. They are optimistic. They can go home when the time comes, no matter what adversity they are in. Of course, these are sources of frustration [for Japanese]. But I can't say which is better or not. When we think about the quality of individual life and the view of life, we may want to agree with them. It is not really true that we, Japanese, think a company is everything. It is probably that we value our family more than a company. However, in reality, we can't show this. So, we end up staying longer at the company. Americans don't have this kind of reality. I think this is the biggest difference. I have been in the auto industry for almost 20 years. I feel this difference. I want to move to a better place if I can find the one.[laugh] I am a very Japanese "*sarariiman*" (salary-man), so I have been staying with one company this long. But I don't think things will be like that in Japan. I don't think the younger generation will be like that. It may be hard for Asians to act like that, and moreover, Japan does not have as much "*kokuryoku*" (national power) as in the U.S. So, in the nation like Japan, people want their security first. In contrast, here in America, although there is a big gap between the poor and the rich, people are freer. They can be like this because there is more national power. Americans here in our company enjoy their lives more than we do, unfortunately. And, I feel jealous of them. We Japanese are not good at enjoying ourselves. If I were an American, I would think of moving to a better company.

The American work ethic certainly includes the notions of diligence and dedication. The perception of loyalty, however, differs from that of the Japanese. In the U.S. loyalty has been traditionally defined by the phrase, "For God, home, and country." The personal, private, and individual precedes loyalty even to the nation. Thus the job and the social groups within the company are far less important to the American than his home and family. This contrast was well depicted in the following conversation with Takizawa of the United GM Glass in Kentucky.

Sumi (myself): By the way, do you think you have a sense of loyalty to your company? It is usually said that workers in America just work for a paycheck, just work from 9 a.m. to 5 p.m., or 8 a.m. to 5 p.m. Do you see yourself different compared to this attitude?

Takizawa: Well, it's more or less the same in the sense that I want to do a good job since this is my work. But, what is different is that for Americans, work and the company are not related very much. Their attitudes toward family is very different from mine. For them, after work, family comes first. For me, work and company are inseparable. So, after work, I go to a Japanese restaurant with other Japanese employees, or go for a drink, and we talk about our work related matters or mundane matters. Or, I keep staying on my job and try to process some unfinished work. The only way I can deal with the difference is to persuade myself that they are American and I am not. I am Japanese.

3. REGIONAL INFLUENCES ON MANAGEMENT PRACTICES

Although not a specific topical concern of this study, I have addressed regional influences on the organizational practices of the Japanese transplants in the U.S. In chapters three through five, I briefly discussed site selection processes by Japanese transplants. The Midwest and the West Coast regions of the U.S. differ radically in terms of their life styles, histories, climate, geography, and racial ethnic compositions. In my process of collecting data in these regions, I was able to perceive a noticeable difference in the success of implanting Japanese work ideology within specific environments of the U.S. Regional characteristics within specific industries and the incumbent history of both the region and the industries themselves have noticeably impacted transplants. Kenney and Florida's study (1993) pointed out the Japanese tendency to concentrate the automotive related transplants in the Midwestern regions, whereas the high-tech transplants are mostly located on the West Coast. In addition, both Kenney and Florida's study and Abo's study (1994) of Japanese transplants pointed out that auto-related transplants in the Midwest exhibited a more Japanese pattern of utilizing of teams and small groups on the shopfloor as compared to the high-tech transplants in California. Milkman also contended that organizational practices of Japanese high-tech transplants in California conformed more toward traditional American patterns of elaborated hierarchies with more detailed job classifications and descriptions (Milkman 1991). My data also conform to these findings.

The American automobile industry was conceived and born in the Midwest more than a century ago. The accessibility of natural resources, coal and iron ore specifically, and the vast expanses of flat land in the region allowed for the rapid growth of the steel industry, and eventually the auto industry itself. The Midwest, thus, built a solid infrastructure for the automotive industries. For more than fifty years, Detroit reigned supreme in the automotive industry on a world-wide level. In the early 1970's, Japanese automobiles suddenly became noticeable on American highways. The concurrent decline of the American auto industry provided fertile soil for Japanese auto-related transplants. Lay-offs by large American auto manufacturers in the area provided large numbers of available skilled workers, and space was available for large manufacturing sites at affordable prices for the Japanese industrialists. The production processes of automobile manufacturing required large-scale assembly line design and a large blue-collar workforce. This provided ample opportunities for the Japanese to experiment with some of the organizational practices of their home plants, such as QC's and other forms of work teams. In addition, the relatively stable workforce in rural and traditional regions in the Midwest certainly appealed to Japanese auto manufactures who expected American workers to remain with the companies for a significant period of time.

On the other hand, California's industrial growth has had little to do with its counterparts in the Midwest. Though there are some auto manufacturers, like NUMMI (New United Motor Manufacturing Inc.), the auto industry in California is not a primary industry as it is in the Midwest. In the northern region, the aerospace industries developed in the 1940's and attracted many high-tech investors, such as Hewlett-Packard and then Apple computers in the 1970's. Certain historical contingencies brought major computer industries into the area called the Silicon Valley. California had already built a solid infrastructure for high-tech industries by the early 1970's when the Japanese high-tech companies started seeking opportunities for direct investment in the U.S. As I mentioned in Chapter Four, the nature of high-tech manufacturing processes does not require a large production area with long assembly lines. In addition, high-tech assembly does not require a large number of blue-collar workers. Coupled with the highly mobile labor market of venture capital activities and the nature of production processes in high-tech industry, Japanese management had little opportunity to instill their home practices in the high-tech, fast-paced atmosphere of California.

In contrast to the mobile workplace of the West Coast, the Midwest in general features a more stable, more slowly changing populace. The tendency toward mobility is certainly evident, even in the Midwest, but there is a more population stability over generations. The organization of production processes is a primary reason for explaining why the auto related transplants in the Midwest have exhibited a tendency to be more Japanese in their business practices than the high-tech transplants in California. In addition, as I have explained, social and cultural elements of these regions also contribute to explaining the differences in the organizational practices between the auto transplants in the Midwest and the high-tech transplants of California.

Although it is not yet possible to make any definitive statements regarding these differences, they appear to offer possible insights for explaining why Japanese auto transplants are located in the Midwest and are more Japanese, while the high-tech transplants are located in California and tend to be more American in their organizational practices. This contrast can provide many possibilities for further research.

4. THE EXPERIENCE OF WOMEN WORKERS

This study has also shown how American women workers have dealt with managerial structures and expectations in Japanese transplants. Both Katie Springer at Suntech and Carolyn Monroe at Nippon North America were successful in their careers at Japanese-owned companies. They both felt, however, that being a woman posed greater challenges and difficulties than being an American in Japanese-owned companies. At the same time, they were able to deal with the social and cultural differences at the workplace in the sense that both of them learned about Japanese expectations toward work, and thus were able to form their own coping mechanisms and survival strategies around these

Japanese expectations. Katie learned how to deal with the Japanese managers in a non-confrontational manner. Carolyn was able to take advantage of the formal structure of Japanese organizations, where employees respected her position and status regardless of her gender. In addition, it is important to note the structural factors which contributed to the success of these women in their companies. Neither of them had children to care for. Katie had an understanding husband who was willing and able to support her career progress at Suntech. Carolyn was a single woman who compared herself to her co-worker who was conflicted by the expectation of longer work hours given that she was a mother. In contrast, two Suntech employees, Sharon Vargas, a line-worker, and Martha Ferrari, a secretary, were single mothers. The necessity of attending to their children frequently conflicted with Japanese expectations of perfect attendance and overtime work.

5. THE ROLE OF CULTURE

In this book, I made an analytical distinction between culture and structure. Employing Ong's definition of culture (Ong 1987), I viewed culture as emergent and shifting meanings and practices within the web of power relations. On the other hand, I viewed structure as the relationships among social institutions and social groups. In the context of workplaces of the Japanese transplants, I dealt with a concept of culture, such as a corporate culture, Japanese culture, and American culture, not as static, monolithic entities, but as a process in which all elements of each culture constantly interact and create new meanings under the influences of the corporate level control (i.e., between parent companies and their U.S. subsidiaries) on the one hand, and the plant management level control (i.e., on the shopfloor) on the other. From this angle, I viewed the processes of change in the corporate culture of Japanese transplants as the differential and often contradictory outcomes of the power relations among the Japanese employees, American employees, and the Japanese management of the parent company in Japan.

It is clear that structural conditions in workplaces in the business environment can change rapidly. Changes in cultural elements of the workplace, however, occur far more slowly than the structural level changes. Frustrations among Japanese with the attitudes of Americans towards work and the company remained relatively constant. Likewise, the dissatisfaction of American employees with Japanese management and the push and pull of corporate structures was consistently evident.

Understanding the process of corporate culture change in light of the power relations at transplants thus revealed that the process was by no means uniform, consistent, or continuous. In the organizational context, the differences of power between Japanese and American managers, between Japanese managers and American workers, and between the parent company and its U.S. transplant can either accelerate, slow down, or sometimes even reverse the process of culture change. As implied in the preceding quotes by Sakamoto and Takizawa, they were unable to internalize the work ideology of American employees because they had to secure their career development at the parent companies in Japan.

This study has offered some perspectives and insights to explain why the Japanese retain their ideologies and philosophies regarding work and the company at the transplants. These managers and engineers may change gradually only when there are corporate structures at the parent company in Japan that accept these changes, and only when the corporate culture of the parent company is willing to deal with these differences. By observing Japanese and American employees within the web of these power relations, and by accounting for forms of control both at the corporate and the management level, I showed in this study that the corporate level structures will probably need to change first in order to initiate changes in the workplace on the level of interaction among individual employees. The successful integration of American and Japanese employees at the transplants, therefore, will likely necessitate a change in the corporate culture of the parent company in Japan. The following dialogue between Takizawa and myself illustrates the reality of Japanese managers in the U.S.

> *Takizawa*: Sometimes my fellow American workers ask me, "Why are you still working?" when they go home.
> *Sumi*: How do you respond to this?
> *Takizawa*: I just laugh. I don't bother to explain anything, and they [Americans] go home after five or six.
> *Sumi*: I can understand. You are so much aware of what is expected on you, as a sales manager and as a Japanese. So, you end up working hard as ever.

Takizawa: Right, right, right . . .
Sumi: This is very Japanese, I think.

Bibliography

Abegglen, James C.
1958   *The Japanese Factory*. New York: Free Press.
Abo, Tetsuo, ed.
1994   *Hybrid Factory: The Japanese Production System in the United States*. New York: Oxford University Press.
Albuquerque Journal
1996   "Olympus America Plant To Close," 4 Star, 2C. August 1, By David Staats
Amano, Matt M
1979   "Organizational Changes of a Japanese Firm in America," *California Management Review*. Spring, 21(3): 51-59.
Baba, Marietta L.
1986   "Business and Industrial Anthropology: An Overview," *Napa Bulletin*. Vol. 2. American Anthropological Association.
1994   "The Fifth Subdiscipline: Anthropological Practice and the Future of Anthropology," *Human Organization*. 53(2): 174-186.
Babson, Steve
1993   "Lean or Mean: The MIT Model and Lean Production at Mazda," *Labor Studies Journal*. 18(2): 3-24.
Bartlett, Christopher and Yoshihara Hideki
1988   "New challenges for Japanese multinationals: Is Organization Adaptation Their Achilles Heel?" *Human Resource Management*. 27(1): 19-43.
Benedict, Ruth
1946   *The Chrysanthemum and the Sword*. Boston: Houghton Mifflin.

Black, Stewart J. and Mark Mendenhall
1990   "Cross-Cultural Training Effectiveness: A Review and Theoretical Framework for Future Research," *The Academy of Management Review*. 15(1): 113-136.

Blau, Gary J. and Kimberly B. Boal
1987   "Conceptualizing How Job Involvement and Organizational Commitment Affect Turnover and Absenteeism," *The Academy of Management Review*. 12(2): 288-300.

Brannen, Mary Yoko
1991   "Culture as the Critical Factor in Implementing Innovation," *Business Horizons*. 34(6): 59-67.

Braverman, Harry
1974   *Labor and Monopoly Capital: The Degradation of Work in the Twentieth Century*. New York: Monthly Review Press.

Brown, Clair and Michael Reich
1989   "When Does Union-Management Cooperation Work?: A Look at NUMMI and GM-Van Nuys," *California Management Review*. 32(Summer): 26-44.

Burawoy, Michael
1979a   *Manufacturing Consent: Changes in the Labor Process and under Monopoly Capitalism*. Chicago: University of Chicago Press.
1979b   "Anthropology of Industrial Work," *Annual Review of Anthropology*. Vol. 8, Pp. 231-66.

Clark, Rodney
1979   *The Japanese Company*. New Haven: Yale University Press.

Cole, Robert E.
1971   *Japanese Blue Collar: The Changing Tradition*. Berkeley: University of California Press.
1972   "Permanent Employment in Japan: Facts and Fantasies," *Industrial and Labor Relations Review*. 26(1): 615-630.
1979   *Work Mobility and Participation: A Comparative Study of American and Japanese Industry*. Berkeley: University of California Press.

Cole, R. and Deskins, Jr.
1988   "Racial Factors in Site Locations and Employment Patterns of Japanese Firms in America," *California Management Review*. 31(1): 9-23.

Coleman, Samuel
1996   "Obstacles and Opportunities in Access to Professional Work
Organizations for Long-term Fieldwork: The Case of Japanese
Laboratories," *Human Organization.* 55(3): 334-343.
Dillon, Linda S.
1992   "Integrating the Japanese and American Work Forces," *Quality
Progress.* 25(5): 44-49.
Dore, Ronald E.
1973   *British Factory Japanese Factory.* Berkeley: University of California
Press.
Dunphy, Dexter
1987   "Convergence/Divergence: A Temporal Review of the Japanese
Enterprise and Its Management," *The Academy of Management
Review.* 12(3): 445-459.
Edwards, Richard
1979   *Contested Terrain: The Transformation of the Workplace in the
Twentieth Century.* New York: Basic Books.
Fruin, W. Mark
1994   "Cultural Relativity and the Study of Japanese Management," in
*Learning from Japan: Improving Knowledge of Japanese
Technology Management Practices.* Appendix C, Pp. 52-56.
Washington, D.C.: National Research Council.
Fucini, Joseph and Suzy Fucini
1990   *Working for the Japanese: Inside Mazda's American Auto Plant.*
New York: The Free Press.
Garon, Sheldon
1988   *The State and Labor in Modern Japan.* Berkeley: University of
California Press.
Garson, Barbara
1975   *All the Livelong Day: The Meaning and Demeaning of Routine
Work.* Garden City, New York: Dubleday.
Gelsanliter, David
1990   *Jump Start: Japan Comes to the Heartland.* New York: Farrar,
Straus and Giroux
Gibney, Frank
1975   *Japan: The Fragile Superpower.* New York: Norton.
1988   *Miracle by Design: The Real Reasons Behind Japan's Economic
Success.* New York: Times Books.

Gordon, Andrew
1985   *The Evolution of Labor Relations in Japan: Heavy Industry, 1853-1955.* Council of East Asian Studies, Cambridge: Harvard University Press.
1990   *Labor and Imperial Democracy in Prewar Japan.* Berkeley: University of California Press.
1992   "Contests of the Workplace," In *Postwar Japan as History.* Edited by Andrew Gordon, Pp. 373-394. Berkeley: University of California Press.

Graham, Laurie
1993   "Inside a Japanese Transplant: A Critical Perspective," *Work and Occupations.* 20(2): 147-173.

Gregory, Kathleen L.
1983   "Native-View Paradigms: Multiple Cultures and Culture Conflicts in Organizations," *Administrative Science Quarterly.* 28(September): 359-376.

Grenier, Guillermo J.
1988   *Inhuman Relations: Quality Circles and Anti-Unionism in American Industry.* Philadelphia: Temple University Press.

Gundling, Ernest
1991   "Ethics and Working with the Japanese: The Entrepreneur and the 'Elite Course,'" *California Management Review.* 33(3): 25-39.

Hamada, Tomoko
1992   "Under the Silk Banner: The Japanese Company and its Overseas Managers," In *Japanese Social Organization.* Edited by Takie Sugiyama Lebra, Pp. 135-164. Honolulu: University Press of Hawaii.

Hamada, Tomoko and Willis E. Sibley (Ed.)
1994   *Anthropological Perspectives on Organizational Culture.* Lanham, MD: University Press of America.

Hatvany, Nina and Vladmir Pucik
1981   "Japanese Management in America: What Does and Doesn't Work," *National Productivity Review.* Winter 1981-82, Pp. 61-74.

Hazama, Hiroshi
1971   *Nihonteki Keiei* (Japanese Style Management). Tokyo: Nikkei Shinsho.

Hirschman, Albert O.
1970   *Exit, Voice, and Loyalty.* Cambridge: Harvard University Press.

Hull, Frank and Koya Azumi
1988   "Technology and Participation in Japanese Factories: The Consequences for Morale and Productivity," *Work and Occupations.* 15(4): 423-448.

Ito, Kinko
1987   *Organizational Adaptation of Japanese Companies in the United States.* Ph.D. Dissertation, The Ohio State University.

Jaeger, Alfred M.
1983   "The Transfer of Organizational Culture Overseas: An Approach to Control in the Multinational Organization," *Journal of International Business Studies.* 14(2): 91-114.

Japan Institute for Social and Economic Affairs
1989   *Japan 1989: An International Comparison.*

JETRO
1992   *NIPPON 1992: Business Facts and Figures.*
1995   *US and Japan in Figures IV.*

Johnson, Chalmers
1982   *MITI and the Japanese Miracle: The Growth of Industrial Policy, 1925-1975.* Stanford, California: Stanford University Press.
1993   "Comparative Capitalism: The Japanese Difference," *California Management Review.* 35(4): 51-67.

Johnson, Richard T.
1977   "Success and Failure of Japanese Subsidiaries in America," *Columbia Journal of World Business.* 12(1): 30-37.

Johnson, Richard T. and William Ouchi
1974   "Made in America (under Japanese Management)," *Harvard Business Review.* 52(5): 61-69.

Jordan, Ann T.
1994   "Organizational Culture: The Anthropological Approach," *Napa Bulletin.* Vol. 14, Pp. 3-16. American Anthropological Association.

Kalleberg, Arne L.
1990   "The Comparative Study of Business Organizations and Their Employees," *Comparative Social Research,* Vol. 12, Pp. 153-175.

Kamata, Satoshi
1982   *Japan in the Passing Lane.* New York: Pantheon.

Kamishiro, Kazuyuki
1985   "Gijutu Kakushin to Rodo Mondai" (Technological Innovations and Labor Problem), In *Gijutu Kakushin to Rosi Kankei.* Edited by

Sumiya Mikio, Pp. 13-43. Tokyo: Nihon Rodo Kyokai.

Kaplan, David and Charles A. Ziegler

1985   "Clans, Hierarchies and Social Control: An Anthropologist's Commentary on Theory Z," *Human Organization.* 44(1): 83-88.

Katz, Harry C., Thomas A. Kochan, and Mark R. Weber

1985   "Assessing the Effects of Industrial Relations Systems and Efforts to Improve the Quality of Working Life on Organizational Effectiveness," *Academy of Management Journal.* 28(3): 509-526.

Kenney, Martin and Richard Florida

1990   "How Japanese Industry is Rebuilding the Rust Belt," *Technology Review.* Feb/Mar, Pp. 25-33.

1993   *Beyond Mass Production: The Japanese System and its Transfer to the U.S.* New York: Oxford University Press.

1994a   "Institutions and Economic Transformation: The Case of Postwar Japanese Capitalism," *Growth and Change.* 25(Spring): 247-262.

1994b   "The Globalization of Japanese R&D: The Economic Geography of Japanese R&D Investment in the United States," *Economic Geography.* 70(4): 334-369.

Kleinberg, Jill

1994   "Practical Implications of Organizational Culture Where American and Japanese Work Together," *Napa Bulletin.* Vol. 14, Pp. 48-65. American Anthropological Association.

Koike, Kazuo

1977   *Shokuba no Rodo Kumiai to Sanka: Roshi Kankei no Nichibei Hikaku* (A Comparative Study of Industrial Relations in the United States and Japan). Tokyo: Toyo Keizai Shimpo-sha.

1981   *Chusho Kigyo no Jukuren: Jinzai Keisei no Shikumi* (Skill Formation in Small and Medium-Sized Businesses). Tokyo: Dobunkan.

Komai, Hiroshi

1987   *Nihontekikeiei to Ibunka no Rodosha* (Japanese Style Management and Workers of Different Cultures: U.S., Southeast Asia, and Japan). Tokyo: Yuhikaku Sensho.

Kondo, Dorinne K.

1990   *Crafting Selves: Power, Gender, and Discourses of Identity in a Japanese Workplace.* Chicago: The University of Chicago Press.

Kuruvilla, Sarosh, Daniel Gallagher, Jack Fioroto, and Mitsuru Wakabayashi

1990   "Union Participation in Japan: Do Western Theories Apply?" *Industrial and Labor Relations Review.* 43(4): 374-389.

Lamphere, Louise
1987   *From Working Daughters to Working Mothers: Immigrant Women in a New England Industrial Community*. Ithaca: Cornell University Press.
Lamphere, Louise, ed.
1992   *Structuring Diversity: Ethnographic Perspectives on the New Immigration*. Chicago: University of Chicago Press.
Lamphere, Louise, Patricia Zavella, Felipe Gonzales and Peter Evans
1993   *Sunbelt Working Mothers: Reconciling Family and Factory*. Ithaca: Cornell University Press.
Lincoln, James R.
1989   "Employee Work Attitudes and Management Practice in the U.S. and Japan: Evidence From a Large Comparative Survey," *California Management Review*. 32(1): 89-106.
1990   "Japanese Organization and Organization Theory," In *Research in Organizational Behavior* by Staw and Cummings. Vol. 12, Pp. 255-294.
Marsh, Robert and Hiroshi Mannari
1976   *Modernization and the Japanese Factory*. Princeton: Princeton University Press.
Milkman, Ruth
1991   *Japan's California Factories: Labor Relations and Economic Globalization*. Institute of Industrial Relations, Monograph and Research Series 55. Los Angeles: University of California Press.
Misawa, Mitsuru
1987   "New Japanese-Style Management in a Changing Era," *Columbia Journal of World Business*. 22(4): 9-17.
Moore, Joe
1988   "Production Control: Workers' Control in Early Postwar Japan," In *The Other Japan: Postwar Realities*. Edited by Patricia Turumi, Pp. 14-35. Armonk, New York: M.E. Sharpe, Inc.
Murakami, Yasusuke and Thomas P. Rohlen
1992   "Social-Exchange Aspects of the Japanese Political Economy: Culture, Efficiency and Change." In *The Political Economy of Japan: Cultural and Social Dynamics*. Vol. 3, Pp. 63-105. Edited by Shumpei Kumon and Henry Rosovsky. Stanford: Stanford University Press.

Murayama, Motofusa
1982   "The Japanese Business Value System," In Lee and Schwendiman, ed., *Japanese Management: Cultural and Environmental Considerations*. New York: Praeger.

Nakane, Chie
1967   *Tate Shakai no Ningen Kankei* (Japanese Society). Tokyo: Kodansha Gendai Shinsho.
1974   "The Social System Reflected in Interpersonal Communication," In *Intercultural Encounters with Japan*. Edited by Condon, J.C. and Saito, M. Pp. 124-131. Tokyo: Simul Press.

Nihon Keizai Shinbun (Japan Economic Journal)
1992   "Nayami Tsukinu Beikoku Shinshutsu" (Investing in America: Endless Worries), June 8.

Nonaka, Ikujiro
1988   "Self-Renewal of the Japanese Firm and the Human Resource Strategy," *Human Resource Management*. 27(1): 45-62.

Nonaka, Ikujiro and Johny K. Johansson
1986   "Japanese Management: What About the 'Hard Skills'?" *The Academy of Management Review*. 10(2): 181-191.

Odaka, Kunio
1975   *Toward Industrial Democracy*. Cambridge: Harvard University. Press.
1984   *Nihonteki Keiei*. (Japanese style management: Myth and Reality). Tokyo: Chuko Shinsho.

Oliver, Nick and Annette Davies
1990   "Adopting Japanese-Style Manufacturing Methods: A Tale of Two (UK) Factories," *Journal of Management Studies*. 27(5): 550-570.

Ong, Aihwa
1987   *Spirits of Resistance and Capitalist Discipline: Factory Women in Malaysia*. Albany, New York: State University of New York Press.

Osako, Masako
1977   "Technology and Social Structure in a Japanese Automobile Factory," *Sociology of Work and Occupations*. 4(4): 397-426.

Ouchi, William
1981   *Theory Z: How American Business can Meet the Japanese Challenge*. Reading, Massachusetts: Addison-Wesley.

Ozawa, Terutomo
1981   *Multinationalism, Japanese Style: The Political Economy of*

Outward Dependency. Princeton: Princeton University Press.

Parkers, M. and J.Slaughter
1988   "Choosing Sides: Unions and the Team Concept," *Labor Notes Book.* Boston: South End Press.

Plath, David
1983   *Work and Life Course in Japan.* Albany: State University of New York Press.

Pucik, Vladimir
1984   "White Collar Human Resource Management: A Comparison of the U.S. and Japanese Automobile Industries," *Columbia Journal of World Business.* 14(3): 87-94.

Rehder, Robert R.
1989   "Japanese Transplants: In Search of a Balanced and Broader Perspective," *Columbia Journal of World Business.* 24(4):17-28.
1990   "Japanese Transplants: After the Honeymoon," *Business Horizons.* 33(1): 87-98.
1992   "Building Cars as if People Mattered: The Japanese Lean System vs. Volvo's Uddevalla System," *The Columbia Journal of World Business.* 27(2): 56-69.

Rohlen, Thomas
1974   *For Harmony and Strength.* Berkeley: University of California Press.
1975   "The Company Work Group," In *Modern Japanese Organization and Decision-Making.* Ezra Vogel ed., Pp. 185-209. Berkeley: University of California Press.
1989   "Order in Japanese Society: Attachment, Authority, and Routine," *Journal of Japanese Studies.* 15(1): 5-40.

Sahlins, Marshal
1972   *Stone Age Economics.* New York: Aldine Publishing.

Sakai, Kuniyasu
1990   "The Feudal World of Japanese Manufacturing," *Harvard Business Review.* 68(6): 38-49.

Sethi, S. Prakash, Nobuaki Namiki, and Carl Swanson
1984   *The False Promise of the Japanese Miracle.* Marshfield, Mass: Pitman Publishing.

Shimada, Haruo
1988   *Hyuman Uea no Keizaigaku* (The Economics of Humanware). Tokyo: Iwanami Shoten.

Smith, Robert John.
1983   *Japanese Society: Tradition, Self, and Social Order.* New York: Cambridge University Press.

Smith, Wendy A.
1994   "A Japanese Factory in Malaysia: Ethnicity as a Management Ideology." In *Japan and Malaysian Development,* Edited by Jomo K.S., Pp. 154-181. New York: Routledge

Starr, Martin and Nancy Bloom
1985   *The Performance of Japanese-owned Firms in America: Survey Report.* The Center for Operations. Graduate School of Business. Columbia University.

Starr, Martin K. and P.A. Hall
1987   *The Performance of Japanese-owned Firms in America: 1982-1985: Survey Report (2).* The Center for Operations. Graduate School of Business. Columbia University.

Starr, Martin K. and Newton Garber
1987   "Business in Japan and the United States of America: Some Implications for Management Science and Operations Research," *International Journal of Management Science.* 15(5): 383-388.

Steinhoff, Patricia G. and Kazuo Tanaka
1986   "Women managers in Japan," *International Studies of Management and Organizations.* 16(3-4): 108-132.

Steven, Rob
1988   "The Japanese Working Class," In *The Other Japan: Postwar Realities.* Edited by Patricia Turumi, Pp. 91-111. Armonk, New York: E.P. Sharpe, Inc.

Sullivan, Jeremiah J.
1992a   "Japanese Management Philosophies: From the Vacuous to the Brilliant," *California Management Review.* 34(2): 66-87.

1992b   *Invasion of the Salarymen: The Japanese Business Presence in America.* Westport, Connecticut: Praeger Publishers.

Sullivan, Jeremiah J. and Nonaka Ikujiro
1986   "The Application of Organizational Learning Theory to Japanese and American Management," *Journal of International Business Studies.* 17(3): 127-147.

Sullivan, Jeremiah J. and Richard B. Peterson
1989   *Japanese Management Theories: A Research Agenda.* School of Business Administration. University of Washington.

1991   "A Test of Theories Underlying the Japanese Lifetime Employment System," *Journal of International Business Studies.* 22(1): 79-98.

Taira, Koji

1988   "Labor Confederation in Japan," *Current History.* 87(528): 161-178.

1993   "Dialectics of Economic Growth, National Power, and Distributive Struggles," In *Postwar Japan as History.* Edited by Andrew Gordon, Pp. 167-186. Berkeley and Los Angeles: University of California Press.

Takeuchi, Hiroshi

1985   "Motivation and Productivity," In Thurow, L., ed., *The Management Challenge: Japanese Views.* Pp. 18-30. Cambridge: The MIT Press.

Tanaka, Akira

1986   "Some Thoughts on Japanese Management Centering on Personnel and Labor Management: The Reality and Future," *International Studies of Management and Organizations.* 15(3-4): 17-68.

Thurow, Lester C.

1985   *The Management Challenge: Japanese Views.* Cambridge: The MIT Press.

Trevor, Malcolm

1988   *Toshiba's New British Company: Competitiveness through Innovation in Industry.* London: Policy Study Institute.

Tsurumi, Yoshi

1978   "The Best of Times and the Worst of Times: Japanese Management in America," *Columbia Journal of World Business.* 13(2): 56-61.

1992   *Japanese Corporations in America: Managing Cultural Differences.* A Report by the Pacific Basin Center Foundation.

Turner, Christena

1991   "The Spirit of Productivity: Workplace Discourse on Culture and Economics in Japan," In *Boundary 2,* Special Issue: Japan in the World. 18(3): 90-105.

1995   *Japanese Workers in Protest: An Ethnography of Consciousness and Experience.* Berkeley: University of California Press.

University of Tokyo, Institute of Social Science

1990   "Local Production of Japanese Automobile and Electronic Firms in the United States: The 'Application' and 'Adaptation' of Japanese-Style Management."

Wakabayashi, Mitsuru and George B. Graen

1991   "Cross-Cultural   Human   Resource   Development: Japanese

Manufacturing Firms in Central Japan and Central US States," *International Business and the Management of Change.* Edited by Malcolm Trevor., Pp. 147-169. Avebury.

Wall Street Journal

1985   "Japanese Firms Set Up More Factories in U.S.," March 29, By Douglas R. Sease.

1987   "Exacting Employer: Toyota Takes Pains and Time Filling Jobs at Its New Assembly Plant in Kentucky," December 1, By Richard Koenig.

1989   "Nissan Workers Reject UAW Bid To Organize Plant in Tennessee," July 28, p. A3, By Gregory A. Patterson.

Watanabe, Susumu

1991   "The Japanese Quality Circle: Why It Works," *International Labour Review.* 130(1): 57-80.

W.E. Upjohn Institute for Employment Research

1973   *Work in America: Report of a Special Task Force to the Secretary of Health, Education and Welfare.* Cambridge: The MIT Press.

Weiss, Stephen E.

1987   "Creating the GM-Toyota Joint Venture: A Case in Complex Negotiation," *Columbia Journal of World Business.* 22(2): 23-37.

Wolf, Eric

1990   "Distinguished Lecture: Facing Power," In *American Anthropologist.* 92 (3): 586-96.

Whyte, William Foote

1987   "From Human Relations to Organizational Behavior: Reflections on the Changing Scene," *Industrial and Labor Relations Review.* 40(4): 487-500.

Womack, James P., Daniel T. Jones, and Daniel Roots

1990   *The Machine that Changed the World.* New York: Rawson Associates.

Yoshida, Mamoru

1987   "Macro-Micro Analysis of Japanese Manufacturing Investments in the United States," *Management International Review.* 27(4):19-31.

Yoshino, M.Y.

1968   *Japan's Managerial System: Tradition and Innovation.* Cambridge: The MIT Press.

1976   *Japan's Multinational Enterprises.* Cambridge: Harvard University Press.

Index

www.ingramcontent.com/pod-product-compliance
Ingram Content Group UK Ltd.
Pitfield, Milton Keynes, MK11 3LW, UK
UKHW020411010325
455677UK00029B/842